DRIFTWOOD PRESS

2023 ANTHOLOGY

EDITORS & STAFF

JAMES MCNULTY
MANAGING FICTION EDITOR
VISUAL ARTS EDITOR
INTERIOR DESIGNER
COPYEDITOR

JERROD SCHWARZ
MANAGING POETRY EDITOR
VISUAL ARTS EDITOR
POETRY INTERIOR DESIGNER
COPYEDITOR

FICTION EDITORS
CLAIRE AGNES
STEPHEN HUNDLEY
RACHEL PHILLIPPO

POETRY EDITORS
ANDREW HEMMERT
DAVID GREENSPAN

GUEST FICTION EDITOR
LYNDA MONTGOMERY

PUBLICITY ASSISTANT
OLIVIA FARINA

INTERNS
DECEMBER VERBOUT
COTY POYNTER
AR SALANDY

COPYEDITOR
JESSICA MAPLE HOLBERT

COVER IMAGE &
CONTENT ILLUSTRATIONS:
OLIVIA SULLIVAN

COVER DESIGN
SALLY FRANCKOWIAK

Independently published by *Driftwood Press*
in the United States of America.

© Driftwood Press, 2023
All Rights Reserved.

Fonts: Sifonn, Josefin Sans, Agenc̶ ther

Published i
ISBN-13: 9
Please visit our website
or email us at editor@driftwoodpress.net.

TABLE OF

Contents

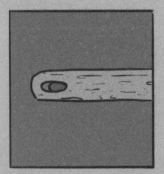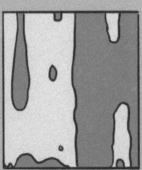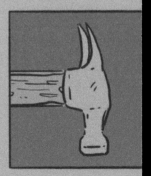

TWIN SISTERS
Michael Hugh Stewart

She was sixteen the first time. They had taught her how to read uniforms so she would be sure to pick an officer. He had acne scars, but she couldn't remember much else about him. Blue eyes? He followed her out of the bar and into the alley. They told her not to look, but she turned around anyway and watched the German approach—green eyes?—, watched Paul stalk behind him, watched the hammer rise and fall. It took several hits.

To prepare, she invented a game. We sat facing one another, she smiled, and I hurt her. If she changed her expression, I won. If not, she did. It was easy to look at myself and cause it harm. I had a lifetime of shared doubts and fears to call on. Often, I talked about our parents. There were no limits. *That would defeat the point*, she said. So sometimes, I did the unexpected—slap her, push a pin into her arm, cut her favorite blouse. Eventually, it did not matter, her expression no longer matched her feeling—her face was independent of circumstance, and she could smile at a man as she led him to his death. Just as the game changed my sister, it changed me. Though perhaps in ways I did not appreciate at the time.

In my sister's Paris, they killed Nazis in the alleys, and the Nazis killed them in the streets. In my Paris, there was rationing and a curfew from nine in the evening to five in the morning. Trucks drove through the city with loudspeakers; I cannot remember what they said, only that they would say it once in German, then once in French.

I have a picture of her from then: sitting at the table with two long men, cigarette smoke partly obscuring her face. Straight hair and a severe look that didn't make her any less pretty. Which is strange to say because I have never been pretty.

For a week, she hid Paul in my apartment. He slept in our parents' bedroom. My sister and I shared a bed growing up, and even after our parents went missing and my sister began to sleep elsewhere,

I continued to sleep in the same bed, looking at the same patch of ceiling that I had stared up at every night of my life. *I thought you would sound the same,* he said to me. *It is strange to hear a different voice in her mouth.*

There are differences between us, little tells, but sometimes when I see her in a room, I feel like a ghost watching myself. If I watch her drink tea, I can almost taste it.

In the evening, Paul listened for messages over the radio. *Athalie remained in ecstasy. We say twice. Athalie remained in ecstasy.* He was a slight man with a thin blonde mustache over thin lips. He mouthed the words to himself while he wrote them down. He was comfortable taking over the apartment. I had to be careful with his laundry—I could not dry it on the line, or I would have needed to explain the presence of a man. After the war, he was arrested for doping greyhounds. He died in prison from an infection.

I asked him what it sounded like, hitting the German with a hammer. *You're a morbid little bird.* He liked to talk. He told me they were lovers, but I doubted that. He told me that she saved his life once. *Pushed the knife in the bastard's eye—smooth as butter.* I know the knife he was talking about; our father used to keep it on a chain next to his watch. I have seen her use it to cut the end of her cigars. Always two wedge-shaped cuts—a cat's eye, that's called.

The last night, I made a cake. He called me sentimental. I tried to imagine the sound that it would make, hitting a man with a hammer. Like pounding chicken? Because of the rationing, I used beets instead of sugar. They stained my hands and the cutting board, and even the blade of the knife. My hands were still pink when I pushed open the bedroom door. The hallway light reflected off of his eyes and made them look wet. I didn't say anything when I uncovered him. He lay there docile but eager as I straddled him, nighty bunched at my waist. I rolled my hips slowly but insistently, pulling her name out of him, making him repeat it while his hands searched my face looking for hers.

AVERTED VISION
A Conversation with Michael Hugh Stewart

James McNulty: "Twin Sisters" is an extremely compressed story; the word economy is extraordinary, and the cohesion and culmination of the many threads of tension is succinct, appropriately ambiguous, and beautifully handled. Much of this interview will consist of lengthy praise for the craft efforts here, and I should note that our editors were unanimous in wanting to publish this piece. For readers who don't know, "Twin Sisters" ended up edging out another runner-up for our 2022 In-House Contest, winning no doubt because of the high-level of craft on display here. All of this to say: welcome to the pages of Driftwood, Michael. We're happy to have you.

Michael Hugh Stewart: Thank you, I am excited to talk to you, and I am flattered to have won the contest.

JM: Despite the compression, this story has a good handful of conflicts and tensions without ever feeling scattered. Nazi Germany is a backdrop, and the sisters' relationship takes the foreground, though we seem to see much of this through the speaker's relationship with Paul. Was this initially a longer draft that you cut down? Talk to our readers a little about the act of writing such a compressed narrative—while simultaneously balancing many threads.

MHS: Writing is often about circling an idea, an image, or a line; it's a matter of accumulating notes and scenes more than developing a narrative. This story started with a Texas restaurant and the Oversteegen sisters.

In college, I worked in a restaurant (with Lily Hoang) called Twin Sisters, and for whatever reason, that name has surfaced in my notes over and over again for years. It led me to vague ideas of echoes and repetitions that, over time, solidified into a question: what if a twin thought of herself as an echo of her sister?

Then, I came across the story of the Oversteegen sisters, who, along with Hannie Schaft, formed a three-person Dutch resistance during WWII. Among other acts of sabotage and heroism, they lured German soldiers from bars into the woods to shoot them.

The combination created something I could orbit: seduction, echoes, violence, and shifting point-of-view.

As for length, I write in a very uneconomical way: I often break my sentence into clauses and sketch dozens of unneeded scenes. A short piece like this might be twenty pages (although there is a lot of white space on those pages) before I start to edit.

JM: I love that you're willing to whittle twenty pages down to two; the tightness of the narrative, the economy of the words, shows this effort. But most writers would hate to throw away so much work and time, not realizing that cutting and throwing away is a necessary part of writing. I'm curious—are your longer narratives as tightly written? Is short fiction typically what you write?

MHS: I typically write short fiction and poetry. I like how each form lends itself to the unsaid and unseen and allows you to read with a kind of averted vision.

Averted vision is a practice in astronomy. If you spend a lot of time looking up at the stars, you've probably noticed that some cannot be seen if you look directly at them. You have to shift your sight, and look a bit off target, so the photoreceptors that work best in dim light, the rods, take over. I love the idea that the only way to see something is to not look directly at it.

JM: This is a lovely idea, and I think it very much shows in your writing: there's more happening just off the page, implied and suggested. As I mentioned earlier, there are a good handful of interesting craft decisions on display here. One is how the story seems to have a sort-of bait and switch within the first two paragraphs. We arrive at the first paragraph thinking it's third person, but the second paragraph reveals it to be first. This craft decision embodies the themes of the piece: the identity, the person, seems to switch. When it comes to very clever uses of craft such as this, where the craft replicates the themes so directly, is it wholly intentional on your part from the get-go, or does the idea develop over the course of revisions?

MHS: Given what I said about averted vision, it probably comes as no surprise that I like to think of early drafts as constellations. When I start, I'm looking for bright moments from which a reader can make a shape. To this end, I sketch dozens and dozens of scenes, often just a few lines each: an image, an action, a detail. In this piece, there were a couple of images that stood out right away: the hammer, the beet stains, and Paul's wet eyes. There were facts I felt partial to such as the Athalie in ecstasy code. And details that, although I could not tell you why, seemed necessary—the wedge-shaped cut in the cigar and Paul doping greyhounds come to mind.

Once I have these initial sketches, the research and revision begin. For revision, I play with the arrangement of parts and the anatomy of the sentences themselves. I mumble to myself for weeks at this stage; I have to hear each line out loud. I listen to how the various pieces come together and try to feel my way through them, if that makes any sense.

Of course, it is not as tidy as this implies. This is a process of discovery less than a well-executed plan. Whenever I uncover a new detail in my research or a sentence shifts in an unexpected direction, I return to sketching. It's a very slow ebb and flow—I wrote the first draft of this piece in 2018—but I'm not in a hurry.

JM: There are some really stunning, stand-out lines throughout this piece. Your word economy—and the punch of each line—never lets up. I think of, "In my sister's Paris, they killed Nazis in the alleys, and the Nazis killed them in the streets," and "…sometimes when I see her in a room, I feel like a ghost watching myself." Of course, the final line comes to mind, too. I'm not sure there's much of a question in this heap of praise, except to ask: how do you come up with these lines? Do they come to you slowly, or quickly? Is it research that inspires them, or perhaps just a lot of time spent drafting, slowly typing out the sentences as they come?

MHS: The alleys and streets line was the first sentence I wrote, and it remained relatively unchanged through every revision. But that is very unusual for me. As I mentioned above, I like to slowly revise and discover the possibilities of a line through experimentation.

One way I do that is by isolating a clause and pivoting around it. For example, with the ghost line, I knew I wanted to end with "a ghost watching myself." So, I took the clauses that led up to it and tried various permutations:

/when we are alone in a room
/when I see her in a room
/when she is in a room
    /I am
    /I feel like
    /I seem
        /a ghost watching myself.

I find the research process aligns nicely with my writing style. I love searching and collaging. For this piece, I listened to French Resistance messages, looking up sugar rations (500 grams of sugar a month) and the recipes invented in response to the rations. Most of my research does not end up on the page. I have a trove of pictures of Persian women in the mid-1940s. I was trying to figure out how the two sisters would dress, and more specifically, how they would dress differently from one another. I read the biographies of several resistance fighters to uncover some details that I thought I would need: where in Paris they would meet, what the Germans blared from the loudspeakers they drove around the city, etc. (Although, I did come across this beautiful detail in Pearson's *The Wolves at the Door,* which has become its own piece: The French avoided eye contact with the German invaders, "who had begun calling Paris 'la ville sans regard' (the city that never looks at you).") I'm sure this work isn't strictly necessary, but it is pleasurable, and I'll take any excuse to go to an archive.

JM: We've been finding lately that many of the stories we select for publication have a good bit of research done while writing them; research helps a good deal with specificity of language and scene, allows the scene to both feel real and lived in—yet still unique because of the specificity. Research also makes the writer more confident in their prose, I suspect.

A few of my editors wanted to ask a question, too; Claire has a question about research and setting.

Claire Agnes: I'm curious about the manifestation of the setting in this story. Was there a certain process of research or experience you used in order to imbue time and place with authenticity? What artifacts and information are you drawn towards, and through what process are details selected? Alongside this story, I'm interested in your larger narrative impulses, and whether the elements of time and place often fluctuate throughout your work, or if this particular setting has consistently called to you throughout multiple pieces.

MHS: I love that you used the word "artifacts." Some objects seem better able to carry ghosts. Some can summon a place or make a person come alive. Most of my research is spent looking for them; my writing is more curation than creation.

My methods are pretty traditional: JSTOR and coffee, reading rooms and a notepad. I also travel and interview quite a bit, though usually that work is not tied to a particular piece but is more inspirational. I can think of no better research advice than this gorgeous passage from *The Allure of the Archives*, in which Arlette Farge talks about the importance of remaining sufficiently open:

> "There are 'quiet,' ordinary documents that can lead you astray and take you far from where you had planned to go or even to understand. Perhaps this is what it is to let yourself soak up the archive; to remain sufficiently open to the forms the archive contains that you are able to notice things that were not a priori of interest. It might be countered that saturation is hardly a scientific method, that the word itself is troublesomely vague, and that this almost childishly naive idea could easily allow faulty interpretations to slip into the research. Of course. But I am tempted to answer with a metaphor, knowing full well that this only makes things worse: the archive is like a forest without clearings, but by inhabiting it for a long time, your eyes become accustomed to the dark, and you can make out the outlines of the trees."

In my research, I endeavor to become more accustomed to the dark.

As to the second part of your question, while I tend to jump around a lot in my writing, I do have several pieces set in or around the world wars. I think this is because I am fascinated by how they have been mythologized. My interest in them is in many ways similar to my interest in fairy tales.

Olivia Farina: There's something very haunting about starting with something somehow simply and startlingly violent at the same time, then ending with a scene of intimate deception. With the opening and closing image being so drastically different, I wonder which scene came to you first?

MHS: The scene with the hammer came first. I was tenderizing a chicken breast for dinner, and the wet, flat sound of the frying pan repeatedly hitting flesh stayed with me. The sound was uncomfortable and intimate, and while the opening and closing scenes are very different, I tried to create in both that feeling of intimacy and discomfort. My intention was for the two scenes to have a similar sort of gravity and passivity—there is violence and deception, but also inertia and inevitability.

JM: Talk to me about some of your influences—both literary and not.

MHS: I am drawn to photography perhaps because, like short work and poetry, it allows the viewer a certain agency. More specifically, I am influenced by the compositions of Fan Ho and Alex Webb, the quiet discomfort of Todd Hido's images, and the lyrical photographs of Rebecca Norris Webb, particularly her work in *My Dakota*, which often layer reflections, glares, and memories. Another photographer whose work has had an outsized influence on me is Masao Yamamoto. Yamamoto ages his prints. He smudges them, carries them in his pocket, rubs them with his hands, giving them texture, history, intimacy. He then arranges them with a generous use of white space. The images themselves are striking, but it is the way they work together that makes me return to them again and again.

As for the literary, I love the writing of Milorad Pavic, Fleur Jaeggy, Anne Carson, W.G. Sebald, and Renee Gladman. And there have been a couple of writers whose work I admire deeply, but whose effect has gone beyond that, who have been kind mentors and without whom I would have never left that kitchen in Texas: Rikki Ducornet, Carole Maso, and Brian Evenson.

JM: Perhaps it's not too surprising that you reference photography first; the specificity of your written images signals a photographer's eye. What're you working on next, Michael?

MHS: Currently, I am writing a longer series that braids some seemingly disparate subjects including St. Lucy, my father's oncoming cataracts, Greta Garbo, early cinematography, etc. Even more than my usual writing, this is a work of assemblage. Finding the various bits of information has been fantastic—the British Library for a doctoral thesis on St. Lucy, Philadelphia's Rosenbach Museum & Library for Garbo's letters to Mercedes de Acosta, online forums to learn how orthochromatic film renders blue, etc. But it has also required me to draw on events from my own life, stories about my father and my grandmother. I am still learning how to navigate the discomfort inherent in any degree of memoir.

JM: Do you feel comfortable discussing the particular discomfort you're feeling? Do you think this discomfort aids or hinders the prose?

MHS: I think it is nervousness about "getting it right." Nonfiction demands a different level of responsibility to the subject and to the reader. Moreover, in this piece, I am interested in belief more than absolute truth. If someone sincerely believed that St-Mercurios' father was eaten by two dog-headed men and acted upon that belief, then I am less concerned with the historical fact of the event and more about what sort of world such a belief creates.

Then there is the vulnerability inherent in using events from my life. All I can say is that it gives me a new appreciation for those who write memoirs.

JM: As we wrap up the interview, is there anything else you'd like to add?

MHS: I just want to thank you, Olivia, and Claire for your generous questions. I appreciate the time and attention you've given my very short story, and the opportunity to talk about so many things near and dear to me.

NEON FISH

Johanna Povirk-Znoy

With his gun aimed at the earth, Dad described our holdings for when the shit hit the fan. The utility shelves in the bunker behind the house were lined with buckets of rice, water filtration tablets, and boxes of bullets. Dad had also buried various necessities throughout the woods. If the bunker was destroyed or became infested by the government, we would be alright.

It was a Saturday morning so we were doing target practice, but Dad was keeping us longer than usual. Maddie jiggled from foot to foot—phones were a distraction so not allowed, and I watched my sister's thumb swipe uselessly along the barrel of her gun. Something small scurried over dry leaves. Dad had us tell him again where the important things were buried and I made my face placid as I pointed to the spots on the map. Inside, I was vibrating.

"Pure precaution," Mom said. "You girls will be fine. We'll all be fine."

Dad's mouth drew tight and Mom cupped her hand on his shoulder.

"I like to have my ducks in a row," he said, holding her eyes.

Mom held his eyes right back.

"Just so long as they don't lay their eggs in one basket," she told him.

Mom's first shot was perfect, right in the center of the target. Her second shot hit the limb of a tree, but it was perfect too even though Dad thought it was a mistake and made her aim again.

Now Dad is in the woods out back making a video about pemmican. This is his fifth batch and he says he has it good enough to do a tutorial. The tutorial portion he filmed in the kitchen; out in the woods he's explaining to his screen about underground storage and showing off the canvas tent that he waterproofed by hand.

Pemmican packed in Ziploc bags sits on the counter. I helped pack it, so I know from touch that it has hardened dense and soapy.

Next to the pemmican is a dish of cracklings for Charley the beagle. Dad fished out the cracklings with a slotted spoon when he was boiling the fat to render it. He used the blender to turn dehydrated beef and blueberries into powder. Then he poured the clear fat over the powder to make things wet again. Unhardened pemmican is a material you could use like mortar. Hardened, it can give life when life is dying.

Pemmican can last fifty years, probably more. Dad doesn't want us to eat much because it's for the future, but I've had a taste and it does not taste good. It took fifteen hours to dry the meat in a low-temp oven and everything smelled like leather. Hardened up and in plastic, all smells are gone.

Currently, the kitchen smells like baking. Maddie is making a cake with vanilla Duncan Hines frosting that she has colored blue and red and a dense black. Over the summer she got deep into cake-making. Maddie watched her YouTube videos at the same rate Dad made them. She likes this one YouTuber who is also thirteen and has a cookbook and a line of spatulas and frosting tips you can get at Michael's craft stores. Maddie didn't buy all that junk; she mostly made do because of how Dad is, though he was surprisingly okay about the Duncan Hines. I think he likes to dip into it at night.

All through August the kitchen was humid with sweet. Maddie cut up yellow sheet cakes to build cities and coral reefs and a dinosaur head for our cousin Josh's fifth birthday. Now she's using the cakes as a project for school. Instead of a diorama, she's explaining the solar system in baked goods form. There is a big ball-shaped cake for the sun and cupcakes for all the planets. Crumbs from the cake are mixed in with the creamy home-style frosting, so it's messy looking and textured like dirt. I think part of the cake thing is she gets to consume vast amounts of sugar as she goes. The girl remains stick thin, so it doesn't bother our parents. She is me a few years ago, all muscle and bone before I pushed out into boobs and hips.

Maddie uses her fingers to paint the cakes in the tricky spots. She globs frosting on her pinky with a swipe up the bowl before coating the sun. Her fingers are constantly dyed at the tips, and the corners of her mouth are smeared with yellow. Maddie wears headphones as she works, but I wouldn't talk to her when she's at it anyway. She turns very proprietary about the kitchen and speaks to me like *never have I ever blended together wet and dry.*

Everything about the house and my family is turning me anxious because of what I have planned for today. I go into the bathroom with the nautical theme so I can pluck my eyebrows to relieve some stress. This bathroom has Mom's magnifying mirror, and I pull at hairs you wouldn't know existed unless you looked this close. The bathroom is warm from the oven being on since morning. Shells and beach rocks sweat under the rope netting on the toilet tank.

I keep the lights low and pour some lavender oil into the diffuser. In the magnifying mirror I catch a glimpse of the pulsing beneath my temples, a soft glow of neon trapped under skin. It's only in the places where my skin is thin and veiny that you can see the fish moving: my temples, my wrists, the insides of my elbows and the tops of my feet. Behind my knees, too, though I have to swivel for that.

I put a finger to my temple and feel a shiver tingle down deep to correspond with the tail swishing beneath my finger pad. It annoys me that the fish turn me on like that because it's a two-way thing; they also come out in droves when I get turned on by events totally unrelated to them. This means they are out a lot. I have trouble not touching a spot when I feel them swimming there. I tell Jack the fish are killing me, but he kind of likes what they do. I guess that's better than him finding the situation too weird to handle. He pushes on the ones behind my knee to make me squirm when we are spooning on the couch and then he laughs. He thinks it's a game. He doesn't know how they feel when I'm under crisp sheets but my inner skin is clammy from them bobbing around and getting unpredictable in their patterns. I can't sleep and I want to scratch them out with my nails. It's a sweaty fever dream and I chew at my wrists lightly, hoping to push the fish deeper inside of me so I can't feel them swim. Jack likes the way they make me needy for him, but he's still agreed to help.

When it started, I didn't know what it was and I spent time online trying to find the answer. Scabies come out at night, which was when the fish were liveliest. I thought I must have got scabies from Jack who is done with high school and sleeps on a mattress in the middle of the floor. His bedroom is strewn with beer bottles and gnawed up chicken bones in styrofoam containers. Still, he is meticulous about bathing and bristled when I suggested his habits had set parasites loose inside of me. "You can be clean and have scabies," I told him. "Like lice on a clean scalp. Kids get them just from hugging." Jack turned off the expression in his face and moved away from me on the couch. I had to make a lot of jokes to warm him up again. Eventually I had to admit that I was both primary and solitary host. I had to admit nothing would crawl through my skin and into his. After I admitted that he was sweet and sympathetic and would touch me again.

The thing that sets them apart from scabies or any other known parasite is the glow. The fish glow so bright you can see them through the skin. They're distinct shapes now, tube-shaped fish with pupil-less eyes, but at first they were hazy, passing clouds of color. Before they were hazy, they were basically invisible. I'd feel the movement of something gliding inside me, but I couldn't pinpoint where because it was so deep, a region of my body I had no reason to know. The doctor pushed on my abdomen. "Here?" he asked. "Here? Do you feel pain when I do this?" His palms were flat and utilitarian. "How about here?"

The doctor thought I was a silly little crazy. I almost felt bad for him. He was so sure that I was making it up, but I knew more than he did: I knew that I wasn't. I paid the copay to a nurse with the driest skin while the fish surged giddy inside of me, celebrating their discretion under the doctor's touch.

I got used to the movement eventually and, later, to the glow, which was like a smudge on my skin that manifested from beneath. There were no side effects beyond my confusion at causation and the way I got kind of horny when I pushed on my wrist and felt a fish bumping against my finger. The internet couldn't freak me out because no one else had neon fish. There weren't any horror stories to hypochondriac about. The closest thing online was the animals they inject with fluorescent protein harvested from jellyfish. I looked at glowing piglets, puppies with light up noses, a bunny named Alba some artist made that goes green under ultraviolet light. Because of the mad science aspect, I wondered if Dad was up to something weird. But those animals on the internet were injected while they were still in the womb. I hadn't always been this way and, to be fair, Dad hadn't always been a way where I'd suspect him of something crazy. I had to let the fish be.

The fish could change color—we saw them do it, so when we counted, there was no way to keep track. Jack and I would lie on my bed and try our best. There could have been nineteen, but also there could have been ninety. We'd call out random numbers to count, "One, twelve, seventy-six, forty," and then I'd get worked up because we'd be touching them as we did that. I'd straddle Jack and the fish would swarm to my inner thighs as we had sex. It looked good with the changing colors, but it was also funny in a slapstick way. The fish would pulse with a rhythm that wasn't ours and we'd lose our pace trying to meet theirs or laughing at the discrepancy. After, they'd recede for a bit to go rest somewhere down in my depths and guts.

Jack was the one who thought they must be saying something. When the fish pushed against my skin, you could see the glow, but also they raised my flesh into gulpy little bumps. The fish would shrink and expand, urgent then lackadaisical. To me it felt indiscriminate. Jack, meanwhile, was sure there was a pattern.

"It must be like braille," Jack said. "The size and frequency are different letters, and they're trying to spell something for us. It's like that guy who was paralyzed and wrote a book by blinking his eyes." He was convinced there was a code we could hack. Jack read books about the Talmud and knew some things about computers. We were some of the last generation to learn cursive and he believed we had all the tools.

"What if it's just how they breathe?" I asked. I used old tights as a blindfold. Then I put my right hand on my left wrist so I could chart the movements without being distracted by the glow. Jack closed his eyes and put the side of his face on my thigh to comprehend the fish through his cheek. "Oh man, there's definitely something here," he said, tapping my knee in time with the information he seemed to extract from my thigh. Jack was getting speedy and excited, but I was slowing down. Under the dark of the blindfold, I felt the fish from my inside and my outside. There were wet waves: a sadness, a satisfaction, an acceptance, all woven together and then, repeat, repeat. The repeat was the hardest part. I wasn't ready for this; I did not want these fish.

I sat up straight, forcing Jack up too.

"I think the only way to read them is to get them out," I said, traitor that I am. The fish slid cool and aloof in response.

I had always liked Jack since we were kids and he was just Megan's older brother. Later, when I was in middle school, he was the high schooler I would flirt with on the back of the bus. The flirting was actually just talking because so many people all in one place made me nervous, and focusing on one person was the best remedy for that. Jack laughs in inappropriate places. He's sweet, but he's also bad because of his parents, so Dad doesn't like him. Jack doesn't really drink or do drugs; at least he's never the one to buy drugs or to drive after he's done a bunch of drinking. He has long hair for his metal band and long limbs to match. When people say something dumb, Jack flicks his eyes around like dim lasers and does not smile back. Unless he likes everyone involved, he won't participate in group conversation.

Still, when we are alone, Jack is my champion. He builds me shape when I lose definition. It is like I am a shape made of fabric and so I flop, but then he's around and I gain edge. I told him this once and it turned him sad and withdrawn.

"It shouldn't be like that," he said after a bit and because he understood that I loved him more.

In the bathroom I pluck an eyebrow hair and something lights up that is my phone, not a fish. Jack is here. I look at myself hard in the mirror. I think, *it'll be a cleanse.* I think, *it'll be just like popping a zit.* I think, *I will be a floppy shape again.* Then I go to the door and let Jack in.

I lie on my belly with my arms stretched out and my fingers gripping the edge of the mattress. The wall is about three feet from the foot of the bed, a wide and open canvas. The fish are streaming through my arms. It's the last light show, it's a code show for Jack. My inner elbow lights up green, my wrist is shot through with orange. A worm-like fish seems to suction its yellow lips inside my vein. Its eyes are beads, illegible, but it is begging all the same. Jack is behind and above me. This is warmer than the kitchen. I feel warm breath in my ear. Jack blankets himself over me, a warm body, extra warm where his penis is jumping. Please, I say, I'm not ready for you. I say this inside, to the fish. To Jack I say, "Let's go." He begins massaging me like we talked about, pushing the fish through my veins with his wide fingertips. If he pushes them toward my wrists, there is going to be build up like sediment in deltas. Or I don't know what, I've never tried to direct the fish.

"Maybe you should push in two directions at once," I say. I mean he could push the fish in my right arm toward my wrist, the ones in my left arm back toward my heart. I think if they don't all get crowded in the same place their exit won't be painful. I close my eyes and the begging fish washes away behind my eyelids.

"You're too nice," Jack grunts. "We have to be forceful if we're going to get them to explain." He still thinks the fish have something singular to say.

Raindrops are fat on the windowpanes and the scent of pear body spray floats through the room. Maddie must have been in here messing with my stuff. The sheets I grip are peach and lemon; everything is spring even though it's fall outside. "Can I?" Jack asks, and I say *yes*, so he is inside me pushing but also still pushing his fingers against my veins like they are tubes of almost-done toothpaste and he is trying to get enough for one last brushing. It hurts because it's scary, but then I get outside of feeling and here they come, thousands of them shooting out through the insides of my wrists and splattering their gelatinous bodies against the wall. They are Gusher fruit snacks if the outside of a Gusher were membrane-thin. The wall is a watercolor, dripping yellow, green, aqua, pink. The drips are moving a little this way, a little that. They form words with letters like nothing I've ever seen, and then the words morph into pictures that have no meaning: Saint Patty's day, a moonlit field, a garland of roses around a horse's head. I watch them go from dumb and distinct to vivid and abstract.

Jack comes on my back and flops onto his own back, eyes rolled so he can study the vibrating mess on the wall. Absently he pulls my right arm onto his chest, begins kneading my wrist as if it was made of clay and he is trying to suture some hole. There is no hole in my wrist. The fish got out without breaking skin. I miss them with a piercing sensation—I am empty, and I have made a mistake. The mistake lasts for the shortest instant. Closing my eyes against the foggy light, I feel a swish down deep. New fish are swimming; teeny babies are getting squeezed out with each heartbeat. I bask and my breathing slows. I tense my muscles to keep them from the surface so Jack won't get to see.

"Neat," says Jack, nodding toward the wall of spent fish. He pulls my wrist toward his mouth and gives it a soft kiss. "You and your little fish."

In this moment, I have two choices. I can either need him completely so bad it hurts, or I can roll him onto his stomach and push him hard into the mattress until he is sucked under and cannot breathe. Instead, I get dressed. When I stand, some excess fish trail off of me like medusa dandruff, squirming. The one I pick up is pink, plumped in its center where the neon juice distends its skin. The fish bursts upon contact with my lips. I take a picture of the wall painted in shifting colors, and then I use my peachy blanket to wipe the marks away.

We clean up to go have dinner. Maddie bounces on a stool, still listening to music and high on sugar. Mom has a night shift at the hospital and Dad is working in the basement—I can hear the whirring. Jack and I drive to Timmy Horton's and load up on bacon and cheese. We listen to something from his friend's band that sounds just like his own band, and I lean into the headrest as I chew. I have no idea what I'll hatch as next. I put my nose into Jack's shoulder so I will remember his details when, someday, I am alone, or when I love somebody else.

All the lights are off when we get back, and the pemmican is gone. I see Dad's muddy boots from being out in the rain and I imagine he has buried it somewhere safe. I could dig up all of his holdings and replace them with air and he would never know. The pemmican will rest below the frost line in its aluminum container. It will remain uneaten by us and impenetrable to worms or bugs.

Jack kisses me deep and soulful, but I keep him in the doorframe. I can tell he's disappointed that I don't sneak him in to stay. Still, sweet and on my side, he does not push when we say goodnight.

With Jack gone, I'm both jumpy and exhausted so I turn on some TV. I fall asleep watching a reality show and am soft and seasick upon half waking. Spawning, the new fish have gained enough mass to transmit a glow. I begin to pull myself to bed, but when I pass the gun cabinet in the room with the dark green carpet I hear the bullets buzzing. The bullets are doing shaky little dances in their respective chambers. It seems clear that we can solve one another's problems.

I prop my left hand on the clean pine of the cabinet and use my right to move the numbers on the padlock to spell out my birthday. Dad has taught me how to unload even though he says an unloaded gun is a liability waiting to happen. I shake bullets from the big gun, the small gun, and the six in-between. It takes a few trips, but I load my palms and bring the bullets into the kitchen. Everything is dark and I turn on the lights that glow inside the cabinets with frosted glass doors. The room gets lit by filtered light and the blender is silhouetted in the cabinet over the sink. I pull it out. The blender controls light up blue when I plug it in and the pitcher still smells like jerky from the dried meat Dad powdered in it earlier. I have to grip the counter because my stomach is reeling, and when I grip I can see the fish moving up my arms. I put my ear to a fish spot, but it's useless unless I close my eyes. Clink clink clink go the bullets into the glass body of the blender. I add warm water and a spoonful of Pepto that Mom keeps on the fridge. When I blend it, the pink will absorb the metal and the texture will be like the inside of an etch-a-sketch. I throw in some cake scraps to help with flavor. The inside of my mouth grows and drips as I imagine this mixture expanding on my tongue.

The blender has many options for speeds and styles. I press the button for grate. Upstairs I hear Maddie toss around in response to the noise. Downstairs the smoothie is better than I could ever have imagined and I drink it sludgy and warm from a pint glass. I smile at my drinking reflection widened on the side of the toaster, then wipe the blender with a sponge and pad up the stairs and into my room.

Night is cool and lake-like around me, and leftover rain drips from the trees. I feel the bullet-blend making its armor beneath my skin. It's a little sad the fish will be hidden to sight, but I will still feel their signaling even if I can't offer them up to be read. I smile at the sensation of one hitting its mushy head against my newest membrane. *Quiet, my pretties*, I whisper inside. *Don't worry, I've got you tight.*

I think when Jack chews at my wrist the metal beneath my skin might hurt his teeth. Sometimes it will, I reason; he may even chip a tooth. At other times, and before we end, I will soften just for him, and be like a pillow to his bite.

EVERYONE IS ALL THE TIME
A Conversation with Johanna Povirk-Znoy

James McNulty: Hey, Johanna! Welcome to the pages of *Driftwood*! "Neon Fish" was an editor favorite over here; it received the very rare unanimous vote cast from four editors. We're so pleased to showcase the story in our new annual format!

Johanna Povirk-Znoy: Hi, James! I'm so happy the story has a home in *Driftwood* and no longer exists just in a file on my computer or the inboxes of a couple friends. Also, the new format is exciting.

JM: When did you write this story, and how long did you work on revisions before submitting it?

JPZ: This story came about in a nonlinear fashion—I did some writing that ended up fueling the piece way back in 2016, but the writing was more like a fragmented dialogue/notes that I put down, very stream of consciousness style, to process some ambiguity with a person I was seeing. They were notes to myself that didn't make much objective sense, and then I found them a few years later and used some of the lines to make the bones of the scene with the expulsion of the fish—I tried writing it like a letter at first, and then shifted away from that. Once the story belonged to a narrator who was other than myself, I began to wrap connecting threads around the main scene and the whole came together fairly quickly. I probably let it sit for a couple months and then did some editing/moving of parts before letting it sit again and then touching it up and submitting it places.

JM: Most stories with odd premises kick off the premise in the first few paragraphs, but you hold yours back for a few pages—instead, you ground the reader by introducing the father and the sister, with cooking and prepping for the end of the world. Talk to me a little about this decision, and why it was important for you to ground the story in the family before moving on to the central premise and the key relationship.

JPZ: Like I was describing before, I sort of wrote this story from the inside out, or from close-to-the-end back to the beginning. I had this very amorphous scene with colorful fish exploding through skin which I knew was climactic and needed to be built toward in order to resonate. I was also going down various internet wormholes related to parasites. I'd been convinced that someone had given me scabies even though I didn't have scabies at all and was just allergic to some cheap soap, and I told my housemate about this. He went to his bookshelf and pulled out *The Empathy Exams* by Leslie Jamison. It was a funny night; he ended up reading an essay aloud to a friend and I about a convention for people who suffer from Morgellons, an *is it/isn't it* disease where people find or experience fibers stuck inside their skin. I started reading about Morgellons and various origin stories that surround it—I ended up on someone's site who thought the government was responsible, and that angle brought me into the realm of the preppers. Prepping itself rests on an odd premise that you can be prepared for disaster when no one else is. It made sense for me to begin the story in the space of something that, while seated in the world, still has a fantastical element. I wanted the narrator to be grounded in a believable space, but I also wanted the space to have an element of anxiety, which is inherent in the prepper mindset.

Maybe I'm missing your question though: after I started describing the father and the pemmican, I happened onto Maddie, I think because I wanted another pole of consumption. My narrator had these fish inside her body. I wanted her to live in a believable world, but I also wanted there to be an echo between her experience and other things which can be absorbed by a body.

JM: During our first round of line edits, I suggested the father's prepping was possibly a reaction to COVID. You responded that you'd written the story before COVID, but it was interesting how COVID meant that "having a prepper as a character has a different weight now." How does the father's prepping play into the heightened anxiety of the story, and has COVID changed any of your thoughts about preppers?

JPZ: I was interested in the contrast between a prepper, or someone who believes that there are solid and plotted steps you can take to protect yourself from doom, and my teenage narrator who is coming to terms with the forever-ness of ambiguity. I think the prepping creates anxiety with its suggestion that there's one (or multiple, but still definitive) answer to a problem. Maybe this allays anxiety for some people, but anxiety itself is related to future-thinking, which seems to be a central tenet of prepper-dom. COVID has perhaps just exaggerated what I already thought about the idea of prepping— while I can empathize with the want, no one can prepare perfectly for disaster because disaster is never going to look the same or just as you imagined it. There's a movie I remember watching a long time ago, *Why Do Things Get in a Muddle (Come on Petunia)*, where the question in the title is answered by the idea that things get muddled, in part, because there's so many more ways things can be a mess than be 'tidy.' We know the abstract shapes of a lot of messes that are coming our way, but just like we couldn't predict a new virus, we won't know the actual mess on a bodily level until it arrives and we have to live in its details.

JM: Sex scenes can often be daunting in fiction writing, and there's so much anxiety packed within your central sex scene here. Could you delve into the craft behind creating this scene?

JPZ: I wrote this scene pretty quickly and without thinking about craft—maybe the speed itself informed some of the anxiety. But I was also thinking about sex that is multiple things at once, or in this case both sex and not-sex at the same time. I did want to build up the not-sex-but-still-sexual fish expulsion before any description of penetrative sex, which itself reads more like an afterthought. But again, I think writing this very fast is probably what set its mood!

I listened to a fiction podcast once where David Means said he had a "preposterous theory" that sex in fiction is always just about communication and dialogue between two characters. Maybe that was embedded in my head along with my fascination about how the same conversation can mean very different things to the people involved.

JM: The David Means theory is, I think, usually true, and I think you internalized that to the point where you maybe didn't need to outwardly, consciously think about craft, but you *were* intuiting it. I think, so often, that the most successful use of craft happens when the author isn't consciously making an effort to think about it—the craft has become so internalized, so understood, that it comes naturally when you write. And if you're *really* in the zone, really in touch with these internalized craft decisions, that's perhaps how you can make new craft discoveries.

You speak about the writing coming fast for this scene; much of the structure of the writing—the long paragraphs, the repetitive sentence structures, etc.—makes it feel almost like a fever dream, this sort of *fast* quality. Can you speak to how long the initial draft took—or usually takes—to write, and what you do to get yourself in the proper headspace for writing?

JPZ: It's hard for me to remember how long the initial draft took, but typically my first drafts for things are pretty speedy even if they're in parts. Maybe I'll spend an hour or so writing a very messy, very fast fragment of a text—the fragment could contain the whole arc of the future piece, or it could just be a portion. I tend to write these by hand. The editing and shaping generally happens when I begin to type things up, and it can take anywhere from a couple of weeks to long stretches—sometimes I think something is done and then I'll rework it a year later. I'm still trying to find my best headspace for writing, but morning seems good, especially right when I wake up or after I've gone for a run—I like to write when I'm not thinking too much yet. Most important for proper headspace is minimizing distraction directly before I begin. I have a hard time getting into a story or voice if I've been looking at a to-do list or getting lost on the internet.

JM: Undoubtedly, many readers will be searching for the metaphoric meaning of the fish, and yet I think you play a little coy with them. There are plenty of leads for readers to follow, especially if you believe the fish have something to do with her anxiety. Could the fish symbolize her uneasiness with growing up—a sort of coming of age manifestation? Or maybe they have to do with her unbalanced relationship with Jack? Perhaps the fish are more foreboding—and relate more to the father's fears of the end of the world? But the line, "he thinks the fish have something singular to say" seems meta in dispelling the reader's search for answers. This line came through revision, and I thought it was a rather genius way to make intentional what previously seemed to be a chaotic—or at least, not unified and *singular*—theme.

JPZ: Yeah, I think the editing helped me to clarify a bit without feeling didactic. I do really want readers to be able to have their own understanding of the fish, probably because that is how I like to be a reader. Also, these fish are constantly shifting: they mean a different thing to the narrator in the earlier part of the story than they do by the end.

JM: The meaning of the premise itself—the fish—is evolving. You don't often see symbols and meaning that evolves, at least not in short fiction. I think of the color green in Updike's *Rabbit Tetralogy*, which shifts over the course of four novels from representing youth and opportunity to regret and loss. What do you think evolving meanings adds to the story? What do you love about readers having "their own understanding," which may be different from the character's or the author's understanding?

JPZ: I've never read the *Rabbit* books, but I like that idea of green's meaning shifting as the character ages. I hope the evolving meanings in my story add to a sense of being in time with the protagonist, who is trying to understand the fish from the ground floor of lived experience.

As for readers having their own understanding—everyone is all the time, right? Like even if you read something where there's An Answer for what some metaphor represents, your associations with the Answer are different than mine. So I guess I enjoy fiction that opens more space for the inevitable *different read*. When a reader has to work for their own interpretation it's more like a conversation, not like an authority delivering information. I tend to remember things better when I discover them via conversation, either spoken or via reading or making. Maybe that's why I'm drawn to fiction that makes me grapple a bit.

JM: I quite like a few craft moves in this piece. Particularly, there's a paragraph near the end where she addresses the bullets as a potential solution to her problem. That sentence is followed by a very long paragraph. The lengthy paragraph immediately following this concerning thought increases the reader's sense of dread and anxiety. There was also a good bit of discussion during revisions with us about how long all of the paragraphs should be. When the story came to us, there were less paragraph breaks. How did you settle where you did? Talk to me on a craft-level about these decisions.

JPZ: Conversation with you about paragraph length was actually quite eye-opening for me, like something I hadn't noticed I wasn't seeing. I think a lot about sentence length and often read things aloud as I go to hear cadence and pacing, but I wasn't thinking much about how paragraph length can also inform rhythm or make things funny or suspenseful. I was being quite myopic in how I looked at the length of things! I ended up making some paragraph decisions in the way that I make sentence decisions—because of the sound and even a visual element.

JM: The ending of the story takes an even more severe turn towards the surreal. Our protagonist literally steels herself against her rising anxiety (which could be coming from her family, her boyfriend, the act of growing up, etc.) by coating her insides with bullets. Could you talk a little about the ending?

JPZ: The ending was another thing that I came to via writing and then edited into something more solid when I understood it better. I think of the interior armoring not as being a guard against anxiety but as allowing for a choice of when and how to share herself. I saw this scene very visually and like it was necessary—writing it I had some images of *Rosemary's Baby* in my head, the part where Mia Farrow is stuffing raw meat in her mouth to feed the demon baby she's growing inside her. My narrator is similarly compelled in this moment, but she's feeding herself. I have a visual art practice which I'm often more concentrated on than writing, and this image of the interior bullet-skin is like something I'd like to make a drawing of but could actually explain better in words than images.

JM: There were a few points at which I pushed you for more sentence variety in the critique, but often times I left it alone. As an editor, my mind screams at sentence structure repetition, and yet I have to quiet my typical impulse, because it really does work in this story. The repetitive sentence structures have a droning, claustrophobic quality that makes sense here and yet so often doesn't work or feels amateurish in other submissions. Could you talk a little about the intentionality here?

JPZ: Well, I'm happy that you found a claustrophobic quality here—I wanted some sense of confinement for sure. Confinement seems like one element of teenagehood to me, a feeling of being contained in your body or in your parents' house and a sense that this will be forever, not just temporary. I think I started finding some of this tone as I described the pemmican, and then I embraced that pacing as the narrator's voice.

JM: You mentioned earlier that you didn't think much about the paragraph size and pacing when you were writing, yet it's pretty clear you thought about the structuring a good bit in other ways. For instance, the story is broken up into sections, usually only lasting around half a page each. There isn't enough distinction between sections to say the story is told in vignettes (they're all still very temporally connected), though at a glance the paragraphing would suggest a story told in vignettes. Can you talk to me about this decision and other structuring decisions you made while drafting and redrafting? What does this structure add to the story?

JPZ: I think I make a lot of decisions in relation to language and sound—some of the paragraph breaks were made because I wanted to give space to the line before the new paragraph. The breaks are a bit like breathing space because even though I like the sense of claustrophobia we were talking about, it can be tiring without a rest. Breaks allow both ideas and sound to resonate. If you make a drawing only with heavy lines, you're not going to feel the weight of a shape the same way you might if the line quality alternated between heavy and light. Without variety it might look like clip art or pure decoration. I like clip art and pure decoration, but I *really* like them in contrast with something else. So writing heavy, dense scenes, I make breaks when it seems like breathing space is necessary to aid the preceding paragraph, in the mode of a punchline making a joke.

JM: What other mediums and genres have influenced your writing? Are there any specific creators who have been influential to "Neon Fish" specifically?

JPZ: I remember reading Carmen Maria Machado's *Her Body and Other Parties* around the time I started this and being bowled over by her writing and how deeply she commits to her conceits. Samantha Hunt's book *The Dark Dark* is a short story collection I love and though I read her for the first time after I wrote "Neon Fish," that's a book I've thought about while editing. She has this internal mirroring within the collection where she begins with one disorienting story with doubling characters and then ends the collection with a different version/potential of the same story. Both stories stand on their own, but they also make a porous envelope for the book and seem to say something about stories having weight because of their ability to shift, not because of something fixed and precious. I think Hunt's collection is very generous to writers while maintaining such strong and inimitable presence. Visually, I imagine some of the Chicago Imagists were on my mind, like Christina Ramberg or Suellen Rocca. Christina Ramberg would begin with images from comics or fashion illustration, usually centered around hair and lingerie, and then crop things so they were both foreboding and familiar. Her paintings tend to be claustrophobic, but her drawings were what I was looking at and they have a sentence-like feeling to them because the same general form will get repeated like text.

Also I do love the whole old horror and psychosexual thriller genre. Recently I've been rewatching some of these movies thinking about arcs, but when I wrote this I was probably just watching them and letting some of that suspense and anxiety absorb under my skin.

JM: Thank you so much for speaking with me, Johanna. Is there anything else you'd like to share with our readers as we close out this interview?

JPZ: I think that's it, just thanks again for helping me bring my story out in the world.

BURNING IMAGE

Vincent Panella

TRAVIS

He eased the pickup down the tractor path and parked along the brook where he sat on the roots of a tree growing on the bank. They called it The Spider Tree because half the roots extended over the water before turning down into the sandy bottom. He'd sat on them as a child and later on when he needed to be alone. When they lived farther up the Branch, Malvina would walk him down here with Caleb in the backpack and she'd nurse Caleb while he bounced on the roots and teased the water with his feet. When they were old enough to fish she showed them how to push a worm over a hook and up the shank. Half the worm would hang down for the fish to suck and you had to wait before pulling up so the fish would take the hanging part and then the hook. In the spring they'd catch baby trout the size of the fingers he imagined tracing circles on Julia's belly ever since that day she came out in a bathing suit.

The tree roots still held when he bounced up and down, but today the usual respite provided by childhood memories was interrupted by the roar of a motor as a truck sped by on the high road with its cab light spinning, a first responder for sure. The sight of the truck as a consequence for what he'd done caused him to bounce harder, and now a town pumper appeared with a honking siren that struck him like a physical blow and soon they'd come from other towns with more pumpers and EMT trucks and the volunteers in slickers and breathing tanks and helmets. They almost never arrived early enough to save anything and by the time they found water they might as well have pissed on the flames, and even though Julia had a pond, the barn was probably lost. He'd been an idiot to believe her, mistaken to think he was more than he was, not just paid help but somebody to fill a gap in her life.

The fire didn't have to be set either because hay smoldered by itself especially when baled a little green and stored under the roof he'd tried to fix. You didn't need to be a professional firebug to fool Ted Scofield, just push a twine aside and jam a pry bar into a bale with spaces between the weed stems and do this while she was out with Betty Ridell in their boots and riding crops like back in England. Drop a match in there and let the stems catch and burn some hair off your arm where Ted would never think of looking, then close the bale because you're not really sure what you want. If it catches it catches, so maybe if they hooked up to the pond right away he wouldn't have this feeling of his insides being ripped out like knotted rope.

He knew about her before they met. He was running the baler when she came galloping along the Branch Road on that gray Arabian with its tail up like a flag and her own pony tail flying behind so the whole outfit looked like two horses, one on top of the other. She'd come up from New York with the gray and then took a rescue horse from that pervert who moved down from Maine. So now she had two horses and a place on Newfane Hill that needed fixing up. She would need hay and help and he imagined a place for himself even before they exchanged a word. When she stopped and tried to wave him down he figured she wanted hay, but she'd have to see Malvina for that and he didn't stop or even wave back because he didn't want to seem too eager. So after she spoke to Malvina he showed up at her place in the dump truck.

He honked the horn and when she didn't appear he got out and looked around. The barn roof sagged on one side and a sign on the door said, Forest Park Stables, Ride at Your Own Risk. The horses were nosing wisps of hay inside the pen. One was the gray and the other, smaller and white, was the rescue horse, showing ribs and hanging back. He leaned over the fence and whistled and the horses stepped up, the gray first, the white a little spooked until he whistled again and they both came up and nudged for a treat so he let them smell the sweat on the inside of his cap, and when they began to nibble at the cap he pulled it away. He called out, "Hello in there!" and when nobody answered he went back and unlocked the release bar. One pull and the bales would fall and the rest would be her problem.

"I'm coming and don't dump that hay!"

She appeared at the door in a two-piece bathing suit, her skin wet as if she'd just been swimming and he realized about the pond behind the house. She was skinny and so white her skin looked transparent. Older for sure and a little spooky like that white horse as if they were images of each other, not young like she looked that day with her pony tail flying, not exactly blonde like he thought but a kind of white he didn't have a name for. Not ashamed either to come out in a bathing suit and with a rack of stomach muscles above the bottom piece. When she stepped into the sunlight his eye fell upon a curl of lemon colored hair spun around her navel before plunging straight down. The sight roiled him for its brazen display and the weakness he felt before a female trick so aggressive that he was tempted to just dump the bales and go home. He'd tell Caleb what he'd seen and Malvina could come for the check.

She signed for him to wait, then went back inside and reappeared in jeans and a loose tee shirt covering that yellowish swirl that continued to register as if time had stopped from the moment she appeared. She held out a bag of potato chips.

"Take some, you need salt on a hot day."

He ate the chips one at a time so they wouldn't break up. Something here was beyond his expectations. She was extra friendly with the chips and the open way she presented herself. Rubbing his chin, he realized he hadn't shaved and that bits of chaff stuck to his neck and arms from loading the truck.

"You need water too," she said. "Throwing bales around is hard work."

She came back with a jar of ice water. He drank slowly, not wanting to spill it and betray the hope for something that might happen in the future. Finished drinking, he gave back the jar then returned to the rear of the truck and gripped the release.

"Can you back up to the barn?" She gestured toward a hay elevator. "Then we can get the bales upstairs. Is your help included?"

"Hay won't keep dry under a roof like that."

"I can cover it later. Can the two of us do it? Is that extra? I'll pay you extra. What do you get an hour?"

He said, "I don't know," and that was the truth. What was he worth? His only measure was the road crew job he'd lost, minimum wage for the first year.

"If you have another job I'll pay what they pay. How's that?"

"My job right now is haying."

"So how much do you want?"

"Just pay me whatever."

She swung open the gate and he backed up, realizing he could have asked for a definite amount, but this way might be better. He stopped at the elevator and said, "Let's get it done."

They sent a dozen bales up to the second floor then carried them to the far end of the barn where the roof was in better shape even though daylight still showed between the shingles. They worked in the heat and barn dust until the job was done and it was nearly five o'clock when she brought out a checkbook and two bottles of Switchback.

"It's beer thirty," she said. "You know about that, don't you?"

She might have asked the meaning of bacon and eggs. This was another sign, and as she popped open the bottles he studied her thin arms wrinkled at the elbows and biceps the size of baseballs. That she looked both old and young only fed his imagination. Old for experience, old for doing strange things down in New York or up on Grimes Hill with that guy from Maine. Why else would she come out like that with her belly in the sun? Old but strong, and for the last two hours she'd matched him bale for bale and never slacked off. She told him the arm strength came from holding back horses and mucking stalls in a New York stable.

"Is that where the sign on the barn comes from?"

"Three years down there until they went out of business. That's where I got the Arabian."

"A horse like that costs quite a bit."

"That's Candy, she's my sweetie, and let's just say she wasn't cheap."

"How about the white one?"

"Loki's an Icelandic, and I got him from a man who couldn't afford to feed him."

"You know what happened with him."

"What they found has nothing to do with a horse he couldn't feed."

"The sheriff was up there."

"But the stuff wasn't his. He claimed somebody else left it on his property."

"Whatever."

"That's right, whatever. Let's just say neither one of these animals were cheap."

He interpreted the remark as an invitation to secrets she would reveal if things worked out, and with the chips and the beer and the bathing suit and what she might have paid for the horses—something other than money—it wasn't so crazy to imagine that his fingers like those quivering trout pulled from the brook might trace that golden swirl to its destination. And drinking beer with her, lifting the bottles together as they'd lifted the bales, confident from an alcoholic push, he figured that even he, Travis Forrett, unemployed and broke and without her education, just might work his way into a job and even a home and something he'd never had before; and he imagined his fingers alive on her belly and his body flecked with chaff tangled with hers in ways she would direct just as she convinced him to help with the bales.

His eye traveled to the house with missing clapboards and a barn door dangling on loose hinges, and from there to a fancy pickup and horse trailer.

"You've got a nice place here," he offered.

"It needs work."

Pointing at the truck and trailer with his beer he said, "That's a pretty fancy rig."

"I worked for that."

"I never said you didn't."

"But maybe you were thinking I have money because I'm from New York as if you want to hold it against me."

"I wasn't thinking that. I didn't mean anything."

"Just to clear things up, I worked down there full-time and saved up my money. Everything you see here I paid for and I'm easy to get along with. Tell me how much to write the check for."

"Just the bales."

"How about your labor?"

"You bought me a beer."

"I can't do that, you don't work for free. Besides that, we already agreed to pay you. Will you take minimum wage?"

"No problem."

"I could use some help around here. What kind of work do you do?"

"Just about anything."

"Can you fix that roof?"

"I can try."

JULIA

She should have listened to her horse friend, Betty, who told her all about the Forretts, how they hayed every field along the Branch, Travis and Caleb, Robert the father, and the mother, a big woman named Malvina who could throw two bales at a time onto the flatbed. The family lived in a sugar house when the boys were born and the story ran that Robert saw the chimney plugged with creosote and they decided not to clean it out. So after the house burned down they collected insurance and built a bigger place up in Wardsboro. The boys were like night and day, the young one had a steady job but the older one never settled. He'd been fired from the road crew after swinging a shovel at Ted Scofield and his fist fights with Robert during haying season were as perennial as the hay they cut and sold. There wasn't a summer when Travis and his father didn't get into it with Robert calling him lazy for daydreaming and it was lucky Malvina was there to pull them apart at least until the next cutting. Betty said they were basically good people and that everybody had stories about those old Vermont families, hinting they were all inbred and a little bit off.

She set these rumors aside because Travis was a young man she could use, simple as that. He seemed like a hard enough worker. She'd been riding on the Branch when she heard the clack-clack of the baler and he appeared further out in the field. Heat shimmered over the tractor canopy as the machine threw out compact bales which tottered and then fell over and lay in yellow-green blocks and she imagined her name on each one. Attentive to his work, Travis took off his cap and ran one hand through his hair to let the breeze cool him off, looking back to check the baler and forward to keep straight along the windrows. He never noticed her.

Unsure of himself with the chips and the ice water, so maybe a little slow when it came to asserting himself, but he was also a man without a job who would appreciate the work and settle for minimum wage which was all she could afford. She'd been watching from inside when he gave the horses his cap to sniff. He'd be gentle with them and that was important. But why did he ignore her that day when he was running the baler? Maybe he didn't stop because he resented people like her because he thought they had money, which she had, but that didn't mean she was rich. Okay, she had enough for the rest of her life but only if she was careful. And maybe she was a little testy about her background and a little too bold when she came out in the bathing suit just to show him she wasn't some Girl Scout. What the hell, she didn't have much left anyway. It was a hot day and she'd taken a dip and didn't want to keep him waiting because he might dump the bales and leave. Then with the chips and the beer thirty she wanted to show him she was just a regular person. How could she know that a few beer thirties later he would stare into his Switchback bottle for the words he needed and say, "That first day," and stop dead.

"That first day what?"

"What you showed me when I brought the hay."

"In my bathing suit?"

"More or less."

"I'm just a stick."

"You were more than that."

"And therefore?"

"What do you think?

"I think you're way out of line, that's what I think."

So was it her own fault for tempting him? Her own fault for not listening to Betty? Her own fault that a fire hose was stuck in her pond and smoke was pouring from the barn? A fireman shouted, "That hay's about to catch!" and with one giant breath the green smoke turned to flame and the fire like a starving beast began chewing its way through a roof repaired over the years with asphalt over cedar and just lately the tar Travis had spread but apparently in the wrong places. So much for the barn.

The fire would cost her the barn and a helper she'd need to replace, not so easy when she couldn't afford as much as Betty, whose man drove a truck bristling with rakes and shovels and packed with every power tool known to man. She looked over the volunteers in their slickers and breathing tanks and tried to find needy faces under their helmets. Would any of them work for what she could afford to pay? And here was Ted Scofield—fire chief and road foreman—asking if Travis had been in the barn and she said yes because she'd left him to shovel out sawdust while she rode with Betty. When Ted suggested that a leaking roof might have wet the hay and caused it to "combust" she told him Travis had repaired the roof and he said, "Well that's the problem right there you've got people with a history and why isn't he here right now he must have something to hide."

MALVINA

The dump truck was too wide for the tractor path so she parked on the road then slid off the seat. She stepped carefully down into the sunken field, setting her foot each time before transferring her weight, minimizing the back pain that was only relieved by cortisone shots the doctor was reluctant to continue.

Through the uncut brush along the brook she saw him at The Spider Tree doubled over in pain. The memory of their old innocence choked her speechless when set against the scene at Julia's house. She'd just been there, and as the volunteers poured water through the second floor windows the popping sound from the hay and the smell of burning shingles cut right through her. Julia was standing in a small crowd of onlookers sobbing into a tissue with Betty Ridell hugging her by the shoulder. Then Ted Scofield came over with sweat running down his face and asked, Where's your son? Where's Travis? If only she could turn it all back. How she'd been young and slender, how life was hard but easier, how she could mow a lawn with one of them in the backpack, walk the mile from the sugar house to the brook and watch Travis ride the tree roots like a hobby horse. She could have done more with him, made him talk for example.

Once on level ground beyond the uncut brush the walking was easier. Robert had mowed this part, but it wasn't worth haying, not with carpets of cut goldenrod among the ferns and bedstraw. The cows wouldn't eat it and no sense bringing down the rake and baler because there was plenty of hay from the other fields along the Branch. The people who owned this little field never came up. The Forretts had mowed it for two generations as part of the haying rights to the ten acres across the road, a thousand bales there and they might get five dollars a bale. That was a big part of their cash flow. To hay the big field you had to mow the little field so it wouldn't grow over with weed trees. Fair enough. Haying was better than owning, you kept the hay and paid no taxes.

So now he was bouncing on the roots like a kid. What to do with him, thirty-eight years old and fired from the road crew after he got into it with Ted Scofield, who'd call the state inspectors for sure. Then what? Jail for arson? A grown man with no job and Julia his only source of income and now he'd messed that up. He'd been a problem from the start, two weeks late, hung in her stomach like lead and almost toppled her forward when she walked. That was when her back pain started along with other complications she didn't like to think about. When her water broke he still wouldn't come out, but when he did she was almost split wide open. A ten-pound boy who wouldn't take her milk and they had to get formula from the Drop-In Center. Wouldn't talk until he was three and she thought there was something wrong with him. Never at peace when he grew up, not like Caleb who would have nursed until the grave. He'd been this way since high school, scratches on his arms he said were from the cat, then one day she saw one a good six-inches long and close to a vein. That's no damn cat, that's for crazy kids, why did you do it? I don't know. She took him to a counselor but he wouldn't talk to her either. Was somebody supposed to open his head and look inside?

He'd always been vulnerable, and when offended drew into his shell and punished himself. He only opened up to Caleb—who reported to her—telling her what Julia had shown him, as if any woman who did that didn't know what she was doing. Caleb said Travis was so excited you'd think he'd seen a wonder of the world. Caleb was the smart one, he saw through it and told her everything.

"He thinks there's a reason she showed him."

"So do I."

"She was up there with that guy from Maine, and down in New York too."

"So he thinks she did something for those horses."

"And she might do something for him."

"She liked that he worked cheap, that's what she liked."

No need to stick around the fire after telling Julia she was sorry about the barn, a half-truth, the other half related to the wages of sin. Wages alright. Betty gave the eye sign for her to leave, and why watch a burning barn when Ted Scofield had the Forrett's history written all over his face? He'd been there years back with that sugar house burning from the top down, the cupola spitting hunks of red hot creosote like there was a volcano inside and the old cedar shingles curled up with age and crying Welcome to the flames. The old place was smaller than a trailer. For septic they dug a hole and filled it with stone. When it smelled bad Robert poured in a few gallons of muriatic acid that burned out the spaces between the stones and a nose-hurting smoke arose like some angry genie down there with a message. Which was to get the hell out of there because you can't have two boys into their teens sleeping in the same bed and going outside to pee every morning. It wasn't natural and that had an effect on Travis she couldn't explain.

Walking was easy on the level part, the weeds already drying under new growth, the near transparent top layer of ferns yet to surrender their moisture. Even with a hayed field, a good fire every so often burned out the chaff and weed seeds and added lime in the ash, like rebirth, like something almost religious. Burn this field in the fall and you'll get some hay next summer. Burn a barn and you'll get a better one from the insurance, everybody knew that. So maybe there was an upside.

Now there would be gossip to add to what she already knew, all the news on the Branch and up in Wardsboro. Did Travis do it or not? They'd never be that specific. Julia's barn was a fire waiting to happen, case closed. So there in the Price Chopper parking lot standing at their four-wheelers she chatted with Betty and certain women who liked to talk as much as she did. She knew the couples having trouble, the kids who were wards of the state, the men both weak and strong. She and her friends would look up to the sky or off in another direction as if the scandalous talk came from somewhere else. After all they minded their own business. Guess who's cutting every tree on his land for firewood. That's all he knows how to do and he doesn't have enough driveways to plow because he pushes the snow right up against your garage. The daughter took off, the one with so many piercings she looked like a Christmas tree not only on her face but places too private to mention. Can you imagine people who want to hurt themselves? Left the kid with the father who never helped out anyway and nobody can find her and in a way she can't be blamed.

She knew what they said about her too, about the Forretts— even though she herself wasn't a Forrett—about their old place with a chimney fire from a family burning wood all their lives who knew better. Well it was true and that house fire waiting to happen wasn't much different than hay bales under a poorly repaired roof. Behind her back they would say that she and Robert had set an example, that the apple didn't fall very far.

Maybe Julia did go up there and do more than buy that rescue horse. Maybe they did watch porno together and do what they saw on the computer. He was a strange one, no job—which meant he sold drugs—one of those braided beards hanging from his chin with a little bow at the end, lived in two trailers nailed together as one unit so he wouldn't violate the zoning. Last spring a turkey hunter found his backpack in a hollow tree stuffed with magazines and videos and who knows what else. He fessed up and the sheriff let him go because none of it was kiddie. What people did these days. All this online business. A few years back Robert met some slut online and came home with STDs and she bore with that. She'd seen it all on his computer before she threw it out and before they all got arrested, women with boobs like pillows and all shaved between the legs. Next thing you know they'd shave their heads too, then men and women would all look the same and you had to see close up to tell the difference. That was how the world was going, all of it sicker than shit. She almost threw up when she saw what Robert had been looking at and maybe Travis and Caleb too. If she hadn't thrown the computer in the landfill after taking a hand sledge to it just in case, he might be in jail because there could have been little girls on it. She wouldn't put it past him.

What was it coming to? How would they get along, what with Robert driving a gravel truck part-time, the best he could do, paid in cash, no social security? Caleb was lucky enough to work for a tree service. He was small and a good climber, but how long before he fell off a pine or cut off his leg with a chain saw? Then what? Unemployment? Food stamps? They had those already, but Robert didn't know it. Now their only cash flow would be from hay because Travis and Julia were finished.

So there was Travis bouncing on the roots like a little kid. She approached through the soft grass, aware of a humming noise coming out of him with each spider bounce as if the roots expelled sound from his lungs. The poor fool was a barrel of hurt with his imagination run wild.

"What did you do to that woman?"

"Nothing."

"What did she do then?"

"Nothing."

"Don't lie. Do you think I don't know what she showed you?"

"I didn't see anything."

"Don't try to fool me. What did you do to her?"

"Nothing."

"Did you touch her?"

"I didn't touch her."

"And you think Ted Scofield isn't going to ask you some questions after that hay lit up? And what made you think...."

She didn't need to finish the thought. He was bouncing, off somewhere.

"You're going to break those roots, then you'll be sorrier than you already are."

THE EAR THAT NEGOTIATES, OR, THERE WILL ALWAYS BE A LINE
A Conversation with Vincent Panella

Stephen Hundley: Hi, Vincent, and welcome to the pages of *Driftwood*. Our editors were drawn to the specificity of place, language, and vocation in "Burning Image," set in the hayfields and family farms of Vermont. We knew immediately that this was a singular story, capable of transporting readers to a stylized, emotionally tortured space as Travis struggles with his choice to burn down the barn and the rest of the community deals with the consequences.

To get us started, what parts of Vermont or New England farm and field culture were essential to you while writing this story, which is so deeply set in that place?

Vincent Panella: I grew up in Queens and came to Vermont in the mid-seventies after having spent six years in the Midwest. Vermont is a mountainous state and much of the flat land tends to be in the valleys. I live in one these valleys where the small fields are flat enough for crops, and since the land tends to be poor, the main crop is hay. Those who own these fields, sometimes newer arrivals, will surrender the haying rights to keep the land open. Usually families who've lived here for generations have hayed the fields because they have the equipment needed to cut and bale the hay and have made agreements with the land owners. The hay can be used for their own small farming operations, or put out for sale. Hay is often a major source of income where the soil is poor and the season too short to grow anything else. Over the years I have watched the fields being mowed and hayed, and have come to know the families who work for those who often have more wealth and education.

SH: The layering of information and scene in "Burning Image" produces a cinematic effect. Was this triptych structure always the plan? How did you arrive at this ordering of the events?

VP: I write from character and let the story find its way. I originally conceived "Burning Image" as Julia's story and wrote long passages about her horse life in New York City. I threw out much of that and focused on the scene where she sees Travis on the hay baler and entertains the possibility of buying the hay he's baling. I then wrote the same scene from Travis's point of view, and how he's intimidated by the sight of her galloping on the fancy Arabian horse. This allowed me to bring Malvina into his thoughts, and I began to see how the story had three main characters.

It seemed natural to begin the story with Travis, but with Malvina and the spider tree and the image of catching baby trout in the brook as a gateway to the scene in which he delivers the hay and Julia comes out in her bathing suit. So I had three characters and a burning barn as the outer frame of the story. The challenge was to make the story move forward with the barn burning and backward with the Travis and Julia story.

To be more specific about the layering, once I decided on three main characters, Travis had to be first. His resentment of the upper classes comes smack against Julia's machinations. Her section had to come next with the explanation of her behavior and her reasons for leading Travis on.

Then I came to Malvina, who had the widest scope of vision. She was necessarily last in the sequence. She occupies the moral center of the Forrett world. As I was putting the sequence together I thought not only of stories like Rashomon, but of those Renaissance triptychs where the large center piece is the main frame, and the smaller panels are complimentary. So I wanted to duplicate a triptych in a way that writing allows, which is linear.

SH: I can see Malvina as the tie between worlds, and I felt the heft of her authority when she was on the page. I was interested in the social pressure exerted by the locals on the outsiders—specifically in the case of the ostracized man from Maine. There seemed to be a certain moral high ground maintained by the working class over their wealthy neighbors, a way of exercising power and judgement. It made me wonder how much control the long-time Vermonters have over their environment.

VP: Since 1976 I have lived in southern Vermont, probably the most liberal part of the state. The moral high ground occupied by native-born Vermonters over what are called Flatlanders—like myself—leveled off over time as the newcomers split their wood and planted their gardens and learned to negotiate the mud and snow just like everyone else.

In the context of "Burning Image," the person from Maine has triggered Malvina's condemnation by mistreating a horse and mistreating the earth by crowding two structures on a plot of land zoned for one. Coming from outside Vermont, and with non-traditional facial hair, he's a target. The pornography hidden in the woods—luckily not 'kiddie' as Malvina observes—offends her sense of decency, which gives her the high ground. Malvina exhibits a snobbishness rooted in pride of place. The Forretts have also mistreated the earth by pouring muriatic acid into their dry well. I can only lay out this irony for the reader to grapple with. Vermont's harsh climate imposes a living expense that makes people take shortcuts. Between natives and outsiders there will always be a line.

SH: The rumor mill was grinding along behind the scenes in this story. I was fascinated by the community of characters readers are exposed to—one of the strengths of this form. How would you describe the community that "Burning Image" takes place in? How did you find this place?

VP: Before moving to Vermont in 1976, I lived in a rented Iowa farmhouse and came to know the local people, and to witness farming in a place where the land was richer and the growing seasons longer. Much of that world was easily transferred to Vermont. I moved here after the farmhouse I was renting was sold to a man who wanted a hobby farm. As in Vermont, he would hire the locals to work his land.

Vermont is a poor state, and while the sixties and seventies witnessed an influx of anti-war types, often from cities, families like the Forretts remain. Vermonters are one with the land. They make their way by plowing snow, mowing lawns and fields, logging, selling firewood, hay, and maple syrup. Those who own backhoes and exca-

work. I am a character-driven writer and can only do my best work if I can also deliver a strong sense of time and especially place. This is why some of my other work deals with Italy and Italian-Americans, yet even within that locus I have managed to incorporate my experience with rural life.

SH: I was struck by the dialogue in this story, which I found textured and capable of being curt, coy, and devious while still maintaining realism. Is this style of character speech characteristic of your work, or was this an experiment?

VP: This is characteristic of my work. Dialog and the rhythms of speech are voices in my inner ear. I try to use dialog to define character and to push the story forward. It has to count.

SH: What or who has influenced your inner ear, and do you express this lyric awareness in any other mediums?

VP: That inner ear is the sum of myself, the ear that negotiates language and listens to characters and creates stories from what it hears. The need to tell stories is a product of my total experience, and getting to the source of all this would also require a list of writers and artists too numerous to mention. I spoke before about the public library and a memoir about the origins of my family in southern Italy. This foundation, American and Mediterranean, has determined what and how I write, and more importantly, why I write.

I grew up in a house without books, where the Sicilian and Neapolitan dialects were languages I couldn't understand and didn't want to learn, not then anyway. This background gave me the advantage of a double perspective so important for a writer. There were two outsides to look in from, and as a way of engaging life and being 'American' I had to not only learn but to master English. And so I became a reader. This love of English and history drove me to the great story tellers beginning with Homer and Herodotus, and moving on to the usual suspects, Conrad, Hemingway, Joyce, Faulkner, Italians like Sciascia and Pasolini in translation. This mix gave me the voice I strive for and which I can only describe as an epic voice, a voice that tells a story from deep down, a voice colored by New York Jewish and Italian rhythms and exemplified notably by Lenny Bruce, whose combination of high and low diction and rapid flow I find particularly affecting.

Writing is my only medium, stories, longer works, an occasional play—one recently performed in local theater. For a few years I wrote for a now defunct site called Vermont Views. These were poems, memories, flash fictions, anecdotes from my bartending life in upstate New York, my short career as a news reporter in Dubuque, Iowa, and my longer career as a writing instructor at Vermont Law School. Publishing online provided me with small victories while I was writing longer pieces.

SH: Thank you for giving us a peek under the hood of this textured, driving story. Are you able to speak to or direct our readers to any other projects of yours, either forthcoming or still in the works?

VP: I have nothing forthcoming right now except the story to appear in *Driftwood Press*. I am busy with stories in-progress and a longer work. I am trying to find publishers for the aforementioned novel and story collection. My web site, vincentpanella.com, is the best place to fill out the picture I have created here. Thank you for this opportunity to talk about my work.

MŌDOR

Izzy Buck

Gren leads the way around the snake nest and deeper into the swamp, water bubbling as they weave through the alder carr and race the setting sun. They must reach home before dark to start the fire. Each night, Gren and Ma wear its smoke like a cloak, keeping the bugs off their skin and out of their ears. Before, the villagers never lingered in the swamp's darkness, the bugs hungry and vicious for their blood. Now, Gren and Ma wade through the water, each movement slow and syrupy through the humid air. Reeds tickle Ma's waist as they reach the small clearing in the middle of the swamp: their home.

Gren works carefully, sharpening his spear on a stone as Ma begins the fire. Her son's hands are scabbed and chapped: not well-watered like the cattails or the swamp grass. Hands unfamiliar to a boy of barely seventeen summers. Ma looks down at her hands as she tends the fire; they're the same. Cracked and bloody. Beggar's hands.

"They've grown," Gren grunts between heavy swings on the rock.

"Oh?"

"Hired an outsider. There are at least fifty new men."

"We've been making an impact."

Gren smiles slightly. "Yes, I guess we have."

The first men they captured died slowly. Tied up with coarse rope like game, Gren had dragged their bodies from the Great Hall, deep into the charred remains of the abandoned village. Blood and dirt melded into a black muck, coating the mens' entire bodies. Initially, Ma had been startled by their wounds: a perforated shoulder, a blood-soaked brow. Gren had never been one for violence, often abandoning the village hunts as soon as duty allowed. Finding excuses to miss his sister skin and gut the game. Never watching Ma roast the animals. Her sweet, gentle boy.

Now, with raw knuckles and tendons bursting from his forearms, Gren stared down at the men. Eyes hard. The pair shouted syllables that meant nothing to Ma or her sweet boy. Were they threats? Pleas? Swears? Pressure built in Ma's chest with each sound, expanding her ribs and threatening to crack the bones. Suddenly, without thought, she grabbed a stone from the ground and brought it down hard on one man's skull. Crack. Blood splattered on her face, but she kept going, his screams becoming more distant with each blow. His partner kicked away, shrieking like a wounded animal, scooting desperately through the dirt with tied limbs. Gren turned to the side and retched.

Ma buried the men in all their glory: golden rings on fat knuckles, woven shirts on sweaty chests, long pendants around necks. She never touched their treasures, for they belonged in the ground. Down, down, down, in the earth from which they were stolen. These pale ghosts of men knew only how to steal. How to take. She buried them by rotting stumps and crispy grass. By stones skinned of moss during the fires and carcasses of animals too slow to escape the destruction. An offering of sorts: to the forest and her creatures, she presented the men who had killed.

———————

Ma watches the fire as the sky trades its pink hues for black. As she looks at her boy sitting across from her, she can't help but notice the damage. Gren's body is stamped with reminders of the raiders. A long mark on his bicep. A crooked third toe. The most prominent: his left eye draped in deep purple scar tissue. Gren notices Ma's gaze and unwraps a cloth from around his belt. Placing it over his eye, he begins to knot it behind his ear. Ma reaches out in protest.

"Let it breathe," she says.

Gren's mouth forms firm lines on his face.

"I don't want you to look at it."

Truthfully, Ma doesn't want to look at the wound. Gren's eyelid was thoroughly ravaged by the burn: flesh peeling and unhallowed. When Gren was born, he had been soft and pink, chin round and cheeks plump. Now, strife had plastered Gren's skin to his skull, bringing out the sharpness of his jaw and hollowness of his cheeks. Aging years in a matter of months.

Ma makes herself meet Gren's good eye with gentleness: "It will heal cleaner this way."

He nods, dropping the stained cloth to the ground. It lands next to a troupe of ants struggling to carry the sunken body of a cicada. Gren stops and watches them work. A straggler creeps up his fingers and over his knuckles to keep up, Gren holding still until it has crossed.

Her sweet boy.

Her flesh and blood.

Ma smiles and wants to touch his cheek, but Gren stands. There is work to be done.

———

When the raiders built the Great Hall, the trees fell and the forest screamed. Polished silver hatches cut into the trees, hacking out bits of woody flesh until the majestic beings could no longer stand. As they plummeted to the dirt, birds fled their branches and rodents abandoned their high reaching homes, their descent celebrated with cheers from the raiders. Hundreds of trees were hauled away with ropes and refined into the hall. Desecrated with gold. Discolored with jewels. The hall stood ugly against the ruins of the forest.

After the fire and the terror, Ma had insisted on burying the dead. She stood in the center of their smoldering village and watched her daughter's blood drool into the dirt. Bodies scattered like falling trees: bodies of sisters and brothers she had been born alongside in the birthing tent, of babes she had watched age alongside her two children. She couldn't look away from their flesh branded with the bootprints of the raiders, trampled as if they were nothing more than dirt. Ma's eyes were stuck on the bodies, gazing inside: at their insides. She could see the splintered ribs poking through Onela's chest like yearning tree branches. The innards hanging lazily out of Wig's open abdomen. The pulpy muscle of Theo's skinned thighs.

Falling to her knees next to her daughter, Ma released a

throat-burning scream. She screamed and screamed and screamed until Gren ran over and held her firmly. The only survivors. Pressure flooded Ma's heart as she looped her fingers through her hair and pulled hard with each sob, begging for an explanation for the destruction. For a reason for the carnage. She couldn't bear to look at the blood or the wasteland that was once her village, that was once her home.

Gren untangled Ma's fingers from her hair and pressed her palms to the earth, eyes steady despite their weeping. His tears were silent and strong as they cut through the grime on his skin.

"They live on," he said. "In the earth."

Ma knew that her brethren would become new trees and flowers and wildlife, but she wasn't satisfied. She could have fought harder. Flailed harder against the grasp of the bandit as he pulled Halga away. Kicked his metal-clad chest with more force. The pain had been sharp when her bare foot collided with the shell, but she could have kicked again. The raider had laughed when her toes crumbled against him, cutting Halga's throat so quickly that Ma only saw her daughter fall to the dirt, clutching her neck. Ma had wanted to peel back the plate of metal and decimate the delicate flesh inside. But instead, the raider stabbed Ma's stomach with his sword and left before she even hit the ground.

As Ma lay unmoving in the mud, she focused on Halga's desperate fingers and gurgling breaths. Her eyes wide with a type of fear Ma had never seen. She reached out with shaking fingertips to her daughter, stretching until her muscles threatened to tear from the effort.

Just out of reach.

Ma felt heavy as the mud clung to her hair and her skin, pressing her deeper into the earth as the gurgling ceased: Halga's last breath.

Vision blurry from tears and blood loss, Ma watched the trees and her people fall. Her body throbbed as her blood trickled into the ground. She felt her roots growing and the world becoming small behind her eyes until there was nothing left.

It took Ma and Gren three hard days to bury the bodies. They pierced the earth with loose stones and charred pieces of wood that had survived the burning, but they mostly used their hands. Hands washed in the lake between burials. Hands that, despite the water, were never clean. Fingers caked in juices from melting flesh. Tired hands, aching from pushing through the dirt to the hidden earth below. From prepping an eternal bed for every relative, friend, and neighbor they had ever known. Broken hands.

"It's time for me to go," Gren says as he stands and surveys the land.

"How many will you bring back this time?"

"I'm not sure. Two. Maybe three."

"I'll be ready."

Ma was always nervous when her boy left. She wasn't afraid to be alone in the swamp; fear for her life had left long ago. She worried for Gren—possible deaths washing across her vision instead of the landscape. She could see Gren on the ground, a group of raiders like a forest around him. They would take turns hacking his flesh, long swords blurring with each swing. Ma could see bloodlust guiding their hands, creating the gashes all over Gren: skin and muscle and nerves curling back to expose white bone. Ma knew that with each attack, she and her boy moved closer to death—their blessings were finite, and each ambush had a cost.

But she knew her sweet boy was strong and smart, his years in the village giving him an advantage on the ruined terrain. These colonizers didn't know the land, nor did they care to learn about the ridges and the rivers. Gren used their ignorance to his advantage, snaring them easily by unscalable cliffs and crushing them with prepositioned boulders, bodies popping loudly under the weight of the rocks. Or, Gren lured them to rivers after the rain, drowning the raiders in the untamable waters, and watching the bloated bodies be taken by the rapids. Gren would often strike down ten or more men during the night, the patrols often ill-equipped to deal with his advances. But Gren knew to take some home for Ma, and those men weren't as lucky.

The killings became easier over time. Ma learned about the body: where to pierce if she wanted the deaths to be quick and where to slice for a slow bleed. She searched each man's face for the raider from that day, a cold desperation taking over each time she spotted Gren trudge up the hill. Each day absent of that face made Ma's rage stronger. Each kill more meaningful.

She spoke softly to the men, knowing they couldn't understand her questions, knowing she would never understand their answers.

She would jam her stone dagger into a beefy shoulder: "Did you find pleasure in killing my daughter?" The man would often cry out. Ma savored the crinkling of skin around the blade, often twisting upon impact. Watching the wound open into something bigger than itself.

"What did it feel like to tear down the forest?" Stone removed quickly, the man would howl as his flesh coated the weapon and was forced into the outside world. Ma would always hold the dagger up to the men. She liked to watch their faces contort at the sight of themselves on the weapon.

The final blow: "Will your gods forgive you? Because ours will not." Ma would plunge the stone into an eye and pull up for the explosion. Flesh and bone splattering on her skin. Over time, Gren learned not to retch. Ma and Gren never touched women or children, focusing their rage on the warriors, on those who had sold themselves to the great-ring giver and builder of that lofty house.

Hrothgar. As his men defaced the land, they chanted the name like a prayer to bless the ruins. Ma and Gren watched his men work, tearing down the trees and their people. Processing the trunks. Building a great mead-hall meant to be a wonder of the world forever: Hrothgar's throne room, the base for the invaders and their stolen treasures. Ma and Gren did not understand the foreigners' tongue, but they knew enough to recognize this name.

Ma waits for Gren's return with light eyelids. She cannot surrender herself fully to sleep when he's gone, content with listening to the sounds of the swamp. She feels secure this way. Ma is still learning how to connect with the swamp's creatures and give back to her new home: eating swamp berries and Basswood buds over game; befriending the squirrels and the slugs instead of consuming them. Hunting men has turned Ma and her sweet boy away from meat.

Ma refuses to enter a new land and kill those who call it home.

Now, as she waits for Gren's return, she listens to the hum of the swamp. A new type of chatter: she is relieved to be surrounded by life again. Her boy always returns before sunrise. Sometimes in the sweetness of dark, sometimes in the blush of daybreak. But he always returns before the sun.

Steady light warms Ma's eyelids as she brushes away the mosquitoes and grabs her spear.

"Just in case," Gren had told her during the first hunt, pressing the spear firmly into her palms: a gift from the trees and etched with his love. She felt more comfortable with the smallness of her sharpened stone, but Gren insisted on the larger weapon. She always kept it near when he was away, in case of ambush. In case of the return of that warrior's leather gloves and armored chest. Hoping she'd never need it but knowing she eventually would.

Ma makes her way quickly through the swamp, ducking under crooked trees with cold bones in the murky water. There's a familiar seizing in her chest as her heart tumbles over itself with each step. She tries to calm it with slow, steady feet, but it continues to race, causing Ma to stop and lean on her spear for support. Forcing herself to fill her lungs completely.

Hidden in the underbrush, her eyes meet the Great Hall: that lofty house. Gold laughing in the sun. But there's something else, something new outside its doors. She squints and sees the haphazard cross made of coarse wood and rough edges. The horizontal piece tips upward, unstable.

She forces her eyes to stop flickering.

His head lolls forward as if he's asleep. Loose and heavy like when he was swaddled many years ago on her back. Long hair now cut in careless tufts. His hair. His beautiful hair that had grown long and strong since his thirteenth summer, marking the beginning of his transition from boy to man. It had been a hot summer, the hottest in Ma's lifetime, but her boy had loved it.

Now, Ma's sweet boy is glistening. Shining in the sun.

Skinless.

His body is deep red: muscles and tendons slowly dripping blood, pooling at his feet like a bloody shadow. He's held in place by his elbows and hands, arms pulled taut on that crooked wood, tightening the threads of his muscles. Elbows and hands pressed hard to the wood, pierced with shining steel. Holding him up. Nailing him down. Skinned: like an animal.

Ma joins the underbrush as it sways slowly in the wind, legs unsteady at the sight before her. She feels the bubbles in her throat before she releases the heat: a scream for her baby. The spear slides out of Ma's hand and she's running, defenseless, to her Gren. In a moment, she is beside him; Gren's bulging eyes loom down at her, the left finally visible without the burnt skin, and she gazes up at the two holes where his nose had been. Fluid splashes on her like rain, sticking to her cheeks and trickling slowly down with her tears. Ma's hands are on him, her fingers plunge deep into muscle and tendons weakened by the morning sun, becoming a part of the horror before her. Flies jump from ripe flesh to Ma and back, entrusting sticky footprints to her skin and incessant buzzing to her ears. Ma's screams match their frequency as she desperately pulls at her boy. She has to get Gren down.

From inside the great hall: footsteps, gathering voices, and clanging. Ma barely hears the noise until the men are surrounding her and the body falls. The moisture is oppressive in the morning air as she tries to lift Gren up. Taking both his arms, she pulls. His left arm slides loose of its socket and she tumbles backward, arm in hand. The group laughs, leaning on their weapons, too humored by the swamp-wench to consider her as a threat. Too fascinated by her dark skin, strange clothes, and foreign tongue to strike her down and stop the show.

Ma's whole body trembles as one man steps forwards: a stranger. She looks up at his blue eyes and they are hungry for the entire world. The stranger reaches toward her and Ma lurches back in the dirt, screaming, crawling, clutching the disembodied arm. She sees the stranger's hands and knows he has done this, immediately recognizing the blood under his nails and in the creases of his palms. They're like her hands—hands that, despite the water, are never clean.

Her vocal cords strain against the power coming from her chest as she releases sounds she never knew were inside her. The stranger steps forward again, and Ma stumbles to her feet, running without looking back. Back through the tall grass and the underbrush until she is splashing through the swamp and the frogs are groaning at the carelessness of her feet.

She falls to her knees: hands, face, and chest stained. She cradles the arm, clutching what is left of her baby. Her sweet, baby boy.

———————

Ma is back in the underbrush before dark. Songs littered with the slamming of mugs and cheers float from the mead-hall and through the wasteland. The raiders celebrate the death of her boy and laud the man who killed him. The ultimate hero. Ma waits until she can only hear the Nightjars cooing before making her way from the underbrush and through the tall grass. Fireflies floating, the light kisses her cheeks as she passes: goodnight, good luck. Her grip tight on the etched staff of her spear, she moves beyond the empty cross and barren ground, entering the Great Hall without a sound. Soon, she is among the raiders. Mead benches pushed to the side, the men lay in drunken slumber. At their heads rest polished timber-battle shields, and on the bench above each man: a towering war helmet, a woven mail shirt, and a great shafted spear. To Ma, all the men look the same with their white skin and golden hair.

Ma is silent, weaving her way through the heavy snores fueled by celebration. Senses dulled from overindulgence and hubris, they believe there is nothing to fear after vanquishing the monster. She looks for the stranger, the one who stole Grendel's skin and cut his hair. The stranger with the hungry eyes. But he is not among the sleepers.

Breathing steady, Ma squats like the bullfrogs of the swamp and looks closely at the face in front of her. He wears weathered leather for skin and light lines around loosely closed eyes. She places a hand gently over his mouth and draws back her other arm. As the spear meets his chest, his eyes fly open and she catches the scream in her hand. He is afraid as he meets death.

The next man dies quietly, never opening his eyes in time to realize his fate.

It's the eighth man who struggles. Kicking over his shield, the timber crashes to the floor and the sound bounces throughout the hall. Ma's breath quickens as the men stir, some slowly, still weighed down by their drunkenness, others jumping to their feet without hesitation. Yelling. The clanging of swords at the ready. Her spear still lodged in the kicker, Ma whirls around and pulls a scrawny man to his feet, grabbing his sword along the way: metal at his Adam's apple. The raiders scream and jeer but they keep their distance from Ma and the man. Her hand is slick on the hilt, her arm shaking from the weight of the iron, but she holds steady. Ma backs away slowly, daring the raiders to follow as the man's burbles of fear press back against the blade.

They don't.

She moves purposefully through the Great Hall and into the tall grass. The man lets out a shriek among the fireflies and Ma doesn't hesitate to press into his skin, creating a shallow warning slice. He quiets, but his whole skinny body trembles until they reach the underbrush. Ma can't navigate the swamp with the man despite his lean frame, so she presses one final time and lets the man drop. Blood spurting back on her. She finally looks at her captive, breath catching in her throat. The man's face is smooth, still waiting to be marked with signs of age, jaw clean and narrow. He can't be older than fourteen summers.

Ma can't understand why the boy was sleeping among the raiders, but the blame quickly turns inward: why hadn't she realized? The shriek in the grass was one of a boy not yet a man. She had held his thin frame against her own and recognized the feeling; Ma knew what it was like to hold Gren when he was a boy. Knew what it was like to hold a scared child to her breast. But in her rage, had chosen to ignore it.

Ma hears the shouts from the Great Hall, but can't move. The earth has claimed her and her knees knot themselves to the ground. She tries to wipe the red away from the boy with her hands, but she only smears the blood deeper into his skin. Desperately, she grabs a handful of leaves and tries again, but the action only makes the body look like Gren's. Like Halga's. Like all the bodies that day, sunken in the mud within the ruins of the village. Stained and broken.

She hears the footsteps before she sees the torchlight. His face is obscured by the fire until he is upon her, sword drawn and tip at Ma's throat. The stranger with the hungry eyes. He looks down at Ma kneeling in the ferns next to the sleeping boy.

Ma remembers when Gren was a boy. During the village hunts, she would often catch him in the woods, watching the deer and the squirrels and the rooks from afar with eyes full of wonder. Full of appreciation for life. When she would prepare the animals for meals, he would never stay, finding excuses to miss his sister skin and gut the game. Her sweet, gentle boy.

She stares at the boy in front of her. His eyes still open, she gently presses them closed.

She closes her eyes, too.

GIVING REASON TO SUFFERING
A Conversation with Izzy Buck

James McNulty: Welcome to the pages of *Driftwood*, Izzy! I'm so excited to publish your heartbreaking reimagining of Beowulf, which is so filled with brutal (yet beautiful) language that I'm sure some of our readers will squeam while reading it.

Izzy Buck: Thank you, James! I'm honored that my first published piece is on display here at *Driftwood*—I was worried that finding a place for "Mōdor" would be a challenge, but I'm so thankful it has found its home so quickly.

JM: Unsurprisingly, perhaps, my opening question has to do with the violence on display in "Mōdor." The story opens with perhaps some of the most visceral and gruesome descriptions in the story. Could you talk a little about choosing to open with this?

IB: Personally, I love a "big" opening in a story, one that unapologetically throws you into the world and leaves you scrambling to figure out the rules—though it causes me frustration as a reader, I'm drawn to the chaos and the challenge of being consumed by the story.
I tried to mirror this with my own opening, while being mindful that beginning directly with such a violent scene could be too overpowering. Therefore, I tried to balance the violence with the initial landscape description to really ground the reader before delving into the horror. A calmer opening was a bit new to me, but it was the right decision for "Mōdor."
Additionally, I think it's only fair that the reader knows what they're getting into—I know my writing isn't for everyone with its level of violence and I respect those who would rather not engage. However, I hope the first graphic scene illustrates the transformative nature of my violence, that it's not there just to shock, but to emphasize the emotions of Ma, Gren, and the pain found in the world as a whole.

JM: To your note at the end here about shock value and sensationalism: surely some of the scenes—or perhaps descriptions within those scenes—skirt the line a bit. How do you decide when and where to pull back? Is your barometer for sensationalism always, *does it emphasize the emotions of the characters?*, as you imply above?

IB: I won't lie, I *do* want to shock the reader, but that's not my only goal. I tend to write out my scenes without holding back and then cut out what's irrelevant. Often times I'm asking myself, *how does this add to a character?*, but if I've created a description that I simply enjoy and contributes to the overall mood of the story, I'll keep it as well. I try not to be too over the top with my violence, but it can happen since it's such a thin, subjective line.

You really helped me during the editing process to reign things in. My original draft had a lot of single sentence paragraphs, and it was really useful for you to note when it was too much. I try to be just as mindful about the white space on the page as the text, but I can get carried away with shape to the point where it undermines my writing. As I'm learning, this can cause my writing to lean into melodrama—you've helped me realize that my writing can carry itself, and that I have to trust what I've created.

JM: If the language is strong enough, there's no need for too much showy formalism; trusting your already strong language to land the needed punch keeps the writing from becoming too stylized and flashy. Could you speak a little to the craft and act of writing horror—and specifically gruesome scenes? What research or mood-setting needs to happen for you to shift into writing?

IB: Writing graphic violence can take a mental toll, so I try to make sure my physical writing space is as peaceful as possible—whether that's writing in a place filled with natural beauty like a park, or even just a lively coffee shop. Being thoughtful with location helps me combat feeling emotionally drained or isolated by the nature of my writing.

I also work best in chunks, for practical and creative reasons. As someone living with chronic illness, brain fog only lets me function cognitively for twenty to thirty minutes before needing a break. At first it was hard for me to deal with these limitations, but writing this way has allowed me to produce vivid imagery and highly focused prose that I couldn't accomplish otherwise.

On the research front, I'm somewhat limited—I'm someone who doesn't handle gore too well, which, I guess can be surprising considering my work. For example, last week some bloodwork of mine ended with me getting sick because I accidentally saw how much they were taking, so any visual research that could take place to improve my horror writing is off the table. This can be a bit of a challenge as I find visual aids really help my writing, but visualization has been enough.

JM: I think the idea of surrounding yourself with natural beauty while you write shows through. I think I mentioned before that some of the brutal scenes are beautifully written; this contradiction shows in your writing method, too. It's also good to hear that you've found a way to utilize your disability, and that you can "produce vivid imagery and highly focused prose that [you] couldn't accomplish otherwise." Taking control of your disability in this way sounds empowering.

You addressed research briefly here, too. Though you may not have researched the gory bits, what research went into this story? Also, why do you think writing gore doesn't gross you out in the way that seeing it does?

IB: I guess you could say I put a semester's worth of research into "Mōdor." I wrote this piece shortly after I finished two college courses: a medieval literature course and another focusing on medieval religious women. These two classes worked really well together, filling in the gaps when the other left things out.

I was first introduced to *Beowulf* in my literature class. I remember writing an essay examining the construction of heroism in the poem (through the use of violence, conflict-seeking behavior, death via battle, and legacy), and though I was focusing on Beowulf, I couldn't help but notice these constructs applied to Grendel and his mother as well. Yet, we never discussed their possible identities as heroes, despite talking about the heroism of some *really* minor characters. I think that's when I became more interested in what was between the lines of the poem.

My second course had a completely different focus: anchorites, female saints, and other religious figures like Margery Kempe. We discussed how women established agency within extremely restrictive gender roles, mostly through religious practice. Though Grendel's mother is almost as far as you can get from these religious women, the class really had me consider how Grendel's mother was able to draw power from her restricted space on the page. I really wanted to explore her character more.

In response to writing versus seeing gore, I think writing gives me a sense of control. I can't always stop that gut reaction after seeing gore, but writing or reading creates a soft boundary. If it's too much for me in the moment, that's fine—I can stop imagining it and save some emotional energy. Or if I'm able to handle it, I'm able to dive right in. But in the end, it's really up to me.

JM: Could you talk a little about finding the beauty in violence? I think of lines like, "the splintered ribs poking through Onela's chest like yearning tree branches," or other writers like Cormac McCarthy. I'm thinking of *Blood Meridian* specifically, where the Cormac seems to relish finding beautiful and stunning description for horrific scenes.

IB: My writing professor who helped workshop this piece said the same thing and urged me to read *Blood Meridian*, but I haven't gotten the chance to tackle it yet—sorry Professor Montemarano!

When it comes to finding beauty in violence, a good amount of my imagery comes from my experience with chronic pain. Chronic illness can be all consuming, which honestly, makes it easy to write about. The line referenced above actually came from a journal entry describing my physical pain that I later adapted to fit the scene. Maybe it's just the writer in me trying to give reason to suffering, when in reality, pain can be meaningless—but giving birth to such visceral images is one way I cope with what's happening to my body at such a young age.

JM: There's a lot of focus on hands in this story. How do you figure hands play into the themes of this piece?

IB: It's so great to get a question that I don't immediately know the answer to! I fixate on hands in a lot of my writing, and I believe it has to do with their multi-faceted nature. Depending on how they are written about, hands can be portrayed as an extremely personal part of the body or as a way for a character to distance themselves from their actions.

The way hands are written about in "Mōdor" leans into this duality. In many instances, they are a vehicle to destroy people and land; they are a way to of dehumanize the enemy by all parties in in the world. Yet, hands are also capable of creating physical wonders like the mead hall, or are used to show love and tenderness between Ma and Gren. I think in "Mōdor," hands contribute to and perpetuate the moral ambiguity in the story.

JM: What do you see as "the moral ambiguity in the story"?

IB: I guess I personally don't view things as super ambiguous, but I was referring to the use of violence by Ma and Gren. Does violence actually help their situation or does it feed a vicious cycle? I'm not a proponent of violence—but in "Mōdor" I can't help but support Ma and Gren. I've never understood why those who are wronged are expected to take "the high road," with their actions. Maybe it would have benefitted Ma and Gren to avoid confrontation, but I view their deaths are somewhat inevitable, so they might as well get revenge.

JM: A harsh view, but you're right about the characters being doomed wherever they go, even if they ran instead of fighting. How much did prior adaptations such as John Gardner's *Grendel* influence "Mōdor"? What were your considerations when choosing to adapt a text that has such a storied adaptation history?

IB: When I started working on "Mōdor," I was vaguely aware of Gardner's adaptation, but I had never engaged with it. I knew it painted a more sympathetic view of Grendel, a type of retelling I'm generally drawn to, but I tried to stay away from *Grendel* to stay true to the vision I had when reading *Beowulf*. I also wasn't aware of the number of retellings that existed when first writing "Mōdor."

As I mentioned before, I fell in love with *Beowulf* during my second year of undergrad but was mostly drawn to what was missing from the text. Grendel's mother immediately struck me as a character who deserved more space in the poem and was the main inspiration of my adaptation; I wanted to expand upon her identity as a mother and warrior. I was also captivated by the natural landscape: who was there before Hrothgar and his warriors? How did the land change with their arrival?

JM: Along a similar line of questioning, where did you choose to depart from the source material? Why?

IB: I wanted to capture the main beats of the poem without being too restricted by technicalities. For example, Beowulf and his men are pagan in the poem, but it was important for me to include the crucifixion of Gren to touch on themes of Christian supremacy by colonizers. If departing from the source material meant further developing themes that I personally enjoyed or found culturally relevant, I had no issues changing things. I am a big proponent of creative freedom and modernization, so I never really felt restricted by the text.

JM: Talk to me more about being "a big proponent of modernization." I think of films like Baz Luhrmann's *The Great Gatsby*, which divided the literary community with its modernization of a classic. On one hand, you have the original author's intention, which is obviously being perverted; folks who believe in artistic ownership probably aren't in love with the idea of other artists taking possession of the work and reshaping it. On the other hand, modernizing a work is a way to bring the author's old work back into relevance and conversation, and the re-envisioning doesn't necessarily harm the original work itself in any way (though it may harm public perception of the work, say, if people are going into Baz Luhrmann's *The Great Gatsby* fresh and it misrepresents the book). Apologies for my tangent here. What I'm interested in with this difficult topic is what it means to be a "big proponent of modernization." Do you strongly feel that the benefits outweigh the cons?

IB: Oh gosh, that movie. Definitely not my favorite, but I can understand what they were trying to do. I have nothing against adaptations—I'm not a literary purist in that sense. Not to be that person, but is any work truly original? Each piece of writing borrows from others, whether its intentional or not. I enjoy viewing other's interpretations of stories, as it's often not the way I experienced the story. I also think it helps rejuvenate interest in the original work, regardless if the adaptation is "good" or "bad." I think I only have a problem if the adaptation isn't doing something new. Then, it really can be encroaching on artist ownership, or using the name of the original to garner attention (I'm thinking of every life action adaptation Disney has been pumping out. The differences aren't drastic enough to stand on their own, nor are they offering something new beyond slightly changing mediums). But when it comes to writing, I view adaptations as a form of collaborative writing on a large scale. I would argue this only helps the writing community as a whole.

JM: Retelling *Beowulf* as if the men are Christian is a pretty intentional thematic move. Do you see this story as an allegory for colonization? How intentional are you when writing themes into your work?

IB: For sure. I don't want to overpower the voices of those who have experienced colonization and its legacy firsthand, but I hope the inclusion of colonization in my story can be an act of solidarity. Ultimately, I'm tired of religion being used to exert control over others and justify atrocities: especially in today's world. I think it's important to acknowledge our sordid history, no matter how painful it might be. It won't fix things, but it's the least we can do.

Thematically speaking, I often have an idea or two I want to convey in my writing, but the focus can sometimes shift as the piece begins to take shape. I allow the piece to grow into itself, and if it turns into something outside of my original intentions, I'm totally fine with that. I also love when others find themes within my work I didn't specifically write or see—it allows me to view my own writing from a new perspective and it makes me happy to have my work resonate uniquely with the reader.

JM: What other mediums inspire your writing?

IB: My method of writing is very sentence-focused, so I've been trying to get more into poetry, but it's still something new to me. Content-wise, I get a lot of inspiration from manga and anime—I'm working my way through *Berserk* right now and I'm understanding why it's such a celebrated series. Some of my biggest inspirations include *Attack on Titan, Dorohedoro,* and *Nausicaa and the Valley of the Wind.* I'm drawn to anything that immerses me in its world, whether its video games like *Breath of the Wild,* art in graphic novel and movies, or a short story.

JM: *Berserk's* first arc doesn't get enough credit in the literary community; literary comics in general are easily overlooked by our community. The Golden Age Arc in *Berserk* is easily a literary fantasy masterpiece, though the series goes downhill quickly from there. It's a very violent comic, though, and from your writing I can see why you'd be drawn to it. What are you working on now?

IB: At the moment, I'm refining some short stories that I've let sit. Once I get my health under control, I'd like to pursue an MFA, so it would be great to have some more pieces published and in my portfolio. I'm a bit of a perfectionist, so nothing is really ever done for me, but I'm hoping having to submit some stories will help me finish things per se.

JM: As we wrap up, is there anything else you'd like to say?

IB: I'm super thankful for this opportunity. To work with you, have a published piece at *Driftwood*, and share "Mōdor" with everyone has been such a great experience.

FOR THE SAKE OF ARGUMENT
Rebecca Starks

Say you're up late moonlighting one Saturday night with a newly broken arm, having talked for an hour on the crisis line with a veteran of the war on terror, a young man stuck on the nothing that happened to him—unlike most of his buddies he came out of it fine, has a young family and a job at a skateboard shop—and after you've gotten him past his evil hour, bonding over Tony Alva and Rodney Mullen, you turn to the subject of your pop—a Nam vet who late in life couldn't be found without a book on D-Day at hand, *The Longest Day* or *Citizen Soldiers* like another place-setting on the table, part of a lifelong project to understand his own dad, just as you struggled through Tim O'Brien and your sister enlisted after 9/11—telling the caller this to make the point that secondhand trauma is still trauma and sometimes harder to get at, as it could be harder to relieve pain in an amputated limb than in one that's intact. What helps in the case of phantom pain is to set up a mirror along the line of symmetry to make it look like the limb is restored and can be moved, and maybe by analogy you have to find a mirror for the psyche, something that makes you feel superhero-whole again, your sense of agency restored, but this you are saying to yourself, still talking in your head, the veteran no longer on the line, it must be the pain meds that make you run at the mouth.

And after you check on your son, who has worked himself half out of the camo sleeping bag he insists on sleeping in, his cherub cheeks flushed, curls damp on his temple, you fill a bong to relax, doing everything slower with only one hand, the other pledging allegiance at the end of your slung arm, the pain starting to punch through the Oxy but it's too soon for more, and when the cravings kick in you forage in the pantry cupboard along barely stocked shelves. Kath's been doing the shopping so she can read the ingredients, ideally none, whatever you eat will ideally have no packaging but be a pure form of earthly life unmodified other than dead, though in fairness she prefers what is living, fermenting—yogurt, kimchi, kombucha, words your dad would have called one slur, his dad another—so in the end you settle on a jar of pickled beets, something Kath canned two months ago and you can't get open, as you sit squeezing the jar between your thighs, wrenching the lid until your hand cramps arthritic and you're only thirty-four, the rubber band tears, the water won't run hot enough to make the metal expand, so you dent the top with a wooden spoon, then knock it on the bald gray carpet Kath means to pull up some day and replace with wooden flooring, aware that if the jar breaks and stains the carpet that day will be now, you'll be living in a construction zone, like with the kitchen, everything in the flux of improvement to fit her specifications and nothing quite lined up when it's done.

And that's when she comes in—you've woken her, she was out at a birth until ten that morning and didn't go to bed until right after dinner, which is how she rolls, she's never less tired than when she hasn't slept, but even had she wanted some shut-eye she would have had to rush back to the hospital at noon to meet you as you were wheeled in, her face chastened of exasperation so that you almost didn't recognize her but now it's back, as she holds out her hand for the jar she pops open with a quick wrench of the wrist before returning to the bedroom, refusing ear plugs as usual because she would strain to hear what she's blocking out, something that might need correcting, if nothing else your grammar talking to your son, if he were still up, her son, your (plural) son, or maybe it should be your sons (singular). That's when you decide for sure, you go in and tell her while she's falling back asleep, and when she says hoarsely *Sebastian has a badge you can wear* you realize she thinks you mean for Halloween, but you mean for real, and as she looks at you, considering, her face relaxes as it does when Sebi settles on a costume that's not too hard to make, though you'd have to pass a written exam, and quit the weed, and you think she approves, for once, but it's merely the softening of her face in sleep.

Say for the last ten years you've worked five days a week at the motorbike shop where you're the cuddly, round-faced mascot, unable to grow even a scraggly goatee, your leather jacket void of chains and skulls, your skin unmarked other than the six inches of ink on your inner left forearm paying homage to Kerouac—the only record of the three months after your pop was shot and you inherited his bike and tools and dropped out of tech school, ditching your plans to become a psych nurse to ride due west alone, twenty-four years old, looking not for goodness in America but for some kind of wisdom. You were thinking to make it to Denver until one afternoon, setting up camp just outside Ogallala, Nebraska, you watched a Ford Ranger with jet skis back too far into the lake and flood its tailpipe, then a Chevy Astro to the rescue back in too far and stall, so you joined the others wading in to push to no avail until someone flagged down a bottle-green El Camino that agreed to be chained to the Chevy chained to the pick-up, and the engines revved and everyone pushed on the count of three and the vehicles evolved back onto the sand. That was when you decided to turn around and head back to Vermont, the blue-black words I AM A GENIUS meaning whatever you needed them to mean as you found work repairing bikes during the day and now, two nights a week, counseling suicidal veterans struggling to control their addiction to controlled substances, about breaking the cycle of control, and already as you shut the bedroom door you feel the nag of withdrawal and decide you'll take one more Oxy and then switch to Tylenol.

Say one morning, that very morning, you and Sebi had been sitting at the breakfast table watching Gargamel be crushed by a boulder dropped by his future self—a moment he uses to justify hating the Smurfs, when it was his own malice recoiling on him—the two of you pretending to be Lazy Smurf and Greedy Smurf, saying *smurf me a smurf* when you wanted more milk or another donut with sprinkles you'd picked up to celebrate having the morning to yourselves, say just then the door latch clicked and Azrael pounced, shutting the laptop and asking if Sebastian had done his practice yet, nothing in her face hinting that she had just witnessed a miracle, the groveling pleading lashing out under torture at last giving way to stoned bliss, when all went well—you've seen it just once but that was enough to know it was always surprising, always a miracle. Instead it must have reminded Kath that her own child is falling behind, still stalled on the tune "O Come, Little Children" after two years of Suzuki, because he can't get it into his head that up bow means to start at the tip and move the bow up in the air but instead he wants to move up the bow by pulling it down—his failure a kind of flexible empathy that goes beyond your own dyslexia, though he has that too—seeming to experience the world like a photographic negative, confusing everything the way most kids do left and right, something you noticed early on in his confident pronouncements, *you stop at a green light and go at a red light,* or innocent requests, *make the music louder,* followed by inexplicable tantrums or sad histories, *the water was freezing hot,* having scalded himself turning the wrong bath faucet the right way or the right one the wrong way, so that when he was four you worried he wouldn't survive long in the world, while Kath worried about his future standardized test scores.

And then you heard, *And you, it's time you did something else, too.* You should be playing him the audiotape of *Great Expectations,* not feeding him crap she'd have to suffer the consequences of. If you hadn't forgotten, Sebi is gluten-free, lactose-free, sugar-free, artificial dye-free, everything but free, in a frantic bid to cure a hyperactivity that's a reaction to being nagged and bullied and yelled at, an opinion you've derived from the restless frustration you recognize in yourself even secondhand, sometimes accompanied by panic you're Sebi's age again and back in the car with your mom after getting a puppy—a pit mix sitting in the passenger seat who when she tries to stop him from chewing on the center console begins biting at her, barking and lunging at her neck, and while he's just a twelve-pound puppy she's sure he will kill her, she's hysterical and trying to choke him with his collar and swerving on the highway and you have to talk her down from the back seat, directing her in a calm reasonable voice to pull over or you'll all die—even as you couldn't help feeling sorry for Kath, seeing already in her face the hangover of shame, both of you caught in a cycle like on the washer, Normal or Heavy Duty or Permanent Press, and over the whine in your voice that morning you heard again: *it's time.*

And leaving your son to his fate you went down the tilt of wooden steps to the garage out back and kicked up the stand of your Supermoto and rode out to the Kingdom, wondering how you ended up with a cager, when that first time she'd ridden behind you—your landlord twelve years older than you needing a ride to her mom's, her car in the shop and her mom not picking up the phone all day only because, it turned out, she had the TV up too loud while watching *The Young and the Restless* and crunching Doritos Jacked—you'd felt embraced in her clasp, not trapped the way you feel now, trapped above all in the voice that had come out of you on the ridge of argument: *Why don't you play an instrument yourself if it's so friggin important?* And that was the worst thing, as for every kid there is one thing, if conscious of, they would spare their own children, and for you it was hearing your parents argue, something being demanded of you and denied you at the same time, while for Kath it was disadvantage, ignorance, a squandering of potential, whatever was the opposite of ambition and that was just it, there was only a blank, self-satisfied was just a cover for fear, self-doubt, defeat, and did you want that for your child, or did you want to set him up for success?

You remembered her elation coming home from Battery Park to report that a woman who put her child in the blue special needs swing next to the black arc of Sebastian's—Kath always calling him by his full name as she calls you Joseph, as do her friends, though all your family and friends call you Joey, the name on your mechanic's shirt, and you call her Kath, a sign of affection and intimacy, though she goes by Katherine, which feels cold to you—on hearing his name had responded, *He won't be pumping gas with a name like that!* And where you would have cringed and tried to laugh it off, Kath had been proud, pleased at this proof the name would appease the fates, though you thought it was the opposite, tempting them with a totem against failure, like the violin, and maybe that is what was hiding behind your dread of argument, that it signaled failure, a lack of confidence that you could go and yield by turns, let her have her way after you've had yours, the clear rules of the road that start in the bedroom, a thought you can't hang up on even two years later, the words overheard while she was in the kitchen with Lydia still a fresh tattoo on your brain.

Say, then, that you headed out in such a hurry you didn't snap your gloves—as you pulled out onto Route 2 you could feel them flapping at the wrists—and it was a day with a faint drizzle, the first rain in a long dry spell, and once you were on 105 you quivered past the starched repetitive corn fields like those Magic Eye pictures that if you roll your eyes like you're about to fall asleep reveal an image in 3D, but instead you thought of the Janus words your ninth-grade English teacher taught you, how fast can mean speedy or stuck in one place, and cleave, together or apart, words folding over a line of symmetry to mean themselves and the opposite. Maybe that's where Sebi belongs, you thought: in a double-faced world where the horizon bends until time swallows its tail and yesterday is tomorrow, your mind skipping from the playground swings to the police station across the street where Oslo had his birthday party two years earlier, when he turned five—Oslo the son of Lydia and Karl, who are now divorced, which after seeing Oslo split down the middle you want to avoid at all costs. The boy looks right through you with a frown when he's with his dad but is all smiles and fist bumps if he's with his mom, and when he comes over to play is a model of politeness until it's time to go, then starts punching his mother in the stomach and kicking at her shins, acting out his dad's abuse, says Kath, whose low opinion of Karl dates from the time she was Lydia's doula and had to tell him to get off his phone when the baby was crowning. You've wondered, though, if there isn't another side to it, because hadn't you overheard Lydia recommend the seeds of Queen Anne's Lace as birth control, telling Kath what she explained to her clients, that if a woman takes it for seven days after sex the fertilized egg won't implant, not unless you want it to—this in the same conversation as, *He calls it cuddling, snuggling, it's like being humped by a teddy bear.*

Even in memory it made you swerve—you had come up too fast on a gray Dodge Ram—and looking for a chance to pass, you serpentined on the solid yellow, waiting for the road to straighten out for a view of Lake Memphremagog through the veil of light rain. It was like it was Kath driving the truck just ahead, close enough you could smell the smoke from her cigarette, except you had it backwards—she was trying to get around you for a view of the mountains—or it was both: you were each blocking the other's view, meaning the other's illusion they could reach the calm middle of the lake or the fire tower on the top of the mountain, a thought that threw you back to Oslo's four-year old party at the fire station. You've always teared up easily, but when Sebi and the other kids commando-crawled across the dirty carpet while the firefighter called out to stay below the smoke and get to safety, Mom and Dad weren't there, you had to suppress a sob and turn away to blow your nose—so that the next year you were on guard approaching the police station where the kids and parents had gathered waiting for some light to come on, some door to open, until you read the notice to pick up the white phone and dial 9.

You did, conjuring from the dim interior two uniformed lady cops moving low to the ground like bowling balls, and you wondered if this was Lydia's doing or just the way of things, these the rookies who had to show up on a Saturday morning to talk to five-year-olds: one a blonde, the other what your pop would wrongly call a black, the ladies greeting the group flatly, speaking as if they had chewing gum in their cheeks as they handed out sticker badges and began show-and-telling the tools cached in their vests: radio, stun gun, extra ammo, evading the taboo answer to each question by holding up something new, this time the handcuffs and keys, asking, *Who wants to try them out?* And of course the hand that shot up belonged to the boy in blue who had promptly stuck the badge on his shirt and announced he was going to be an officer when he grew up, not the boy who when they asked, *Do you know what arrest means?* said, *Yes, it's when you're a-laying down*, the parents smiling repeating it to each other. But when the cuffs were snapped on, the boy in blue began tugging madly against them, impeding the efforts of the cop to work the key in the lock to release him, so that you were aware of his internal struggle and growing reserve as he was shown the lock box for weapons in the hallway and the cells where people were kept overnight—the officers encouraging him to flush the toilet using a big black button outside the cell, a power flush that made the girl peering into the toilet jump back three feet and run to her mom—and last of all the changing rooms with the tall blue lockers that prompted a kid to ask, unanswered, *Why do you have locks on your lockers?*

So that you weren't surprised when, after being ushered back into the hallway where they were given goodie bags with 911 magnets and a picture of a police car to color in, as the kids burst through the tinted glass doors into the overcast but still brightly limitless expanse of day—Sebi running off to climb on the cannon aimed out at the lake—the boy in blue could be heard saying in an aggrieved voice, *I don't want to be a police officer, I want to be a astronaut*, and you joked with a dad, *Next year, the post office?* And he, *I was thinking the sewage treatment plant*, but the next year Oslo's birthday would be under Karl's watch, so you'd never know. Weaving over the yellow line behind the Dodge Ram, you remembered how you'd felt at home inside the police station: safe—it was the feeling of being a chimney, the thing that protects a house from its hearth fire but is all that's left standing when a house burns down—and that's when you got off, noticing too late the piece of failed metal on the road and, jerking to avoid it, feeling the front wheel slip on the slick asphalt and yourself land skidding on your left arm and side, and more than a fracture and road rash you were being flayed, your wrist bleeding out until the lady EMT in the Dodge Ram saved you with a tourniquet.

When you take off the cast a month later—the cast right now too snug with your forearm's swelling, making you claustrophobic as you lie down next to Kath, who stirs in her sleep to pat you on the shoulder—your tattoo will read I AM A GEN, which the guys will riff on at the shop, guessing, *Genie? Genital? Agent 007?* while all you can think of is Agent Orange exfoliating the brilliance of fall.

Say, finally, a year later, you're showing your ink to the cops interviewing you—making a joke of it, now that you've studied and passed, barely passed, the written exam and passed the PAT, running alongside the police car at the front of the pack after doing the push-ups (push-downs) and bench presses (push-ups) you'd built up to over a couple months while Sebi copied you or cheered you on and Kath watched YouTube videos and fingered chords on a used guitar—and they like you, you can tell, they want to give you the job, and you want the job. You've never felt so comfortable—it's the yes sir, no sir, having nothing to hide: you're one of them, believing of them what you want to believe of yourself, seeing everything for exactly what it is—a toy a toy, a phone a phone—deliberate and unprejudiced, not seeing color, reasonable and bringing out the reasonableness in all the crazies stepping out of cars holding a gun to their heads or storming from the house waving a snow shovel like your dad, in the last minute of his life, before a bullet could fold back the steel like the corner of a book you have to put down, fatigued from trying to unjumble the dancing letters. But then they ask the question, and you know it's over but still can't shake the feeling it's going well, they'll make an exception, you've already told them your greatest weakness is that you think everyone is good.

And you aren't going to lie, though Kath will tell you later you were stupid not to. You hadn't gotten stoned for over a year, but then the month before, sitting at the table with Kath's friends who liked sit-down dinners, the talk had turned to raising kids, how hard it was, and you'd said, *All they need is love,* like the Beatles, reaching over to tousle Sebi's hair, and Kath had added, *and a good education*—and one of her friends turned to you and said, *I hear you're changing careers, Joseph,* and behind the skepticism that cops could be good people you heard in her voice the skepticism that you were good enough to be a cop, and after saying that nothing was definite you left the table, waiting for Kath to clear the plates so you could hiss, *you promised,* because like sex or any secret embryonic dream it was between you and her and nobody else. Then you went to your room and put on headphones in the dark listening to P.O.D. until Trav and Jessie stopped by and you went out back and took the hits they offered, you didn't care, and when Kath found you and mimed hands-up dismay, you passed her the joint and then you were smoking together like Adam and Eve—that was how it was best between you, both of you high, she picking out chords on the guitar and you crooning, *I threw it all away.* But the cops wanted to know where the kids were, and you shrugged, they were inside, asleep or playing, and it was the wrong answer, you saw their gentle disappointment—you should know it's not okay to smoke at a party where there are kids—but as they shook your hand for the last time, in the precinct, they encouraged you to stay clean for a year and try again, and you knew you could, they would take you, but what you needed was to change your life now—not in a year, not pickle and can it but eat it now, fresh with the dirt still on its bloody root, sharing it with your wife and son while you were whatever you were that wouldn't last.

A KIND OF VORTEX
A Conversation with Rebecca Starks

Stephen Hundley: Hello, Rebecca, and welcome to the pages of *Drift-wood*. Our readers were captivated by the pull of this story, which you generate and maintain with minimal punctuation (not counting acronyms—I never knew P.O.D. meant Payable on Death). By the narrative's end, I had seen the character want, try, and fail. The tension of his striving carried me clause to clause.

Rebecca Starks: I'm thrilled and grateful to have this story in *Driftwood*. I'm drawn to its vision of fiction that pays attention to the rhythm of sentences and considers them integral to a story's narrative drive.

SH: Thank you. We take great joy in rhythmic prose. One of the things we liked best about this piece was its attention to sound. Do you also write poetry or music or other modes? How have you developed your ear?

RS: I do read and write poetry, and I've always been drawn to the physicality of language, whether poetry or prose, written or spoken. I don't write music, but I'll sometimes notice myself breathing in the rhythm of music I've listened to and am carrying with me. While writing, I'm captivated by the way sounds subconsciously draw similar sounds to them, but I'm most interested in the idiosyncratic inflections that can be given to language—a kind of music of consciousness and personality. When Frank O'Hara writes, "Leaf! You are so big!," for example, I can access a childish part of myself while staying aware of an adult, ironic detachment. When I work on poems, I can become a little obsessive about pattern, so I find prose freeing, as well as more outward-facing.

SH: I appreciated how this story subverted my expectations for a pattern and moved through time easily. It is, as you say, outward-facing in its delivery, yet still I felt very attached to the narrator and their intrinsic desires for change. You've written a fine, loving striver. How do you impart love to your characters, or how do you depict love?

RS: I think it is something that's come slowly to me, letting a character express love that isn't ironized. I've had to lower my own defenses. I think our initial impulse as children is to love, not to judge or worry or try to prove something. In preschool, I'm told, I hugged my teacher around the leg and kissed the back of her knee, startling her, and when she asked why I said, "Because we love you so." Maybe that's the best answer I can give—that love is shown in spontaneous gestures and a carelessness of the self. I've been re-reading *Frankenstein*—actually, listening to it with my son—and through all the talk about love in that book, the love that feels most convincing is the monster's for the family he observes, because he forgets himself when watching them, enough that he can imagine they will reciprocate his love. A character who loves is especially vulnerable—they forget to hide from others, and themselves, how they feel.

SH: Our editors were charmed by the hope and wistfulness in this narrator's story. How did you arrive at such a character?

RS: In some of his biographical details, Joey is an amalgam of several people I've known, and his psychic life emerged through projection and extrapolation. I think partly he took off because I let him be critical of some aspects of myself that I'd rather distance myself from. I suspect there are a lot of parental couples like him and Kath: the one who just gives love, and the one who wants to make something of their child. The narrator himself wants both to be loved and to make something of himself—well, who doesn't?—and his striving creates the hope and the near-miss. An earlier draft ended, "Say, for a moment, you felt loved." I decided that was too heavy-handed, but I hope that feeling is there: that yearning to be loved even in failure, not to have to earn love.

SH: I think that feeling is certainly alive in the story. Can you speak to your drafting process while writing this piece? Because of the pace I adopt while reading it, it takes on a sort of breathless "run at the mouth" quality. Did you write this in short or long sessions, and how cluttered was your cutting room floor? Did it take much trimming to reach this condensed form?

RS: I had an arc in mind of someone trying and failing to become a police officer, and I remember starting to assemble the machinery of a story and not getting very far. I needed to understand the main character behind the story. At one point, I set him on the phone and let him spin out his thoughts, and the story came out close to its final form, in a single sitting. Later, I cut a few details where I got bogged down, and I kept revising the ending. I've since had to work on clarifying the timeline of events and on punctuation, putting it in sometimes only to take it out again. So, I've managed to spend a lot of time on the story without changing it dramatically—which is closer to my process with poems than with fiction.

SH: Initial drafts of this piece used scant punctuation, though more has come in during revision. This produced a raw, intimate voice that slid easily from paragraph to paragraph. Have you experimented with grammatical rule-breaking like this before?

RS: For me it's a way of giving up narrative control and not "knowing too much." I've turned to it when I'm bored with how I'm writing, when I'm falling into a formula, and it lets me shake up linearity and create a kind of vortex that draws in memories and potential plot developments I might not otherwise have had access to. In this case, it allowed me to feel my way into a narrator—a hypothetical, at first—who is up late at night, on pain meds after an accident, and who feels trapped and wants to feel more whole. He's someone who doesn't have control over his own narrative, his motivations, his subconscious—not that I think any of us really do, but he doesn't claim to, and I think self-interrupting, wide-net-casting sentences convey that better than short declarative sentences would. In the editing process, I was persuaded to add just enough punctuation to improve reading clarity without, I hope, impeding intimacy and momentum.

SH: "For the Sake of the Argument" makes references to specific books, groceries, vehicles, tattoos, and more. These crisp, tangible details served as ties between the deeply interior world of the narrator and the world we know. To your eye, what makes a detail essential to a piece of short fiction?

RS: I've read (and written a few) opposite kinds of stories, whose characters don't have names, only roles, and whose settings are undefined, and I think that can be very effective, but this story felt like it wanted to be almost cluttered with such details. Maybe they helped ground me in a world different from my own. I'm not someone who notices vehicles, for instance, beyond "big gray truck," but a character who works as a mechanic would likely note specifics. I have him read Tim O'Brien, and now that I think about it, *The Things They Carried* creates its world and its tragic sense almost solely from such details—the type of can-opener or radio or rifle or foot powder, and how much each thing weighs. For me there is talismanic energy in such specificity, and joy in the sounds of certain place names, brands, and bands. But again, I think to feel essential, a detail has to be rooted in what the character would care about and notice.

SH: Fiction Editor Claire Agnes praised the story's "beautiful and commendable restraint afforded to emotionality, which results in a believable depth and resonance." How did you balance and deliver the powerful emotions in this piece without swamping the narrative?

RS: That's a wonderful compliment—I think I lucked into it, because I didn't know where the story was aiming and was just trying to "land" it. I felt a sympathy for the narrator's character—and for the others in his life—that helped me suspend judgment, and the counterpoint of memory and forward motion kept me (and Joey) from dwelling too long on any single emotion. The difficult things in his life are dropped in incidentally, but as the story unfolds they are revealed to be driving his decisions, and maybe that leaves space for emotions to resonate.

SH: Can you speak to how you manipulated time in this story for dramatic effect?

RS: I didn't know how the different elements—the idea of second-hand trauma, Joey's desire to change careers, his son's learning disabilities, his wife's overcompensation, and his father's death—were going to connect. So, in some ways the drama emerged from the jumping around in time. What I did do consciously is withhold information until Joey could face certain memories or had to; until the arc of the narrative bent back on itself—to use the metaphor he thinks of regarding his son and "Janus words." "Police" becomes one of those words for him, able to hold two opposing meanings.

SH: This piece and its protagonist are deeply rooted in service. Veterans, mechanics, police, and midwives appear. You delve into these working-class folks with a veracity that makes them feel embodied and occupied; at times, they are bored, at others, they are pressurized. What is your relationship to or affinity for men and women in these types of fields?

RS: This question stirred up a lot for me as I reflected on it. I wouldn't have thought of this as an autobiographical story, but I'm recognizing that it gets to the heart of some essential quarrel in me, over where I'm from and where I've been and find myself now. I'm familiar with service professions through my family in Kentucky and Ohio, through jobs I had before and during college—where, incidentally, I worked sixteen hours a week for the campus police—and through my current social circle of neighbors and other parents. Despite a privileged education, I felt more at home working as a delivery driver than studying literature in graduate school. Academia didn't feel grounded in the kinds of struggles I was aware of, growing up, and the way people turn—the way I turned—to books for salvation, for answers, as naïve as that sounds to me now. I finished my degree but never felt I belonged. I trace these feelings back to my father, who looked at his education as an escape from a narrower world, even as that world kept a hold on him. He was determined for his children to have the same opportunities he had, but also, I think, didn't want us to lose touch with his roots. He might think he failed, in that regard, but it's in me.

Also, for the last ten years I've lived in Vermont, where my husband is an academic neurologist and I work part-time as a writing consultant for medical students and a workshop leader for older adults, and it's been a new landscape for me in terms of class. Early on I would find myself being surprised by people I met, and I realized I was coming up against implicit biases that had formed in other environments. Communities here are small enough, democratically active enough, and integrated enough socio-economically that people know each other through multiple connections—school bus driver and synagogue member, for instance—and aren't generally categorized by their working roles. Maybe this is common, or a function of having children, but somehow it was new to me and very welcome. For three years we lived in a co-housing community alongside people from a range of service and academic professions, from postal worker to astrophysicist, and that mix has come to feel natural to me, whether I'm playing in an amateur orchestra beside a housepainter or slow-jam fiddling with a Vietnam vet. Vermont has a strong political bent toward egalitarianism, and I've come to think of class difference as much in terms of values—valuing community and connection over achievement, say—as of skills and opportunities. That said, the question is emotional for me partly because it brings up inequities and divisions in this country that feel as intractable as its systemic racism, and I'm aware that I'm implicated in, and buffered from, significant suffering that results from a lack of such opportunities.

All to say, I feel I can't really do justice to the question, but I'm glad for the chance to struggle with it.

SH: Thank you for the struggle. It was moving to read your searching, and your community in Vermont sounds quite romantic in its unity. To push into place, do you feel that living in Vermont has influenced your voice or opened you to new writers and possibilities? What kinds of things changed for you, as an artist, when you changed your place?

RS: It's taken me a long time to accept that I won't be an urban writer. Living in Manhattan and Brooklyn for four years in my twenties energized my writing, and I've since been a little in mourning, moving to ever smaller cities—Portland, Oregon, then Burlington, and now a town of 4,000 in Vermont. Partly I think this is mourning for being single, without children, freer to be reckless and to end up in places I don't belong. I remember reading that you know children are in the right learning zone, at the edge of something new, when they happily repeat a task over and over, and for me that's the zone of inspired writing. Vermont feels very comfortable to me, domestic, and I'm still not quite comfortable with that. That said, I'm aware that I carry with me a perspective shaped by the demographics and politics of other places I've lived, and I think that difference has helped me discover my voice and look for what I'm missing. Living far from home, and from later homes, has also given me distance and privacy to work with material from the past.

In terms of influences, Vermont has been an incredibly rich place for me poetically—the roster of Vermont poet laureates includes many of my most-loved poets—and I had the opportunity to edit a journal, *Mud Season Review*, through which I met Robin McLean and Genevieve Plunkett, two fiction writers I'm still learning from. This might have happened anywhere I lived, but as I've left academia further behind, I have a renewed sense of readers who are looking for something primarily emotional, rather than intellectual, from a piece of writing; even as I still believe in form and formal experiment as ways to preserve and access richer emotional experiences.

I've also returned to my first love of and immersion in nature, and probably the most obvious change in my writing is the strong imprint of the natural world and rural settings. The small-town trade-off for Henry James' glimpse through a doorway—or a passing subway car—is the possibility of a deeper knowledge of people, their characters and their fates. Aleksandr Solzhenitsyn said something about that, regarding his exile in Vermont, but I can't find the quote. Also, a side note—I don't want to overromanticize where I live, as behind every utopian ideal lies plenty of conflict! Which is good, if you are looking for stories.

SH: Can you speak more to your time in adult community workshops? How do you see or experience writing's presence in your community? Do you see people in your workshop, likewise, struggling with their image of the country, policing, pressurized love? How has this workshop moved you?

RS: I first entered a Vermont writing community through the Burlington Writers Workshop—which provides free workshops, led by volunteers—and I was impressed by its openness to writers at all stages and by the quality of feedback from participants. They treated a piece of writing with the care they would show a community member, and that was new to me.

Separately, I began teaching workshops through UVM's lifelong learning program and a local independent living facility. Now I regularly teach private poetry writing workshops, but beyond that I've taught workshops on contemporary political issues—how democracy dies, the partisan divide, the 1619 Project, the Supreme Court—and on short fiction, memoir, and poetry. I've learned a lot from older adults—the majority of whom are women who came of age in the 60s—in terms of their longer views on the country and on feminism, racism, socialism, gender issues, and climate change. I find the historical perspective they bring enlightening, whether they fought for civil rights but didn't realize the GI Bill allowed them to get mortgages and accumulate wealth Black Americans could not; or are passionate about reproductive rights because they remember a roommate who needed an abortion before Roe v. Wade. It's challenging to tackle these topics in memoir, let alone in a lyric poem, and I admire their introspection and engagement, their openness to new information and perspectives, and their embrace of the upcoming generation.

I've been moved to meet women who didn't write for fifty years because they were told by a male writing instructor—one verbatim, and others with something equivalent—"I can't believe a woman would think that way, let alone write about it." Separate from the political, I've been moved to observe that traumas don't diminish with time, that an unspoken tragedy in childhood still haunts and demands artistic expression seventy years later; that parents and the deaths of parents loom as large to someone who is seventy-five as to someone much younger.

SH: Thank you for your time and for your commitment to seeking out the powerful and difficult forces that animate this piece. Are you able to speak to or direct our readers to any other projects of yours, either published, forthcoming, or still in the works?

RS: For fiction readers who don't avoid poetry, *Able Muse Press* published two books of my poems in the last couple years, *Time Is Always Now* and *Fetch, Muse,* and I am working on a third. In terms of recent fiction, I have a story ("Where Lemons Bloom") in the winter 2022 issue of *Epiphany*. I'm hoping to publish a collection of stories that was just a finalist for *The Journal*'s Non/Fiction prize, and I'm revising a second collection that would include "For the Sake of Argument." This year, I've also plunged into working on a novel. I always have too many things in the works, and my book publishing seems to lag about ten years behind my writing. It takes much more work than I anticipate to "harden off" a piece of creative writing; it's like preparing a greenhouse plant to withstand the sun and wind.

REBURIAL

Victor McConnell

The hole was deeper than I'd expected, and, though my brother stood on top of the coffin, only his head protruded above the surface of the earth. It swiveled as he surveyed his surroundings, like a gopher or some other underground creature returning cautiously from below.

I flashed the light twice in his direction so he knew it was me. We'd left the wheelbarrow in the truck while we dug, thinking it would be easier to run without it if we were caught before we finished. When I reached the edge, I pulled the black cotton sheet out and climbed down into the grave.

"You ready?" he said. I nodded, looking toward the road as a pair of headlights passed. My breathing was shallow and tight until it was clear they weren't turning, and the feeling reminded me of drinking in an empty field as a teenager and being afraid that each passing car was a cop. Danny said something, but I missed it.

"What?" I said.

"Goddammit. I said I'm going to do it now."

We had talked just after the funeral about opening the coffin lid and what he might look like. I'd proposed at first that we just take the whole coffin, but my brother told me that I was an idiot and that we'd need a forklift or something to do that. He said we just needed to open it and pull the body out. He made it sound so simple, so I didn't mention my fear of the smell of our father's corpse or of how it might feel wrapping my arms around his body. Instead, I'd just said, "Fine. But you're opening the lid." He'd stayed quiet.

Danny reached down and pulled. For some reason I expected it to be locked, but it swung open easily, just as it had in the funeral home, when the mortician had opened the casket prior to the service.

"Turn on your flashlight," he said.

"Why?"

"You really want to take the wrong body?"

I turned on the light, wondering if he was really concerned about that, or if he just wanted me to be uncomfortable. Jokes about whether he could read the name on the headstone came to mind, but I couldn't get one out before my father's face became visible, staring up at me, eyes closed. He'd always worn hats when he was alive, and it seemed odd to see his thin, gray hair combed and uncovered. He somehow seemed more dead than he had the morning before at the funeral. Perhaps the skin had less water in it now.

I inhaled, and the only smell was that of upturned soil, still damp from last night's rain. I shined the light at my brother and it lit up the dirt and sweat on his forehead. He was five years younger than me, but the dirt and shadows aged him a decade. He waved his hand at me.

"Alright," he said. "Turn it off."

The plan was to slide the sheet beneath his body and then hoist him out, wrap him up, and roll him in the wheelbarrow back to the truck. Danny insisted a sheet was strong enough to hold a body. *How could you know that?* I'd asked, but he'd just shrugged and said it was obvious. I thought about that while gripping one corner and sliding a hand beneath his shoulder as my brother did the same with his legs. We lifted one side and pulled the sheet halfway around him, as if swaddling an infant. The flesh along his back seemed mushy. I swallowed, and then we shifted to his other side and pulled the sheet a little farther. It wouldn't slide with all of his weight on it, so I leaned over and wrapped my arms around his torso and lifted while Danny situated the sheet and closed the lid.

I shut my eyes and squeezed tight, thinking about how rarely Dad told us he loved us but how he'd always hugged us. My face mashed against his shoulder, and emotion started to well up in me. Then a faint rankness rose to my nostrils. I dropped the body and turned away from the coffin and retched. There wasn't much room in the grave and I had little choice but to do it at my brother's feet.

"You alright?" he said.

"Yeah," I said, surprised he didn't curse at me. "I'm okay. Sorry."

"It's fine. I think you missed my foot. And at least you didn't throw up on Dad."

I didn't laugh.

"Anyway. It's a good thing I'm driving," he said.

I hadn't had much to drink and wasn't sure if he really thought I was drunk or not.

"Shit," I said. "I could use another drink, actually."

Danny pulled a flask from his back pocket and handed it to me. I drank and returned it to him. The body lay between our feet on the lid. The ground was shoulder height, and when we tried to hoist him out while prone on the sheet, we couldn't get him high enough. I almost dropped him on our second attempt, losing my footing and slamming to my knees. Danny finally grabbed beneath each armpit and told me to lift at the waist. I did, and the body folded over my brother's shoulder. He stood, and I tried to help by shoving upward from the soles of Dad's feet, but his legs collapsed, limp and useless. Then I clambered out of the grave and pulled from above, dragging him part of the way out, bearing his weight for a moment until Danny could join me and we could each clasp one arm and pull until he was flat on the ground. There wasn't much noise other than our grunting, but it felt like someone would hear us, and I looked around.

"What is it?"

"I don't know," I said. "Nothing."

He waited for me to elaborate, but I didn't.

"Alright," he said. "Next step."

We rewrapped him in the sheet and lifted him into the wheelbarrow. His legs flopped over the ends, and I thought about whether it would be better to arrange him in a fetal position or to leave him as is, looking like a cartoon drunkard being carted home.

"You wheel him back. I'll start on the hole."

I nodded and started to wheel him toward the truck, deciding against trying to move him. I'd parked at the back of the cemetery, behind a grove of cypress and mesquite trees, where the truck was invisible from the road. My brother said that I was paranoid, that no one would come to a small-town cemetery in the middle of the night. I asked him how many times he'd been to a cemetery in the middle of the night, and he said that was precisely his point. I parked there anyway. He shook his head and said, "Well, you're on wheel-barrow duty, then."

The headstones were barely visible as I began wheeling through the cemetery. The nearby tree line blocked the half moon, and I was afraid of someone spotting my headlamp if I turned it on. The first collision was the most violent. The wheelbarrow halted unexpectedly against the granite slab, and I slammed forward between the handles, terrified that my father's body would go tumbling out onto some stranger's grave, as if that would finally push things into the realm of sacrilege. It didn't, and the bumps were milder from there, the body still safely in the wheelbarrow when I finally reached the truck. I considered returning to the gravesite to fetch my brother to help. But something seemed wrong about leaving my father alone by the car, and I thought it might impress Danny if I loaded him on my own. I squatted down and lifted, wobbling and turning, then pushing and half falling forward. I grabbed the top of the car door as his body slumped into the seat, then worked to maneuver him until the seatbelt could buckle across his waist.

"We'll have you home soon, Dad," I said. The sound of my own voice didn't settle me or make me feel connected to him. Instead, it just seemed small and thin, like it did during a dream, words cast forth into darkness with nothing tangible to bounce off of. I quickly tossed the wheelbarrow into the truck bed and set off toward the gravesite. I felt more afraid on the return journey, quiet as it was and with no load to bear.

The dirt pile was half gone, and Danny leaned against his shovel as I walked up. He was sweating and breathing even harder than I was. Both of us were past forty, and neither of us did much to take care of ourselves.

Took you long enough," he said.

"Looks like you're taking some recovery time, anyway." I couldn't see his face but knew he was glaring at me.

"Just get the other shovel and help."

I said nothing and grabbed the other shovel and started working. Just as we finished leveling the dirt and replacing the squares of grass, a set of headlights rolled in.

My brother and I dropped flat behind our father's headstone and watched as the car stopped at a grave near the entrance. Whoever it was left their headlights on. We were too far for the car lights to cast shadows, but I still worried that we were somehow visible.

I couldn't tell whether it was a man or a woman at first, but when they stepped forward and knelt, I could hear a woman's voice. She was singing. I couldn't make out the words, but the tune was a child's song, something familiar. An old lullaby.

"I think she's singing to her kid," Danny said.

"Yeah," I said.

She finished and set a flower down, then stood up and left.

"Fuck," my brother said.

"Yeah," I said again.

We both laid there and watched the woman's car recede down the road.

"We could've just done that."

"You mean sing to him and leave a flower?" I said. "Maybe a song. Dad would've hated flowers on his grave."

"Well, Mom would've suggested something like that, anyway."

***

I thought about Mom as we drove. He was right. She would never have let us dig Dad up if she were alive. If we had told her, *we're just doing what Dad wanted*, she would have said, *what he'd really want is for his sons not to go to jail*. It wasn't illegal to bury a body on private land in Texas, but it was illegal to rob a grave.

We had taken some precautions, though. We had an unsigned note from Dad. It didn't say much, just that he was sorry he hadn't decided sooner but that he really did want his boys to bury him at Catfish Point. We hadn't found it until the night before the funeral when we were sorting through his dresser drawers. The body was already at the funeral home and we weren't sure what to do, so we'd proceeded with the cemetery burial. Danny and I had come to the same conclusion by the time of the service, though. My only uncertainty was whether or not we should forge his signature. I'd decided maybe it was more believable without it. I expected my brother to argue about that or the whole idea of moving his body, but he didn't. We'd stood off to the side from everyone else at the service, talking, and he'd told me that he slept on it and thought we should do it. I told him I thought maybe a sympathetic cop would let us off if we brought the note with us. He agreed.

It was a twenty-minute drive back to our father's place. It felt like we were speeding, but every time I leaned over to look, the speedometer showed otherwise. Danny told me to *stop being paranoid, goddammit, and just let me drive.* I tried to think about the farm, about where we were taking Dad.

It wasn't really a farm anymore, but Dad always called it that, and that was still how I thought of it. His father and grandfather had both farmed it. When we were kids, there were still a few head of cattle, some chickens, a vegetable garden, and a few fruit trees. Dad worked in landscaping and general maintenance for the city in the Parks Department. His workdays were spent mowing and trimming and planting, and he did the same thing at home on the weekends. There were a few flower beds around the house, but those were Mom's. Dad didn't like flowers. He said he spent half his days planting flowers in parks and that he wanted to grow something useful at home. He seemed perplexed by the whole thing. I remember him shaking his head after a day of tending public flowers and saying, *people like them,* as if there were no accounting for such taste. But he loved the family land and, I think, secretly loved Mom's gardens, too.

There were around three hundred acres, originally. Over the years he sold off all but the fifteen that surrounded the house. Paying for college for us, paying for Mom's medical treatments. What was left included the pond out in front with the big live oak tree that grew on a small peninsula we called Catfish Point, so named because my brother caught a fifteen-pound catfish there when we were children. Fish congregated in the shade of the tree's low hanging branches, and Dad always leaned against that live oak in the morning with a cup of coffee, watching the sunrise for a few minutes before he had to leave for work. That was where he wanted to be buried.

I turned and stared at the lumpy sheet in the backseat. He laid on his side, strapped in with the middle lap belt so he wouldn't roll off when we braked. His limp body sagged on either side of the nylon strap, bent in a sort of half-fetal position so that he could fit on the back seat. Danny hadn't acknowledged that I'd gotten Dad set up in the car on my own, and I looked close to see if I could see his expression. He faced straight ahead, but in the corner of his eye I thought there was some redness. He must have felt me looking at him.

"Can you believe we're actually doing this?"

I wanted to tell him that it was okay to cry.

"I don't know." I paused. "I mean, I'm glad we're giving Dad what he wanted."

Danny nodded and rubbed his eyes. "Goddamn long night already," he said.

I had heard Dad say he wanted to be buried there for the first time the year I graduated from college. I was home for the summer and we were fishing early one morning. He'd motioned toward Catfish Point and told me to bury him right there. I'd responded to him light-heartedly that I'd do it, no problem.

It didn't come up again until one night more than a decade later when my brother and I were both home. Mom was in the hospital with her second bout of skin cancer and would be dead in a month. The three of us were back from the hospital, gathered round the kitchen table. It was late and we were drinking and the talk turned to death. Dad told us that he didn't want to be buried in a cemetery.

"It's unnatural," he said. "Chemicals pumped through your veins, sealed up in a box for all eternity. I don't want that. Put me in a sack on Catfish Point. I don't mind the worms eating me. I'll wind up part of that pond. Only right after all the fish I've pulled outta there."

He took another drink. "Y'all boys will know I'm there. And better in the pond than in that cemetery with my own parents, just all sealed up in a box forever. Unnatural, like I said. Y'all put me in that sack and within a year there'll be nothing but bones there. Even my marrow'll be gone." He smiled when he said that, as though he had been preparing his marrow for some special critter.

"Hell, maybe some flowers will grow above me," he said, and he laughed. My brother and I laughed, too. The conversation then drifted to other things, and we all went to bed fairly soon. Before falling asleep, though, I thought I could hear sobbing through the wall that separated Danny's childhood bedroom from mine.

Dad backtracked the next morning at breakfast, telling us not to put much stock in what he said the night before, that he'd had too much to drink, that if we did bury him on the farm we'd have to disclose it in the deed and it'd make it that much harder to sell if someday we did need to sell. He said his parents had picked out a plot for him long ago and if it was good enough for them then it was good enough for him. I wondered later if he'd have said something different if he'd known that Mom wouldn't wind up in the plot that would've been for her.

★★★

We didn't pass a single car between the cemetery and the farm, and it was almost 3AM when we rolled down the dirt driveway that stretched a quarter-mile from the county road. The house was empty, and I wondered how long it would remain so. Danny and I hadn't talked about what we would do with the place that night, though we'd argued about it before. He and I both lived in town, twenty-five miles to the east. I knew that my brother and his family had no interest in living there, and that I couldn't afford to buy his share. I didn't want to guilt him about selling the place even more now that we'd be selling our father's secret burial site with it. We both needed the money.

The family moved to the farm the year before I was born. Grandpa had died, and our parents had to sell our place or his place. At the time, my parents were living in a two-bedroom cabin on Fairfield Lake, which was a half-hour east of town, an hour from Grandpa's. My father said we couldn't sell Grandpa's land. It had been in the family for a hundred years. So, we sold our cabin and moved to the farm. Over the years I never heard my mother say much of anything about that decision. When she died, though, her will instructed us to cremate her and scatter her ashes on Fairfield Lake. I knew Mom wanted to be cremated, but she'd never talked about where we should scatter her ashes. I figured we'd scatter them in the cemetery or on the land somewhere. I was surprised and a little hurt. I knew that Mom had liked it on the lake, and I remembered her talking warmly about their three years there. She mostly talked about the summers. She was in college, and Dad was already working for the city. On his days off they would water ski until dusk, which fell after 8PM in the summertime. Then they would rush off the water to a country store up the road that served fresh fried catfish until 9PM on summer evenings. I imagined them young and tan and in love, eating at wooden tables, the drips from their bathing suits forming pools at their feet. But I was still surprised that she wanted her ashes scattered there, a place we'd never lived as a family, a place she'd only lived during a time before my brother and I were alive. We never even visited the lake. My father said there was no use in visiting since they'd sold the motorboat. He said that the fishing was better in the farm ponds anyway. Mom would grow silent when he said that, and I never heard them argue about it, but it seemed like she got the last word when we read her will. My brother and father and I rented a boat and carried her ashes out to the center of Fairfield Lake. My father stood, steadied himself against the rock of the boat, and then held the urn like an offering out over the water. We were all silent, and he upended the urn and the ashes fell out, sprinkling the brown surface below. It was a still day, and the ashes seemed to hover above the flat water, separated from the wetness by the magic of surface tension. The three of us stared at them for a minute. Then my father started the boat, and the disturbance caused a small swell to swamp the ashes and break up the mirrored water around us. I watched as some of the ashes began to sink, swallowed by the murky lake. My father pretended not to see and turned the boat back toward the public dock without saying a word.

The night when he'd first brought it up, when we'd been drinking at the house a month before Mom died, Dad had told us to make sure his burial spot wasn't noticeable, that the ground was flush. He said we shouldn't put a cross or any sort of a tombstone, just a big sitting rock. *That way,* he explained, *anyone who comes out will just think it's there because that's a good spot to sit.* It was funny that he said that because he hated sitting. For leisure, he leaned. The only time I remember him sitting was during meals. He liked laying down even less than sitting. I figured that was why he asked to be buried upright.

My brother and I had dug the hole with a posthole digger the evening before we went to the cemetery. He'd told his wife that he and I were going to have a brother's-only, private wake for our father. That we'd drink and talk, that he'd be home in the morning. I asked him if she believed him. *Of course,* he said. *She said that was good, that the two of us ought to talk more.* I told him that I guessed we'd have some time that night. He'd just nodded.

We both showed up at the house around sunset. Danny pulled out the posthole digger and said he'd start, that we could go down a ways with that and then use shovels to widen it. We swapped every fifteen or twenty minutes. A few hours later, we had our hole. Eight feet deep, two feet by three feet across. Our father would stand upright, facing east, just like he wanted.

★★★

Back from the cemetery, we parked beside the house and Danny and I pulled our father out in the sheet, trying to avoid banging him against the edge of the car as we put him back into the wheelbarrow. The flesh of my hands was raw, but I grasped the handles anyway and pushed forward. A bump caused the sheet to fall off my father's head, and I turned my headlamp onto his face. It looked whiter than it had at the funeral home, as though he were as afraid as I was. I had read that dead people look pale because gravity makes the blood pool along their backs, which therefore looks dark and bruised. I didn't want to see his back, and I reached down and covered his face, noticing that, despite the exhuming, his hair remained neatly combed. *I should commend the mortician,* I thought, remembering him saying, "*If you don't want an embalming, I'll just comb the hair, wash the body, and close the eyes.*" He said the last part again, quietly, while spreading his fingers and dropping his palms as if he were playing an invisible piano. "*Comb the hair, wash the body, and close the eyes.*"

The edge of the pond was flanked by small cypress trees and a willow. It was still but not quiet when I reached it. Frogs croaked from the shallows, and some insect I didn't know buzzed from the live oak tree where we planned to bury him. Other noiseless creatures lived below, things that might eat at him once we planted him beneath the surface. I let go of the wheelbarrow handles and turned to my brother, feeling irritated all of the sudden. He carried the shovels, while I carried our dead father.

"How do you want to do this?" I said. "We can't just dump him in."

"Did you hear me suggest that?" he asked.

"What?" I said. He said nothing.

I blew through my nose. "Well, are you going to help?"

He moved forward, allowing our shoulders to bump as he brushed past. I took a step back, off balance.

"You know," he said. "We shouldn't piss each other off around these open graves. It'd be an easy cover up." He smiled after he said it, his grin a caricature of something strange in the light of my headlamp. I didn't smile back, but I could picture lifting my shovel up to the sky and then bringing it to bear on his forehead.

"Funny," I said. "Let's get this done. I think I'm fucking losing it out here."

We each wrapped our arms around him. Our heads were close but we avoided each other's eyes. I held my breath this time. We tried to lower him slowly, but we ended up half-dropping him into the hole, and he thudded into the bottom and crumpled over, knees buckled and neck crooked to the side as though it were broken. The sheet was half off of him, and he looked somehow alive and disfigured, slumped against the earthen walls of his new tomb.

"Shit," my brother said, pulling at his belt and breathing heavy. "Are you fucking kidding me?"

"I know," I said. "We can't leave him like that."

We both laid on our stomachs and reached our hands down into the hole and gripped beneath his armpits. I had a crazy fear that his arms would tear off–but said nothing. As we pulled, his head lolled back and pointed straight at us. His mouth hung open, and I avoided shining my light inside, afraid to see rot or maggots or whatever was happening in there. I was glad his eyes stayed closed. I closed mine, too, and pulled harder.

We finally got him back above ground and then both stood

there, staring at the hole. Eventually, we decided that if we narrowed it and tapered it like an ice cream cone, so that he was leaning slightly against one wall, he would stay upright. I got down into the hole and looked up at my brother. He stood above me with his shovel, and I thought about the image I had earlier of my own shovel crashing into his forehead. He shoveled and I tried to maintain my balance and avoid the dirt as it came down, leaning to the side and packing each new shovelful against the walls, trying to figure how much was needed. After a few minutes, I thought it was sufficiently narrow. I paused, but my brother either didn't notice or pretended not to. More dirt showered atop me, sticking to the sweat on my face and neck. I finally said, "hey," and he stopped and slung the shovel over his shoulder but stayed quiet. I climbed out, gripping the edges above me and worming out of the eight-foot soil tube.

We lowered the body again, and this time, he slid in snug, like a cork in a bottle. I thought that it must be good to have one's grave fit one so well, walls of earth pressing around, cooling in the summer and insulating in the winter. We had removed the sheet as we slid him in, and soon he was standing in his best suit beneath the earth on Catfish Point, just as he'd asked. His head remained flopped to the side, and we decided that we'd pack dirt around it at the end. We set to shoveling and I focused on the sweat beading up along my hairline, the ache in my hands and back, and not the fact that each swing of the shovel dropped dirt onto my father's body. The hole grew narrower and narrower, and we had to eventually drop the dirt directly on top of his head and let it filter down into the gaps. Soon all was covered but his face.

His eyes were still closed, but both of us thought he'd want to see. We debated who would lift the eyelids. I imagined the eyeballs already rotted, that we would pull up his eyelids and see empty holes and things already eating inside his skull. I figured that body decomposition probably didn't happen that fast, but I didn't want to carry the image of my father's vacant eye sockets around with me. I sensed that Danny was having some of the same thoughts.

"You know," he said, "he'll open his eyes if he wants to. At sunrise, you know? He was never much of a night owl."

I agreed. The thought our dead father opening his eyes of his own volition was somehow more appealing than us opening them. I cradled his head while my brother packed the dirt tightly around the base, gradually covering the back. He couldn't bear to press the dirt tight against his face, so we left it exposed and then stood up and cast the last few shovelfuls without looking. Then we smoothed the remaining dirt around and patted down the surface as though nothing was resting beneath us, as though we did not just plant our father's body uncovered in the ground.

All that remained was the limestone block that we hauled from the dry well on the north end of the house. We squatted on opposite sides of the stone, and I slid my fingers in its cool, water-worn grooves and lifted. We shuffled it a few feet over and dropped it atop the grave. The block was heavy, and for a moment I didn't think I could straighten out, that I might be forever hunched with the strain of the night. I finally did straighten, my spine popping. I placed my hands on my hips, arched my back, and looked up at the live oak tree looming above me. Then I twisted to the left, to the east. My little brother was still bent over beside me, hands on his knees, and I couldn't tell if he was resting or grieving. He caught me looking at him.

"Well," I said. "Now what?"

He moved his mouth like he was chewing.

"I don't know," he said. "Go home, I guess."

He spoke softly, as if he were waiting for something. The night seemed quieter now. I looked down, brushing at the loose soil with a boot. I laid a hand on his shoulder in silence, expecting him to shrug it off. He didn't, though, and we both stood there. Then he straightened and turned away from me. Behind him, dawn wasn't far off, but the moon was still high, casting nighttime shadows across the pasture.

CREATURES WIRED FOR STORIES
A Conversation with Victor McConnell

Claire Agnes: From my first read of this narrative and onward, "The Reburial" stood out as a memorably weird, yet remarkably subtle rendering of obligation through the lens of grief. We experience the obligation of sons to their father, of brothers to one another, and of family members to a home. What catalyzed this narrative? Are the characters, settings, and emotions presented rooted in experience or exploration?

Victor McConnell: Experience. I'd love to say it really happened, but it didn't. At least, not yet. But it is rooted in reality.

My parents moved out to the country after I grew up in town, and my dad said in passing once that he'd like to be buried by the pond next to their house, with a posthole digger. He likes flowers, though, and currently is still "above dirt," as he'd say.

CA: It sounds like many of the story's grounding details have remained the same as their real-life inspirations. Can you speak to your decision to keep the story so close to home?

VM: Well, I don't know how to parse out "close to home" versus not. Certain scenes and places may have originated in something I saw once, but as in any story, they sort of morph into their own places with the same sort of independent existence that a dream landscape might have. And so I don't feel like I am actively deciding which pieces of the story should be closer to the world I can touch versus the world in my mind. I just kind of close my eyes and try to see it and feel it.

CA: In terms of process and inspiration, do you often mine personal or lived experience for narrative insight?

VM: I don't know who said it originally, but I've often repeated the joke: "Fiction, non-fiction… it's all half true." We're creatures wired for stories, and I can't help but be on the lookout for them. Snippets of conversations from a bar. Meeting someone briefly at the coffee shop and imagining their life, their world. Sometimes the relationship or experience that prompts a story is longer and more complex, but often it is a relatively small moment.

CA: As you mentioned earlier, the idea of burying your own father by the pond next to his house is thankfully currently an idea instead of a reality, though I can imagine rendering these potential events through realistic scene might still come at great emotional cost to the writer, the pages often only possible after much introspective inquisition. However, writers commonly cite both personal catharsis and realism in emotive narrative depth as benefits of grappling with painful realities and complex nuances of emotion through narrative. Throughout your writing process for "The Reburial" and other works, how do you ratio your balance between authorial distance and mining personal connection?

VM: I don't really try to create a wall between my life and a story. I'm not sure if I could. I will literally just sit at my keyboard and close my eyes and try to imagine a scene, or what someone might say or feel. How much of that someone is me? That's tough to say. I mean, I'm the one who is feeling everything, in a sense—there is no one else in the room.

Though, to be fair, I guess I do draw a line sometimes at writing things that might be hurtful to people I care about. That's one reason I'd probably never write a memoir.

CA: This is a compressed story, focusing on two brothers on one particular and significant night. Was the narrative always this acute? Or did earlier iterations of the piece include additional characters or extensions of time?

VM: I first wrote it back in 2008, I think, and it sat dormant for the last fourteen years. It always existed in this form, though. I remember thinking about putrefaction, about reading about the bacteria that produces sulfide, methane, cadaverine, putrescine. Ultimately, the science angle didn't really play a role in the story. If you're going to dig up and re-bury a body, better to do it quick.

CA: What was the extent of your research for this piece? Was the scope limited to corpse science, or did you flesh out the story with other supporting materials or information?

VM: No pun intended with "flesh out the story," right? Sorry—couldn't help it.

On a more serious note, it's been over a decade, so I don't remember exactly what I read then. Generally, I think I tracked down a handful of academic publications on corpse decomposition—how it happens, how fast it happens, and so forth. I don't think there were other supporting materials involved, as the place and people in the story already felt "known" to me.

CA: For a story in which our central characters spend more than one scene inside of graves, it is a pleasantly humorous piece, skirting the potential melodrama of the macabre through the restraint practiced in the prose. I'm curious as to how you honed the narrative tone, and by what processes this particular voice emerged.

VM: I don't know. Like any voice I write in, I guess it comes from some complex stew of experience, relationships, and neural wiring.

CA: Are the tone and voice of "The Reburial" fairly representative of your other written and/or creative works thus far?

VM: I generally don't write in first person, so this is a little bit of an outlier in that regard. And I don't consciously try to change my tone, but I'd like to think it varies somewhat depending on who the main character is (for example, the voice of an 80-year-old woman versus that of a 20-year-old man). There are commonalities in my work, of course, some known to me (such as moons—I like moons) and others that I'm probably unaware of.

CA: The image of the father being buried upright has stuck with me ever since first reading this piece. How and when was this particular detail introduced to the narrative?

VM: That image embedded itself in my brain, too, when my dad made that comment about having his grave dug with a posthole digger. Thinking of humans "laid to rest" after death is so common, but planting a human upright seems a good jumping off point for all sorts of thought bubbles.

CA: It's certainly an image that adds to the story's memorability, as those small, telling, weird details often have the power to do. Is your writing process typically catalyzed by overheard or experienced moments?

VM: It's pretty frequent for me to hear someone say something that strikes me as funny or strange or memorable or sad. Often it will just become a verbal story that I'll tell to people for a few months before it fades. Sometimes, though, it seems like something that belongs in a work of fiction (or that serves as a springboard of sorts).

CA: Can you speak to your process of forging a single detail or conversation into an entire story? Do you move transition from the point of inspiration into considerations of character, plot, setting, or otherwise?

VM: I usually don't create structured outlines or character sketches. It depends upon the idea, though. Sometimes it will inspire a subject matter that I'll feel I need to research a bit. At this point, the research may lead in unexpected directions. Usually, though, I'll have an idea and will sit down and just quickly write—almost freewriting—and have a very rough, fairly brief version of the story. Then, when (days, months, years later) I actually write the story it may change as I enter the world more deeply.

CA: From biblical tragedy to modern comedy, fraternal relationships have a long history in storytelling. Were there any particular portraits, in literature or elsewhere, that inspired or otherwise informed the characters of the brothers in "The Reburial," or the nuances of their dynamic? How did you go about rendering their relationship within the specific context of this story?

VM: I do have a brother, though these fictional brothers aren't very much like the two of us. Other than, perhaps, being comfortable with dark humor. But when I'm writing a character, I just try to think about what they might say, think, and do. Of course, there are pieces of myself or those I know within them, but as the story grows, they become more distinct and I have a feel for who the characters are, even if I don't know all the details of their lives or how their minds work.

CA: Thank you for sharing this story with *Driftwood Press* and our readers. Where else can we find your work? Do you have any forthcoming projects or events our readers should be aware of?

VM: Thank you for publishing it, and for the thoughtful back and forth.

As for other writing, I wasn't writing much from 2010 to 2020, but I'm working my way back. I have a couple short stories that will be published on a website later this year (like "The Reburial," pieces I wrote years ago that I'm only now seeking to publish). *Kallisto Gaia Press* published a story earlier this year (hard copy only), and I do have a recent work of flash fiction published online in the *Los Angeles*

Review. And one bit of basketball fiction that I wrote about fifteen years ago that I believe is still online somewhere, as well as one or two other pre-2010 pieces that would be hard to find. Working on some other things, both short and long, but no idea when they'll be done.

CA: Thank you for taking the time to speak with me, Victor! Looking forward to reading more of your work.

TANK
Jenna Abrams

AFTER (PRESENT)

T leans over the ferry's railing and spits into the Atlantic. She turns to press her cheek into the metal, watching Darby at the other end. Darby's hair, red and glittered, flops and shakes with the ferry's rocking. From behind, Nate slips his arms around T's waist. She can smell the weed, so she knows it's him before he touches her, knows how the smell will stick if she remains close, especially in the Battery tunnels. Nate kisses her cheek, a thing she perceives more than feels. The sea is choppy, gray and irritated, as the ferry churns toward the Battery's island.

Maybe there isn't a word for the feeling that possesses her body around him, a feeling growing since last year. Her skin used to feel right when it was next to his. This is no longer true and yet it still is: both a memory and a present experience. But she can't distinguish between the two anymore. He still makes something shoot through her body to her brain—it's just, the motivation for the response in her nervous system has shifted. She knows there's a difference in the why of her body's reactions now; she is aware.

It's early spring in Massachusetts, cold and damp, that foggy time at the end of winter when everyone is still waiting for something. This morning, the Cape is coated in a thick, dewy mist. At the end of the coast, the only place to go is out to sea. In the center of the last little island, the only one with inhabitants, sits the Battery: an enormous military compound long abandoned to flood and rust. Beyond, there's nothing but ocean, and if T ignores the mainland left behind, she can almost believe nothing else exists at all.

Off the ferry and onto the island's beach, the wind is urgent, whipping the blanket draped around T's shoulders out like a cape. The three of them slip into the woods, through pitch pine and black huckleberry, a path you'd only find if you already knew it was there.

Buried in a grove of black gum trees, the path opens, and there's the Battery. To T it seems to appear suddenly, unexpected; an immense steel monster surrounded by scrub oak and sprawling early virgin's-bower. An observation tower and three dead guns sit atop. T pulls the blanket tight around her. Facing them, an enormous tunnel yawns, dark and apparently toothless.

The Battery consumes light only a few paces in, leaving the world a shrinking half-moon. Inside, the dampness and silence make the opacity claustrophobic, viscous. It clings to them. Like being inside an eclipse.

To T, it feels like entering the Battery has rendered time irrelevant. In the absolute darkness, there is no way to distinguish between the experience of the Battery's tunnels now and the experience of a year before, or any other. She tries to slow her erratic breathing as they walk. The tangle of tunnels winds around the Battery's center, surrounding the large room at its heart. A maze, the whole thing. Built to confuse enemies in an invasion, T figures. She drags her fingers along the wall, over the crevices and rough bits of concrete, feeling how they might leave an imprint in her skin if she pushes too hard.

Every spring, the Bloom Festival transforms the Battery. For weeks before the art-and-performance event, organizers navigate the winding tunnels, painting walls and building scaffolding for performances. The tunnels, impassable from November to February, thaw sufficiently by spring break, and an ever-growing group gathers in the Battery to party and perform, in awe of each other for one long night.

The Battery is too enormous to decorate completely—once they reach the inner circle, temporary lighting designs will guide their way, but in the outer tunnels, they must fend for themselves. In all that blackness, her sense of space dislocated, T considers which body parts, if any, she can actually feel. Darby, digging for her flashlight, calls, "Have you guys ever been in a sensory deprivation tank?" Of course T hasn't; of course Darby has. Darby's done everything cool, everything she's wanted and nothing she hasn't. Nate only laughs.

"I did it over winter break," Darby says. "The water is super high in salt, so you float, but it's regulated so it's the same temperature as your skin, and there's no sound or light. So you can't see or hear anything, and you can't tell the difference between the water and your body."

"Freaky." Nate drags the word like he does when he's high. He puts a hand on T's ass, a hand from nowhere. Then she truly isn't sure—when are they, which time? She's dizzy, her blood jumping irregular with her muscles, which pucker and tense inside of her.

BEFORE (ALL OTHER TIME)

T and Darby met Nate, officially, the morning after the festival two years ago, but he'd always been on their radar. He was famous in the local scene, someone everyone liked and sought approval from. As they crowded onto the return ferry, Nate was next to T, held her gear while she jumped the dock gap. Darby, never intimidated by anyone, invited him to join that afternoon to explore the empty factory by the Truro pier. She asked like he was just anybody, even though he was a few years out of college, freakishly good-looking with a double nostril hoop on one side and a stud on the other. He made big, weird art installations with rigged blowtorches and scrap metal. He was loud, opinionated, stubborn—he took up all the space around him and more, and T loved it, wanted to be like that. When they met he was sporting the black denim uniform of all post-college punks who lived in Providence and bartended to make ends meet. Later, T flipped over inside when he whistled with admiration at the speed with which she picked the rusting padlock on the factory door. He smelled like weed and eucalyptus oil. Inside, Darby led them to the top floor. The last four white metal stairs were gone, but the guardrails remained; the missing stairs like knocked-out teeth.

With Nate's help, Darby scrambled up, cursing approvingly over the view from the splintered windows. Nate turned to T with cupped hands. When he hoisted her over the missing stairs he was gentle but solid with his fingers on her waist. She felt the weight of a thick ring he wore on his thumb against her hip. He asked for her arm to pull himself up. When his fingers circled her wrist, she felt a crush form almost instantly. She felt so lucky, then, that he returned her feelings. They were hanging out all the time by May. He came to see her at school on weekends. He brought her a denim vest of her own, a heart-shaped patch sewn under the breast pocket. When he wasn't there she barely slept, fantasizing about him. When he stood close to her, before, all the blood in her body used to zip and sing.

Before the Bloom Festival, in middle school, T was starting to dip her toes into what her mom called "weirdo stuff": costumes, acrobatics, shouty music. It was initially Darby's enthusiasm—she was always at T's house putting elaborate makeup on their faces, encouraging T to practice handstands and try hanging from silks, or taking T to youth circus performances or ska shows in her brother's friend's garage. If Darby stayed for dinner, they'd eat with faces covered in silver spirals. T's mother would shake her head; she spent most of T's teenage years doing that. But the world of weirdos (as Darby affectionately called it after hearing T's mom say "weirdo stuff" so many times) embraced T, gave her a space to exist. So she stayed there.

T had attended the Bloom Festival since high school, but the year they met Nate was her first time performing. She did freestyle suspended movement with aerial silks, creating shapes with her body. But she'd never taken real lessons, always forgot the lexicon, secretly didn't care about that as much as she was supposed to. Performing was Darby's idea, a nudge for T to be a little bold. And she'd enjoyed it, maybe not as much as Darby wanted, but she would do it again, especially after Nate offered to help with choreographing her set the next year.

But in the beginning, what T loved most was practicing alone, in the basement where her dad installed the setup after she'd soothed his safety concerns. She kept it dim, only this one seventies-era lava lamp of her mom's glowing, its movements fluid and relaxed, a guide. She swung and flowed through her hips and her fingers. She felt herself in every inch of her body, its movements palpable, unplanned, instinctive, boundaryless. That was before.

"What's the point of the tank?" T asks Darby. "It kind of sounds like meditation."

"You could say that. But I've heard it can center your balance so you can transport, mentally, to alternate universes. Your body is the vessel and also the universe, unbounded by this plane." Darby sounds like she's reciting from a book. The echo intensifies T's dizziness. It takes her a moment to orient herself, to remember that she is experiencing the present. But the further in they go, the harder it becomes to convince herself that time is a real thing you can move forward through at all.

"Okay, but what did it feel like?" T pushes. Darby has found her flashlight, but still they move carefully, palms flat to the wall. "Could you really not feel where your body ended? Did that mess with your head? Did they talk about it being used therapeutically?"

"Whoa," Nate laughs. "You writing a paper or something?"

"I don't know about any of that shit," Darby says, swinging the flashlight into their faces. "But I could see it being therapeutic, yeah. I didn't feel numb, really. That wasn't it. I felt hyper aware of myself but also like, soft-edged."

"Sounds like a drug experience," Nate chimes in.

"It wasn't drugs, though," Darby insists. "It was the tank."

T has more questions, waterfalling from where she's been storing them a year. What is the effect of blurring the boundary between your body and the world? Can too much disassociation from a body make you unable to feel it at all?

By the time T has formed something that sounds reasonably sane to ask, she's fallen behind. She hurries to catch them, drawing close to Darby's light. It's easy to get lost, despite the markings slapped on the walls in fading paint, indicating the way to the Battery's heart, where the biggest performances are staged. They pass a dimly lit room where something involving pool noodles is under construction. A green mohawk grins and salutes. "Radical adult playhouse," he says, nodding enthusiastically. "Come back in an hour!"

When it's quiet again, T leans close to Darby. "Try to explain again. Please?" she says. "About what the tank was like."

Darby turns to T with a question on her face. She tries, thinking. "I don't know how else to describe it. Like, my body had no boundaries at all. It existed everywhere. Like I was limitless. The only thing in the world that existed or mattered."

What T needs to say now is formless. She senses Nate closing in behind her. Okay, something happens then. Her heart is speeding, nervous system reacting; something is piercing her barriers, demanding panic, and her body is obeying. Nate's hand appears again, this time touching her waist. There is an explosion of light in her head, a painful headache against the dark, and then she is running, shouting that she'll race Nate and Darby to the main room. She's running faster and faster and the flashlight is fading and fading. She's ignoring their layered, ricocheting shouts that call her back, only running, her boots making hollow slaps on the damp cement.

THAT TIME IN THE BATTERY TUNNEL

It was here and almost exactly one year before now. It was raining, the tunnels spitting as they trudged in, all soaked through and talking about floods. There was no real flood—it would have to pour for days to make the Battery dangerous—but it was good to fear something.

The festival was a thing everyone knew about but was also secret. You couldn't technically enter the Battery—it was government property, albeit abandoned—but inside was fine. Cops would interfere if they were on the island (rare) and caught you heading there, but they wouldn't follow anyone inside. Both illegal and sanctioned, forbidden and permissible. This used to be T's favorite part. They weren't supposed to be there, and they knew it; this knowledge transformed the trek from the ferry dock, through the island's kettle hole swamp dense with red maple and black gum trees, from a mere walk into a mission. On the way there, there was danger. But once inside the Battery, you were supposed to be safe.

That time, they trudged through the muddy tunnels drinking shitty vodka, boots making thick, echo-y sounds in the puddles, everything absolutely pitch black except for the glow from Darby's flashlight. It was T, Darby, and Nate, plus Mark, another bartender from Providence, and Maya, Darby's friend from school. They carried a small generator, fire batons, armfuls of silks, lawn chairs. They were charged, light and full of momentum.

It was fast, what happened. The rest of the group got ahead. Nate put his arm around T's waist and dragged her into a side tunnel. She kissed him back when he kissed her but said they should get on to the main room. He put his tongue in her mouth while she was talking. She could taste his need on her lips. She could feel it in his fingers, his thumb ring cold on the back of her neck, when he pushed her onto the muddy cement and yanked down her jeans.

The story here can become anything T wants. She's told herself the story in many ways, a million versions in her head, but even a year later, the story is constantly evolving.

She remembers the mud on the floor of the tunnel, which sloped upwards and was wider than the one they'd come from. The floor was cement and cold and wet with the mud. It was a thin layer of mud, that's what T remembers, and how the pattern of the cement ate into the meat of her palms and stayed there for a while, crosshatched in her skin like an enormous fingerprint. Her knees were stiff when she unbent them to stand. She slid her jeans up. They were wet from the rain. Everything was wet and covered in mud, everything in the world. Before she could say anything, Nate spun her, grinning. He said: *That was so hot. Spontaneous. Hot.* He kissed her numbed face. She knew because she saw his lips come toward her own; she was spatially aware of contact being made but she did not actually feel anything.

AFTER (PRESENT)

T hugs the Battery's cool, damp tunnels, going by touch again without the aid of Darby's flashlight. Her heart is so loud it makes its own echo. At the bottom of a long slope, her feet hit a puddle, and the splash of her own body startles her. She retreats to a defensive position, flat and rigid against the wall.

THAT TIME

One way T tells it to herself is she put her hands behind her and said, "Stop," and he did.

Another way she tells herself is basically what happened, but with her willing participation—when she nodded at his '*That was so hot. Spontaneous. Hot*', she meant it. In this story, T is who Nate thought she was; okay, who he wanted her to be. This is the only version she has allowed herself out loud.

AFTER (PRESENT)

T stops and folds herself in half, arms bisecting her chest, head between her knees, the way her mother instructed her to do when she was nauseous as a child. She puts her hands to the damp ground. The sensation is obscured, blurry, like it can't exactly penetrate. She can't slow her heart, and now she's gasping in the darkness. She lowers her forehead to the cement. Still, it's like it isn't really touching her.

THAT TIME

Another way she tells the story is that she initiated: Nate was her boyfriend, and she was hot and spontaneous, wild and exciting. So of course she did.

There's the way she tells it where she put her hands behind her and said *STOP* or maybe *stop* and he just didn't hear her. This version could be true. She has trouble convincing herself. This version becomes about how she should have said it over and over, screamed like what was happening was an enemy invasion and not Nate, who everyone admired. Or it becomes about how she should have liked it, about how a girl cool enough to be with Nate would have, and what's wrong with her that she didn't? Should, should, should. Fuck these fucking thoughts. She doesn't want to think them.

AFTER (PRESENT)

Darby's laugh is echoing, Nate's stoned chuckle trailing. T hears him call her name once, twice, but then the tunnels fall silent again. She tries to focus on her lungs as she inches forward. She folds herself into a room and holds her inhale while they pass, watching the glow of the flashlight approach and then fade. When it's dark, she breathes again.

THAT TIME

Somewhere in all this is the real version, but she isn't certain what it is anymore. Given so quickly after, his assessment—*Hot. Spontaneous. Hot*—had killed the potential for further consideration. Before her mind could form the word, he had produced other words—his— and then there was no room for her own words of what it was. This is how she has passed through the year: all these versions of the truth. Layer on layer on layer. An armoring, or something.

T remembers the rest of that night like watching a film, with the safety of the screen between her and the hours afterwards. She can watch it like this, in pieces: Nate's palm on her back as Darby twirled flaming rods onstage. The crowd a flash of color, the biggest room in the Battery packed with people in bright clothes, homemade fanny packs, painted extremities. Nate's face when T, fueled by the shitty vodka she'd downed, announced she would perform without her gear. No helmet, no knee pads. Of course it wasn't smart. That was the point. Before she got onstage, Nate asked if she was excited. She looked at her body, covered in the paint she had applied, but also the mud. Because she couldn't talk, she nodded.

"Good luck, baby," he said, and she bit into her lip hard enough to taste blood.

She did well until the vodka pooled in her head and she fell— quickly, briefly, hard. She heard the ground as it connected with her head and she saw brightness and then darkness and then nothing for a minute, until she opened her eyes to Nate and Darby. Okay, the minute could have been a year. She couldn't tell. Time died then and was reborn when she opened her eyes.

THAT TIME, BUT ALSO AFTER

It could have been worse. A concussion, a head wound deep enough to require staples, but she would be fine. It bled in a way that made it seem worse. Nate and Mark and Darby helped her to the beach. She was fortunate, at least, that an organizer had brought his own motorboat, because they'd missed the last ferry by hours. As they loaded her in, Mark stabilizing her head, she reached for Darby's arm. Darby squeezed her shoulder, eyes on the mainland. "You're okay. Everyone drinks too much before a performance. Don't be embarrassed. We'll go to a hospital, and everything will be fine." Her voice was soothing, convincing. Nate appeared over T, his unkempt eyebrows knitted in concern, and reached for her hand. She shut her eyes, and did not open them again until they had reached the other shore.

T has always wanted to be more like Darby: prepared to protect herself against anything, prepared to express any loud noise growing inside her. Darby, who believes powerfully in her own perceptions. When they were thirteen, on the travel soccer team, they lost the regional championship. After, Darby lay on the field screaming for a long time, screaming at the top of her lungs. It was super weird. They all knew she was a weirdo. But also, she was right, and T knew it even back then. That's what they were all doing, inside. But only Darby wasn't afraid to let everyone know what the feeling sounded like. Only Darby could scream for fifteen minutes without thinking twice. But T has no idea what will happen if she opens her mouth.

They had to shave a portion of her head to put the staples in. The doctor demonstrated how to clean the wound. Nate squinted and nodded at what the doctor was doing, like maybe he'd have something to say about it. He sat with her until it was done, and then he dropped her off at her parents' as the sun was coming up, kissing her gingerly on the cheek. At home, later, when T showed her parents the wound and explained the care, her mother worried and fussed, but after watching T clean it herself a few times, she left her alone. T returned to college with a doctor's note and strict instructions to limit her computer time.

For weeks she rose, went to the dorm's bathroom, removed the previous dressing, and tilted her head to examine the bald pink spot, off-center on the top of her scalp, about two inches. She cleaned it with the alcohol pads and applied the Bacitracin with a Q-tip, going gently around the fat silver staples. She covered the pink space with a square of clean white gauze, using medical tape to hold it in place. She looked at her work in the mirror, satisfied; a thing done well, a healing action completed. Good.

Nate stayed close to campus for two weeks and kissed her gently all around her bruised head and held her in his lap and read to her from her favorite books since the concussion made it hard to read. He brought her candy and liquor, and though she wasn't supposed to drink with a concussion, he scoffed at medical paranoia, and she agreed she was probably being too cautious, lame, so she drank, and he was also careful when he moved her head on his dick, careful not to touch the space covered in padding, and she thought, *all this is caring, this is being cared for.*

Once he stretched his arms wide, comically straining, saying, *I love you this much, I can't even reach far enough.* She looked at the space between his hands. She knew what he meant, yet what she saw was how small the space was, how short a distance, so maybe he didn't understand the symbol he was using. Or maybe she couldn't feel the symbol right.

When he returned to Providence she was sucked by a great gravitational force into her room, barely making it to class. When Nate called about another visit she said soon, school was so busy, and that felt true, because everything took twice as long as before; when she pushed him off again she said it must be the concussion. Post-concussion symptoms were real, she'd looked it up. He showed up at her dorm anyway a week later, armed with flowers and a funny Frankenstein figurine, its metal staples tiny replicas of her own, and she decided he, the person in front of her, really did care in his way. Later in her room, when he trailed a hand across her stomach, she smiled with what she hoped was well-conveyed exhaustion and put her hand over his. He looked at her.

"You good, baby? What, you didn't miss me?" he teased. He kissed her in this kind of deep, meaningful way. She had missed him. She was pretty sure. In the square cinder block room, the hand continued on its way.

In the months afterwards and the entire year since, a year that has been one year but has also somehow been her entire life, T has felt her skin create a barrier between itself and the rest of her. Like when you fall asleep on your arm. It started in the tunnel, but after, it spread. Even now, it persisted, like her body had gone to sleep but never woken up all the way. Her mother had taught her, when the arm is asleep, to knead her fingers up and down forcefully, coaxing the blood back into its natural spaces, refilling what's lost. Since the tunnel, T has relied on this kneading to remind her body of itself. In the gray, mildewed dorm shower, after the water is off, she kneads her body from her feet to her scalp, fingers lingering on the scar, massaging the tough skin until it's painful, a little closer to awake.

She can see the shape of it now, sort of. The disparity between their two experiences of the same event. She wonders if they would differ on all elements. Would Nate insist the mud was warm and not cold? The floor metal, not cement? Could he actually have had a different sensory experience? Did he hear her make noises she hadn't made, of approval, encouragement? Or did she make them, and forget? Was the mistake her own? Should she, at least, have known what she was allowed to say to him?

When she got home from Urgent Care that morning, her parents were still asleep. She was dry but freezing. She took a bath. There was grit and mud in the tub from her legs and face. The water went murky after she lowered herself in. She couldn't see her body under the water, so she kept pulling her knees up to make sure they were still there. Each time, she placed her chin into the "V" space her knees made when she pressed them together, then lowered the knees back into the bath's blurry obscurity, watching that part of herself disappear. The grit at the bottom of the tub pressed into her ass and thighs. It hurt. She remembered that.

BEFORE / AFTER

Once, she felt this and could've told Nate every day: I sweat for you, I feel relief when you arrive, I feel nostalgia for you even when you're with me. If we're separated, look for me in the factory near the pier; if I'm not there, it's only because I couldn't bear to crawl up the broken stairs without you. Here is what factories smell like: your sweat. Eucalyptus oil, cheap. Your hands on my waist, the weight of your ring on my hip.

Now she feels this: the profound feeling of unfeeling. Also, the Battery's floor pressing into her knees and palms. Cement, mud, cool and slick against her face. A ring on a hand from nowhere, icy on the back of her neck. The knowledge of an empty body behind her. If she concentrates, she can feel that all the time.

PRESENT

Nate's performance is one of the most anticipated of the night. By the time T has found the heart of the Battery, a large crowd has gathered in the room, shadowy and rounded at its edges. In the crowd, Nate's face appears for a moment and blends away. T stays back against a cool wall. Onstage, a musician plucks a handmade string instrument while two people in rainbow bodysuits balance impeccably on each other, holding positions that seem impossible. T sees Darby's hair bouncing, her face beckoning through the packed room. T steadies her chest before releasing her body to the crowd.

Nate's routine involves contorting elaborately on a metal chair he's welded, suspended by cables. Suspended around him are a dozen papier-mâché moons. He's explained before: something about hard and flimsy materials, something about touching the impossible. She doesn't remember now. It's too loud, too many voices, hard to breathe. She shuts her eyes tight. When she opens them again, the moons are blurry and she's sweating. All these stories and versions of the truth. Layer on layer on layer. Not just an armoring—a burying, too.

On her scalp, there is a small raised ridge where the staples used to be. T strokes it firmly, absorbing the sensation of her fingertip as it skims the uneven scar, building up layers of feeling. When she thinks of care, actually, what comes to mind is the head wound. How she had to clean it so carefully, how precisely they shaved her hair to make room for the staples. When she thinks of care, it's her own hands on her own head: wiping, clearing, smoothing, taping, fixing.

T pushes through the crush to Darby's glittered head and grabs her wrist. "What?" Darby shouts, her attention shifting from Nate. But it's still so loud, still his stage, the crowd's admiration reflected in all the awestruck gazes—suddenly it seems absurd to T that she is in this room at all. What is she doing here? There is a hard knot in her throat, a word maybe, but she is choked by Nate's pull on every set of eyes.

Not Darby's, though. Darby is looking at T. Her expression is not enraptured, not concerned with what else is happening. She is waiting. But the knot in T's throat pulses bigger.

T drops Darby's arm and stumbles backwards through the crowd toward the exit, through the exclaims over Nate, over whatever is happening with him and his body and what his body can do. She shuts her eyes. She slips past the people, the shouts, into the nearest tunnel, blending into the shadows.

"Wait! Where are you going?" Darby's voice is close. She's followed T, but it's hard to tell where she is; her shouts bounce everywhere. They are once again in inky, unintelligible darkness. T keeps her eyes closed as she pushes deeper into the Battery's maze. Darby shouts again, still too far behind T to touch her. "Stop! What the fuck happened? Tell me!"

T resists the urge to drag her fingers along the walls. Instead she lets each footstep choose her path. At the end of a long tunnel, the air opens up into what must be a wide room.

Now, from wherever she is in the Battery's sinuous system, T can't hear anything at all. When she finally stops and unclenches her eyes, she has gone so far that the darkness is as dark as her own shuttered eyelids. The only clue to Darby in the room a moment later is the sound of her footsteps, ceasing as she senses T's presence. She doesn't say anything. They stand there, shoulders close, not quite touching. T counts her breaths, inhaling and exhaling. Then she stretches her arms wide and starts to move. Darby slips out of the way. T moves her body the way you do in water—loose, languid, unconcerned, like there are no walls, no floor. She moves unencumbered, until she is spinning wildly, limbs flying, until her body is no longer contained to itself, until she occupies every inch of the room and everything else; every tunnel in the Battery, everything in the world. As she expands, miraculously touching nothing, she feels every atom of her body and the air around it as one entity, limitless; all the same kind of open, lightless space. She's breathing deep, adrenaline flooding the room, flooding the body she can't see but can now palpably, perfectly feel: every nerve, every cell. She listens carefully to herself as she moves. She can't hear anything but her own heart, beating in this unbelievable darkness where T can't see herself or the Battery or anything else—as if it is beating without a body around it at all, free.

BLURRING THE BORDERS
A Conversation with Jenna Abrams

Rachel Phillippo: Hi, Jenna! Congratulations on the publication of your short story "Tank"! It is a tense and beautiful story, with the sort of emotional charge and striking imagery that is sure to resonate with readers long after their first read. I'm looking forward to hearing a little about how "Tank" came to be.

Jenna Abrams: Thank you so much. In the collection I am revising, this story is the one I've been submitting the longest. It's a whole different feeling to have a story like that picked up. I'm thrilled to have it published in *Driftwood*.

RP: It certainly is rewarding to have your persistence pay off! And we are thrilled to offer "Tank" a home. "Tank" really is the perfect title for this story, in my opinion. Because of juxtaposition to the setting of the Battery, the image of a military tank is briefly brought to mind, but of course we know after reading that the title refers to sensory deprivation tanks. What inspired you to include the concept of these tanks in this story? Did your research include trying one out yourself?

JA: Part of what I love about this title is that it touches different elements of the story. The tank references the setting, of course, but besides that and the sensory deprivation tank described, there's also this foreboding quality to that military word, and what T experiences is a kind of attack. It's also a claustrophobic-sounding and heavy word, in terms of its sound, a word that lands very final and hard, and that felt really correct to me. I had two other titles before this and never felt like they were right. At some point this title clicked.

I've never been in a sensory deprivation tank. The concept of the tank came to me very early in the story. I knew what had happened to this character and where she was going to be when she relived it, or faced it, and I was doing all this writing trying to capture the feeling of both detachment from and grounding within your body, trying to express being numbed from yourself so powerfully it becomes physical. I thought about the borders between our bodies and the world, and how intense an unwanted violation of those borders is. From there came questions about what blurs those borders, what softens the borders of our bodies. I knew that, in part, what my character wanted was relief from the excruciating truth of those borders being violated.

I knew what sensory deprivation tanks were, and then I did the thing that I tend to do when I lock onto an idea that I can feel is going to be thematically important to a piece, and I got a little hooked on it. I was just thinking about it all the time. I read all these articles about them and watched videos of people describing their experiences, and did this rough writing about it, which eventually got developed and whittled down to what ended up in the story, which isn't much. But I think all that writing informed how I wrote T and her body and her relationship with it before and after the assault, so it was really useful in developing the whole thing, not just the parts where a sensory deprivation tank is explicitly mentioned.
I would love to do it one day.

RP: Even while writing about the disconnection and emotional numbness that you've mentioned, you successfully keep us very close to your protagonist's psyche and experience. "Tank" is such a deeply personal story of trauma and of lost and found autonomy for T. What is the significance of giving this character only an initial?

JA: There is a quality of disintegration that is important in the story. These narratives that T has told herself over and over start to fall apart once she enters the Battery and can't escape a more visceral reliving of the previous year. I wanted shifting, disintegrating explanations of what happened or didn't happen and how it can be spun, and T at the center, only a letter as an identifier. The way the narratives disintegrate is mirrored in the way the sections get much shorter in the middle of the story, when T is flashing through all the ways she could tell it. Giving T only an initial was a way to include T herself (her vision of herself, her confidence in herself, her sense of self in general) in the disintegrating. It was also a nod to victims' right to

RP: Part of why "Tank" is so successful is your treatment of Nate. It would have been easy to let Nate entirely play the villain, yet you really allow his actions (and lack-there-of) to speak for themselves, leaving space for the reader to fill in their assessment of his character. Did you find it challenging to write this character in this way?

JA: Yes. Nate's character was a good lesson in letting space talk. I was wary of him being flat if he was too vilified, but it was challenging to write him with restraint, even though I knew it was important to the story. T's conflicted feelings about Nate are at the center of what she's going through—there is something magnetic about Nate; his role in the community and the way others see him, and the way T sees herself because she is with him. It's complicated, and that's part of her tormenting herself. To make Nate a simple villain would undermine that tension. In earlier drafts, I also tried allowing Nate enough space to really show his charisma, show what might draw T and everyone else to him, but it didn't work to give Nate so much space on the page. So I whittled the writing about him down to a few details I thought got the point across, and left a lot of empty space for the reader to fill in their own perceptions. I tried to leave enough to sketch him, and I feel that the reader can rely, otherwise, on T's assessment of his pull on her.

RP: I think your instincts are really on-point here, allowing T's perceptions to guide the reader. My favorite moment in the story is T thinking of her own gentle care of her wound, and how that act rewrites her definition of "caring." Can you talk about the theme of caring in this story, and how important it is to T's arc?

JA: T's concept of 'care' changes over the course of the story. There is a shift in the way she perceives care before she enters the Battery in the present, and the way she perceives it by the end. There is a passage about Nate's visit to her college after the accident, how he stayed close by and spent time with her, doing some things that sound genuinely caring and some things that don't, and T assesses this behavior with a similar degree of muddiness/confusion as she does most of her own perceptions at this point, ultimately deciding that he does "care" for her. She's questioning things, to a degree, but ultimately Nate's narrative is more powerful than her own.

But after the fall, T has to care for herself in this specific, physical way. There is a ritualistic quality to caring for her body—she has to change the bandages and apply the ointment every morning and examine the injury and watch it heal up into a scar. When she's in the Battery near the end of the story, watching Nate contort his body during his performance (importantly, watching him have total agency and control over his body, and be admired for it), she is touching the ridge on her head from the scar. A thing T did by herself, for herself—caring for that wound. It clicks for her, I think, the agency she has over her own body, that she is capable of caring for herself the way she deserves, and that's part of what makes her question what she's doing there, and sends her running out of the room.

RP: It's such a beautiful ending to the story, with T being freed (at least temporarily) in the "unbelievable darkness" of The Battery. The Battery itself is an immense presence in the story, perfectly suited to the themes and tone of "Tank." Is the Battery a real place? And if so, how did you learn of it?

JA: There is no abandoned military battery on an island off of Cape Cod. But the Battery is loosely based on a real abandoned military battery on an island off the coast of Maine. I explored it about a decade ago, when I was traveling around the Northeastern US. I was staying with people in the area who had been there before. We spent a long time wandering around in the dark and exploring the tunnels. The whole experience—getting out there, and being inside—made a huge impression on me.

RP: In contrast to the Battery is the Bloom Festival—a celebration of color, life, and frivolity. You do a lot, successfully, with dichotomies in "Tank." (Darkness/color, hurt/unfeeling, etc.). Is this a conscious move?

JA: Yes, definitely. In early drafts, some of the language was doing that already, in how I was writing about the area (most of that writing I ended up cutting, but small Cape Cod towns have this really interesting summer/winter split in culture, appearance, and mood), and I leaned into similar dichotomies intentionally as I developed the story. I felt the contrasts between darkness/light and feeling/numbness were important to an overarching understanding of T's experience, which is characterized by this moment when time changes for her after the assault.

RP: From the Battery to sensory deprivation tanks, there are so many fascinating elements at work in "Tank" that it would be difficult to list them all. Are there any other aspects to "Tank" that you'd like to discuss?

JA: I think just to expand on your last question a little more—I was interested in the way time is split after a trauma. How perceptions of the world and even sensory experiences can shift dramatically. I used the section headers to make intentionally un-subtle that split experience of time, how stark it is, the before and after of T's consideration of the world and her experience of being in her own body. I think form is a wonderful way to play with doubling down on or mirroring themes.

RP: You mentioned earlier that "Tank" is part of a larger collection. Can you tell us a little about this collection and anything else you may be working on?

JA: Sure! "Tank" is part of a collection (seven stories and a novella) I am revising that draws on both physical and psychological abandoned spaces. Characters contend with what they've buried or avoided, and most stories enter neglected spaces in their worlds: abandoned hotels, forgotten lighthouses, the military battery in "Tank". The stories explore injury and recovery as characters try to heal or resist healing: An artist living 'hyperbolically' for a project tries to forget her ex-lover, but she's tattooed her bite marks across her body. A woman in denial of her own self-destruction seeks her estranged sister at an abandoned lighthouse. A bike messenger recovering from a brutal accident moves in with the woman responsible, and begins obsessively re-examining what she sees as her greatest sins. I'm in the end stages of revision, I think.

I'm also working on a novel. I don't want to say much because it's still an early draft, but it's a multi perspective novel, a bit speculative, that follows two Jewish women in different time periods, set between what was once a Jewish vacation area in upstate New York, and what is now Lithuania.

RP: That sounds like a fascinating collection! Thank you, Jenna, for taking the time to discuss "Tank." It's a beautiful and resonate story, and I am looking forward to seeing it in print.

THELMA VS TIME
Marcie Roman

On Thelma's last day at Faber's Confections, after forty years as a quality control tester, she received a silver pin in the shape of an F. Management issued these on occasion: for highest sales in a quarter, or best new candy design, and once to the employee who single-handedly fixed the conveyer belt motor and saved a day's worth of production. Given that the pin arrived two weeks to the day from a pink slip, Thelma couldn't help but think that in her case F stood for Fired. F for Future unknown.

While she waited for the bus home, she removed the pin from her blouse and dropped it into her bag. It joined the heart-shaped box of Faber's Assorted her supervisor had handed her at the end of the shift. "To remember us by." As if she didn't have a cabinet full of chocolate boxes, her employee bonus for every major holiday. Stanley used to bring them to the appliance factory, but they'd accrued in the five years since his passing.

On the bus, she took a seat reserved for older passengers after a middle-aged woman stood to make room. Thelma couldn't recall when the switch had happened, from being the one who gave up a seat to one who received it, but her tired feet and swollen ankles expressed their gratitude. The doors whooshed open to let on a stray passenger, along with a wave of humid air. Thelma fanned herself with her paycheck envelope. A cloying sweetness emanated from her hair and clothes, a workday souvenir she would have gladly left behind with her lab coat, clipboard, and employee ID.

The bus lurched. The standing passengers grabbed poles for balance. As a reflex, she gripped the armrest even though her arthritic fingers could no longer be trusted to hold on. Yet another casualty in the ongoing battle: Thelma versus Time.

Over the years, her view out the window had also transformed. A corridor of family-owned businesses displaced by a skyscraper. A block razed for a monolithic warehouse known as a fulfillment center. The bus exhaled and inhaled passengers in an area once used for animal slaughter that now attracted urban professionals. A sign on a brick façade advertised *Affordable Upscale Lofts*. Below it, in weather-beaten lettering, *fireproof storage since 1927*.

The seat-volunteer exited at Fullerton and a burly man in a Cub's shirt took the pole, blocking Thelma's sightline. She held her bag on her lap and listened for her stop to be announced. The street names served as a more reliable marker, anyway.

The bus let her off near a yellow-brick apartment building where a friend from elementary school had once lived. Nowadays, it seemed to contain more residents than units with moving vans appearing nearly as often as garbage trucks. A Spanish station blared from an open window. A pack of boys loitered in front. Too young, she assumed, to head to the park where even adults had been warned to be on guard. While she waited for them to step aside, one of the boys slurped from a Styrofoam cup and tossed it to the ground. He might have been seven, or maybe eleven—she had no basis for judging children's ages—but surely old enough to know the purpose of the city trashcan, just a few paces away. The smell alone announced its presence.

A path opened and she hurried through with a small shake of her head.

On the sidewalk in front of the graystone three-flat where she'd lived her entire life, she spotted a fast-food bag next to a splotch of red. Ketchup, she assumed. Such a challenge it had become to keep litter at bay.

She climbed the stairs and inserted her key into the lock, but before she could push the door, it flew inward with Thelma grasping the handle. She caught her footing and found herself face to face—practically kissing distance—with her upstairs neighbor of two months, Mr. Rhodes.

"Oh dear," she said and stepped aside.

"Not a problem," he replied, his voice gruff.

Before today, she'd only seen him from afar. When he exited, she noticed that his neck skin sagged like hers did, as if an internal glue had lost its adhesion.

The entry smelled of damp paper, onions, and something medicinal. She fished for the tiny mailbox key and inserted it into the middle door. The mailbox to her left displayed the remnants of peeled masking tape. To the right, a brand-new label-maker strip identified her neighbor by last name only. From what she could tell, Mr. Rhodes lived alone and worked odd hours, the squeaking stairs announced his comings and goings. She assumed he did something mechanical and could imagine the urgent, late night calls. A plumber perhaps. Or an electrician. As if to support her claim, she spotted a hardware catalogue on the floor, its cover espousing the virtues of pipe wrenches and u-bolts. Thelma resisted the temptation to read the first name of the addressee. *Keep your nose in your own business,* her mother used to say. Her mother had been on a first-name basis with the entire block, but those were different times.

Thelma sorted the mail as she ate her usual dinner (tomato soup, buttered toast). The stack contained solicitations from credit card companies still addressed to Stanley and a telephone bill that she set aside. But, ah, a nice surprise: a postcard from Miriam. Thelma's up-stairs neighbor for over two decades, Miriam had migrated to Florida a few years back, "like the old bird I am."

The postcard contained images of palm trees and flowers so brightly colored, Thelma felt she should wear sunglasses. But on the back, Miriam reported the familiar, so even though Thelma had nev-er left Illinois, she felt comfortable in her assumption that day-to-day life wasn't all that different across state lines.

For dessert, a sliced pear, soft enough to drip juice on her chin. The gift of chocolate had gone straight into the trash can (the pin lost amid the tissues in her purse). When she opened the lid to deposit her napkin, her mother's voice returned, as if the walls had absorbed her sayings along with decades of cooking grease. *Waste not, want not.* But surely her mother would understand that all Thelma *wanted* was to have a future as barren of chocolate as a desert is of water.

After dinner, she cleaned: mopping the heavily-traveled areas, a scour of the sink and counters, a light dusting of the spare bedrooms. One contained the old radios Stanley liked to tinker with. The other held her mother's belongings, who'd lived with them till her death.

"You might consider downsizing," a distant cousin of Stan-ley's said, when he stopped by to express condolences. But Thelma wouldn't hear of it. Three generations of her family's history had transpired within these walls; she was its last preservationist. Plus, the landlord hadn't raised the rent in over ten years.

Thelma carried the bucket and mop outside. She removed a rubber-banded menu and brought it with the fast food bag to the trash bin on the side of the building. Then she got to work, mopping her way from porch to stairs, the soapy water running toward the sidewalk in a temporary waterfall. Miriam and the other neighbors used to commend her for how clean she kept the stoop. "It's our front yard," Thelma would say, echoing her mother, who would have been on hands and knees with a sponge.

All of them were gone now. Moved away like Miriam. Or joining her mother and siblings on the other side. Stanley, too. His shift that Monday had started at six, and Thelma had been enjoying the gentle pace before she left for work. The slow boil of the kettle. The broadening pool of light on the hardwood floor. Until the jangle of the phone burst in like an intruder. Two words, "We're sorry," and her prior life came to a halt, with no map for how to proceed. But she did. Letting herself be carried forward on the currents of routine: work, clean, sleep.

Thelma flipped the bucket over the curb. Hamburger wrappers and cigarette butts took a murky journey toward the sewer. She heard raised voices. The kids from earlier approached on the sidewalk. One of the boys snatched a baseball cap off the head of another. A skirmish and the hat soared into the path of an oncoming car. The hat owner sprinted across the street, waving the reclaimed object over his head as the car horn blared. The rest of the boys followed, dodging traffic to a cacophony of horns and squealing brakes.

How dangerous, Thelma thought. Even more so as the summer light faded. Several streetlights were out. They had been for months. She'd been meaning to call someone at the city about it. Now, she supposed, she'd have no problem finding time.

At least her evenings retained the same structure: the cleaning that led to a few hours of TV. She and Stanley used to watch the news together, and she'd enjoyed the game shows that followed, the volume turned low as Stanley dozed in his recliner. In the early years of their marriage, they'd owned a black and white set, and she still had the habit of picturing two worlds: her everyday reality with green peas for dinner, blue bedroom slippers, and the orange juice she sipped in the morning for vitamin C; and a black-and-white fantasy place, where game hosts were kings, and pretty girls jumped in excitement when told to "Come on down." Thelma would have liked to step into the television set, to be part of one of those game show worlds. But only as an audience member. She harbored no false hope, even in fantasy, that she ever would have been the one to *come on down*.

The reddish splotch from earlier still marred the sidewalk. In the dim light, it looked like dried blood, but she preferred to think of it as nothing more than a blend of tomatoes, sugar, and vinegar. She swiped the mop over it and watched the concrete darken, the water staining it clean in a way that left a satisfied feeling in the pit of her stomach.

She wondered if Mr. Rhodes recognized the work she put in to keep their home looking nice. Not like the empty frame house next door—the Kolacki's old place, foreclosed on with the last owner—with its rotted siding and yellowed newspapers composting on the porch. The only other time she'd conversed with Mr. Rhodes—if it could be called that—he'd been watching the workers replace plywood on the boarded-up windows.

"Good to keep the squatters out," he'd yelled over the hammering. "Hope there's no need here." He'd gestured toward their building where the For Rent sign in the first-floor window had faded to a dusty pink.

"Don't believe so," she'd said and hurried to catch the bus.

Under the darkening sky, patches of light illuminated the sidewalk, like markers for the occupied buildings. She did wish there was a light in the first-floor unit. Another set of watchful eyes. Her right knee locked. She rubbed it until she could bend again. These twinges had become as tenacious as a pesky bee, stinging her knees in a seemingly immortal fashion.

Across the street, the boys raced each other up a chain link fence that boarded a grassy, bottle-strewn lot. The winner swung his leg over the top and began to climb down the other side. She imagined him trapped in his trespass, a taste of being behind bars, but then felt a different sort of twinge, as if her personal bee had stung her right in the conscience.

A siren sounded. A car revved its engine as it sped by. The boys sprinted back across the street, closer this time.

She gave the concrete one last swipe and pledged to check it in the morning in case bleach was needed.

"Hey, Gramma. Why don't you let me clean for you."

The boy who'd dropped the cup stepped forward. One of his friends pushed him on the shoulders. Another yanked his t-shirt, the fabric already stretched so thin it looked close to tearing.

Thelma pulled the mop handle to her chest.

The boy held out his hands. "How about I borrow it then. I'll make my place pretty too." He gestured toward the yellow building.

The other boys hooted. It was clear she'd entered the game. The mop as much of a lure as a stick to a golden retriever.

"Leave her alone."

Startled by the unseen voice, Thelma dropped the mop handle. She bent to retrieve it then used it to push upward as her eyes traveled over scuffed work boots, dungarees, an untucked t-shirt, and on up to the sweaty face of Mr. Rhodes.

"You heard me," he said. "Go on with you."

The smell of fried chicken wafted from a take-out bag as he swung it in the boys' direction.

The boy shrugged and headed the other way. "Whatever. Just trying to help." The others followed with a chorus of "Yeah."

Thelma opened her mouth to thank Mr. Rhodes but all that emerged was a gasp. She hadn't realized she'd been holding her breath.

Mr. Rhodes nodded. "You should get yourself in."

A bead of sweat dripped from his eyebrow. He flicked it aside.

Thelma hurried up the stairs as her knee continued its protest. In the entry, Mr. Rhodes bent to pick up the catalogue. She searched for words to express her appreciation, but when none came to mind, she continued up as the mailbox squeaked open below.

In the kitchen, Thelma put down the bucket, washed her hands, and collapsed onto a kitchen chair.

"Oh, my goodness."

She fanned herself with Miriam's postcard. Her friend would surely tell her that every kind act deserves one in return.

Thelma scanned the room. A tip of gauzy pink ribbon dangled

from the trashcan lid. She retrieved the chocolate box—a slight ding on the bottom but otherwise who could tell—slipped out the door and started up the stairs. Silly that she'd waited so long to make a proper introduction. The lightbulb on the top landing flickered as it did at times. A whiff of chocolate caught her nose, but she couldn't be sure if it came from her person or the chocolate box. One sweaty palm gripped the banister while the other stuck to the cellophane packaging as if it were flypaper.

Miriam's door knocker had been removed. Thelma rapped twice with an open palm, her knuckles too swollen from heat to be enlisted for duty. From the apartment, she could hear the voice of an exuberant news announcer. As she raised her palm to knock again, Mr. Rhodes spoke on the other side of the door.

"Who is it?"

"It's Thelma, from downstairs."

The door opened halfway.

There stood Mr. Rhodes, a napkin tucked into his shirt, a chicken leg clutched in his hand, his chin shiny with grease.

"Yeah?"

Thelma sensed his irritation as if it had been emitted into the air like the musk of a skunk. She waited for him to offer his first name. Call me Al, he might say. Or Hank. Or Fred. When he stayed silent, the imbalance made her feel as if she were still standing with one locked knee. She hid the chocolate box behind her, grateful for the width of her hips.

"I thought," she stumbled. "I mean, I appreciated your help outside, and wanted to thank you."

"Was nothing, but you should be more careful. Them foreigners are going to do us all in."

He shifted position. Behind him, the living room appeared dark except for the blue glow of the TV. Thelma thought of the evenings she'd shared with Miriam in that room, sometimes with spouses, sometimes "just gals." Or when old Mrs. Steelman used to live there, and Thelma could barge in uninvited to borrow an egg for her mother.

"With their gangs and drugs, they'll end up shooting themselves to pieces." He brandished the chicken leg. "'Course if they keep getting in, we'll be run out soon enough."

For a second time that day, Thelma gaped like a wide-mouthed fish.

She wanted to object, "They're just children." She wanted to say, "Weren't we all foreigners at one time?"

Her fingers clenched the box. The air in her home felt tarnished and she wanted it cleaned. She straightened her back, lifted her chin, and spoke with the authority of a Quality Control Tester.

"I disagree, Mr. Rhodes. They are our neighbors, and you—" Her heel found the stair as she delivered a phrase she'd had four decades to rehearse. "You have made a mistake."

Mr. Rhodes slammed the door. Thelma walked downstairs. At the landing, she paused to steady herself. Soft light leaked from her apartment onto the welcome mat. Inside were the things that made her feel safe: Stanley's chair, and her shows, and a cup of tea, and the family photographs seen too often to still really be seen. The images of the ones who'd made it over. The ones who'd found a place to call home.

She loosened her grip on the box. The smell was stronger, the candy in battle with the heat. She would take it straight to the trash bin.

She continued down the stairs, out the door, and into the thick, night air. She could hear the boys' laughter, but the sidewalk was clear. As she reached the walkway to the trash bins, the laughter grew into unfettered guffaws: the sound of youth enjoying the freedom of a summer night. She changed course, plodding down the block before her nerve evaporated with her sweat. She stopped in front of the yellow building. The boy who'd tried to take the mop sat with his back against the wall.

"Here," she said, offering him the box. "I had some extra chocolate and thought you kids might want it."

One of the boys jeered. "Hey, Carlos, your girlfriend's giving you candy."

When Carlos didn't reach out, Thelma stepped forward and placed it into his hands.

"I hope you enjoy it."

She turned to walk home, her back stiffened against the possibility of a heart-shaped projectile aimed at her shoulders.

"Hey, Chocolate Lady."

The voice was not unkind. She turned back.

The boy held up the box like a trophy. "Thanks."

She smiled even though it was too dark for him to see. "You'll want to eat it soon. For best quality."

CREATIVE COMPOST
A Conversation with Marcie Roman

Claire Agnes: This is a highly compressed, swiftly paced narrative that excels in its emotive restraint, yet manages to touch upon a number of important and evocative issues—bigotry, widowhood, individual identity and utility, and the bonds of community. How did Thelma emerge as our specific navigator of these tensions?

Marcie Roman: Thanks, Claire. Emerge seems like the perfect term to describe Thelma's arrival on the page. She introduced herself to me in 2005 as part of a writing exercise on character. The instructor passed around a basket of paper strips that listed occupations. My selection read *factory worker*. And then it was as if Thelma had been in queue at an open casting call. She stepped forward and announced, "It just so happens I work in a chocolate factory."

I can't recall how I landed on that setting. For all I know, the person next to me had a half-eaten bar on their desk. Or perhaps I'd been reading *Charlie and the Chocolate Factory* to my daughter. What I do remember is that Thelma's voice came effortlessly, and the experience—which I've learned to cherish in the years since—felt as if all I had to do was listen and take notes. She shared that I was meeting her on her last day of employment after forty years as a quality control tester, and that she felt unsteady in the liminal space between what she knew and what lied ahead. Grateful to have produced the requisite 1000 words, I turned in the assignment and thought our meeting would be like an encounter with a friendly stranger on a plane—pleasant enough company, but then we'd go our separate ways. That wasn't the case with Thelma.

A few years later, I was flipping through a book of historic photographs of Baltimore (where I'm from) and came across a snapshot of an older woman scrubbing her front stoop with a sponge. The caption explained this was a cleaning ritual throughout the city. And here was Thelma again, stepping into the spotlight to share that her mother had a similar routine at their apartment in Chicago. Not only that, but Thelma still lived there and tried to carry on her mother's work. Would I be interested in visiting? (She was, after all, still stuck at the factory, and, I imagine, eager to get home.) Without knowing where the writing would lead, I answered, "Yes," and Thelma boarded the bus, which, in both literal and metaphoric ways, started her journey from fragment to story.

CA: As a teacher, it is always so interesting to hear that responses and connections to the smallest assignment or activity can spur the genesis of character or story, even years after the original due date. What was the process of molding this intersection between a previous writing assignment and a found photograph into full-length narrative like for you as the author?

MR: When I start new writing, it's without any agenda or plan. An editor friend recently designated me as a "pantser," as in someone who creates by the seat of her pants. In those early drafts, Thelma and I spent a significant amount of time exploring the apartment—I believe she shared what was in her fridge and long digressive stories about her family—but there were clues in her walk from the bus to the building that there might be more at stake. Her environment invited a number of those issues you referenced, which I'd been thinking about at the time, along with observations I'd made about the neighborhood I lived in.

I think of these elements as the creative compost that grows a seed of an idea into something more robust. Thelma's story seemed to develop on the time scale of a tree, with long periods of drought when I'd set it aside, and I've abandoned stories that address similar questions, but for some reason she kept popping into my imagination (and herein lies the mysterious factor that causes some characters to have stronger life forces than others). It's only in hindsight that I recognize how much her tenacity—as a character in a story, and the story of her story—has guided my approach to facing challenges in both writing and day-to-day life.

In particular, Thelma showed me that, while you can't keep the rug from being pulled out from under you, there's always a choice to be made in how to respond: stay on the floor; or stand up, grab a mop, and try to make the hardwood shine.

CA: It's clear that you have a strong authorial affinity for and personal connection to Thelma's character. Has she appeared elsewhere in your work, either as the protagonist or as a background actor?

MR: That's such an interesting observation and one I hadn't considered until now. I think the affinity must arise from knowing her for such a long stretch of time. I've written about other women in her age bracket since that helps address my own anxious thrum of needing to know "what comes next," not unlike learning from older relatives. That being said, Thelma herself seems to be unique to this story. To your question of Thelma appearing as a background actor, it's almost as if she's been under contract for this long running project and her contract includes a clause that prohibits moonlighting. But there are aspects of her personality that show up elsewhere. As noted earlier, there's her tenacity—that Midwestern ethic of pushing through at all costs—as well as the ways she has surprised me as a writer, thwarting any preconceived ideas I might have had of her character at the start. And then, there's that butterfly effect quality to her actions, in that there's potential for her small gestures to have a much larger resonance. That theme has definitely appeared elsewhere in my work, both to beneficial and negative outcomes, depending upon the situation or story.

CA: Could you speak to these positive and negative outcomes of theme a bit further? I'm specifically interested in how this thematic thread has materialized in your other narratives, the impact of a beneficial or a negative outcome on your writing process, and if any instances of a "beneficial negative" have occurred.

MR: I probably need to apologize to my characters for this, but I think even challenging outcomes are beneficial negatives, because it's those uncomfortable reckonings that create the greatest opportunity for self-discovery, whether or not the character feels ready to contend with that aspect of self. Not unlike the way facing our own personal challenges can propel us to grow and shift our thinking or behavior.

For example, a story of mine that appeared in the journal *CALYX* begins with a woman in a grocery store lying to the cashier so she can get a (slightly) cheaper price on a product. This small but deviant impulse leads her to commit more significant theft, which she justifies as a move against capitalism, but ultimately forces her to contend with her fears about failing as a parent. I didn't know what direction the story would head in when I began writing it, but it's so interesting to look back now and consider how that one writing impulse acted like a footstep on a frozen pond that sent cracks all along the surface. It benefitted me as writer by creating access to plumb the depths of her memories and learn her secrets. Although experientially things got rough for her at the end, I'd argue the character benefitted through greater self-awareness.

More generally, I think this theme emerges from my own desire, as someone who doesn't view themselves as particularly powerful in our modern societal structure, to recognize ways in which small actions can effect change. This brings to mind one of my favorite final sentences. It's from the novel *Middlemarch*, "...for the growing good of the world is partly dependent on unhistoric acts, and that things are not so ill with you and me...is half owing to the number who lived faithfully a hidden life, and rest in unvisited tombs." In my writing, I'm always on the lookout for ways this might present, and it seems to be the organizing principle of a novel I've been working on for the past few years.

Since I do write about more ordinary characters, being open to the rippling effect of small acts encourages close observation and helps me avoid the trap of passivity or letting characters ruminate for extended periods on what they might eat for lunch (although I can still be guilty of both). While I always hope beneath a character's surface I'll discover undercurrents of kindness and empathy, to avoid sentimentality I do need to make sure that doesn't translate into being too kind to the characters themselves. Rather, in revision I might note that the ice could use another stomp to keep the tension rising.

CA: In the version of this story originally submitted to *Driftwood*, the exact city of Thelma's residence was not specified. In the current iteration, Thelma lives in Illinois, presumably Chicago. I am curious as to both your intent within the original ubiquity of place, as well as the eventual decision to root Thelma in a more specific setting. What part does specificity of place play as you are conceptualizing, drafting, and editing your work?

MR: The Oscar Wilde quote about taking out a comma and putting it back in very much applies! In the first drafts of this story, Thelma was identified as a resident of Chicago. Although the photo I mentioned earlier is from Baltimore, the chocolate shop where she worked is based on a long-time Chicago institution—anyone passing through that area would get a whiff of melted chocolate. During a later draft I took out the identifier because I thought that might allow readers to bring more of their own perspective into the storytelling.

On the flipside, specificity gives the words on the page more of a chance to breach the reader's and writer's imaginations. As I worked through your (very thorough!) editing suggestions, I realized that the best way for me to re-imagine a story I'd been with for so long, was to place myself in Thelma's shadow, which meant traveling through the actual city and seeing the view out her window, hearing the sounds, and smelling the corner trash can. Place can also lure me into the storytelling, in the same way I get curious about a person, inviting me to "pull up a chair and listen." One short story I wrote came about because I would pass a very understated apartment building on my way to work that, for whatever reason, kept waving at me. My novel-in-progress is centered around a failing strip mall in another Chicago neighborhood. This could also be influenced by the work I used to do for film and TV. One of the things I loved about the job was the way a broadly noted setting in a script, APARTMENT BUILDING or STREET CORNER would transform into a wholly realized environment once it got assigned a location and the Art Department performed its magic. I too love how I can still clearly visualize my own imagined settings from favorite books, almost like flipping through an album of vacation photos, which allows me to revisit the reading experience. I suppose I'm always writing toward creating that sense of reality in my work, even if many of the details don't make it to the page.

CA: Your background in the narrative world of film and television is intriguing! Have these experiences informed or shaped the perspectives of your written work, either through the tangible lens of setting the scenes themselves or the more subtle undulations of plot and character?

MR: Funny you should ask since I've given a lecture on this very topic! The focus was on how to enlist the film crew of our imagination to enhance character development and world-building. As I mentioned earlier, I tend to write quieter, ruminatory characters, and often the character is the first thing I become curious about (although, again, a setting can assume that character-like quality). So, as a way to start writing, I'll place that character into a specific location/set or conversely try to people a setting that called to me. This creates the play space in which I can start asking, "Who is this person and what are they worried about, and what is it they want?" Meanwhile, various departments are running in props and set dressing, or building new sets or casting new players, as the characters start to navigate their space. I think a lot of this is happening subconsciously, although I can picture a director in my head with a megaphone shouting "Show, Don't Tell."

During revision, I might take a more tactical approach. If I sense a need to go deeper into character, I'll call on the prop department again to add a significant item, which might serve as an objective correlative. If I'm having a hard time visualizing the character, I'll call in wardrobe and the makeup/hair department to add a few unique details. For a more dynamic environment, I might enlist Extras, or picture cars, or add in sound effects. (I've noted a lot of my stories contain planes, Els, or cicadas.) Like film, most of these details don't make it onscreen, but I've found that characters are more likely to act authentically when I create verisimilitude in my visual renderings, in the same way that an actor has more to work off of on a fully decorated and peopled set versus an empty sound stage. I also read the dialogue aloud to consider how it sounds.

On a more aesthetic level, I'll consider how lighting or music can be employed to set the mood through a narrative's tonality and sentence rhythms. There's also the impactful way scenes are edited together. So, I might use quick cuts and shorter sentences to heighten tension, or longer sentences for more reflective passages. And again, because my stories sometimes need a prod toward movement, when two characters need to be in an extended conversation, I might re-shoot the scene as a walk and talk, which is a switch that also gets made on films. Like most directors, my rough cuts (i.e. early "finished" drafts) are much too long, and through revision I attempt to narrow focus to the beats that most support narrative flow and clarity.

All of this is working toward creating Robert Olen Butler's idea of "the omnisensual cinema of the mind," and John Gardner's "vivid and continuous dream." By creating this experience for myself as writer, I'm also hoping to provide enough clues for a reader's personal film crew to get to work. I consider it such a gift that we get to create these visualized stories in our minds, both as writers and readers, knowing that no two versions will ever be the same.

CA: The timing of the story is, to this reader, one of the strengths of the piece. We meet Thelma on her last day of work, providing a pressing immediacy to the scenes. A bit further on in the narrative, we learn that Thelma is also a widow. Other writers might have felt the compulsion to explore Thelma's experiences of nostalgia, grief, and isolation through the lens of her husband's death, but you intersect these same emotions with Thelma's loss of productive utility, not the loss of a shared, intimate home life. This creates a compelling connection between ideas of identity and value in a capitalist economy and culture, especially with consideration to the story's setting and the scenes presented. Could you speak to this decision? Were there earlier iterations of this story that began elsewhere?

MR: From a process standpoint, I imagine it's because my introduction to her was through that slip of paper with her occupation. The way we might get introduced to someone at a networking party: "This is Jane, she's in Sales." The first line of the story is the first line that came to me, which placed her firmly on the floor of the factory where she'd worked for so many years. Although I ended up cutting the earlier scenes that showed her at work, the clock has always been set to this specific day in Thelma's timeline. Thelma is someone who tries to control her environment by keeping it predictable. This final day created a seismic shift in her routine, which in turn created a portal for me as a writer to explore more vertically those earlier losses, that of her husband and mother, and her experience of the neighborhood. As both a reader and writer, I enjoy these types of turning points that occur after the "explosion"—in whatever form that entails—moments that move a character away from asking, "What happened?" and turn characters to instead face the question, "What now?"

I find this can lead to the discovery of the more subtle questions that lie beneath the surface of plot. In the case of this story, the visible question is how Thelma is going to fill her time, now that she doesn't have work. On a deeper level, it's Thelma asking herself how she'll find meaning and a sense of purpose once this final layer of identity is stripped away.

In hindsight, I recognize that writing the story helped me sift through questions I'd been having about my own career identity. I'd been ready to take a step back from that higher stress environment I'd been working in for many years, but didn't know what might come next. It was one of the reasons I'd ventured back into an academic setting. Writing had always been a passion, but I kept hearing the voice that said I should pursue something with better economic prospects. So, like Thelma, I had to answer two questions: the practical one about where I'd put my energy, but then the broader consideration about the value of making non-commodified art in our current culture. I've finally found my way to Lewis Hyde's *The Gift*, which is helping to answer that question for me as a writer. I can also see how Thelma might identify herself at the end of the story as a gift-giver, sharing a clean stoop, empathy, and a cabinet full of chocolate boxes.

CA: The books that resonate with their readers have this incredible power to motivate both external and internal change. While *The Gift* solidified in your commitment to the craft itself, were there any other books, stories, or works that aided in honing your authorial voice?

MR: Absolutely! But first I should confess that I haven't actually finished *The Gift* but rather was drawn to the premise and have since been dipping in and out of it. I tend to be a horizontal reader, reading multiple books for longer stretches, although I still welcome the immersive experience of a book that can't be put down.

Back to your question though, my earliest impulse to write came from connecting with the voices of writers I admired and then wanting to enter into conversation with their work. I can recall trying to match the rhythms and humor of Shel Silverstein poems. As an adult reader, I listened closely to the voices of writers I admire such as Grace Paley, Virginia Woolf, and George Eliot. Over time, their voices taught me how to be a better listener and, I hope, a better conversation partner.

Switching back to an earlier metaphor, I think any piece of writing that gains entry into that inner sanctum of imagination becomes part of the creative compost for voice. If I were to take a soil sample of my work from year to year, it would likely contain evidence of the writers I was reading at the time. Along with the writers I noted above, that might include Elizabeth McCracken, Tessa Hadley, Elizabeth Strout, or Yiyun Li, to name a few. Yiyun Li was actually the one who gave me the idea of viewing our relationship with other writers as a conversation, since she noted how several of her stories evolved in conversation with those by William Trevor.

That might also speak to how "Thelma vs Time" has evolved over the years. Now that the story has passed through so many seasonal cycles of my life as a reader/writer, its growing environment is (again, one can only hope) much richer. That's something else that makes writing and reading so exciting, because we're always absorbing new ideas and techniques and language and no one knows what might emerge next!

CA: I am fascinated by this idea of conversation as a means of describing the symbiosis between writers and the voices of the writers who read their work. Individual identity within a community, whether that community is a readership, a workshop group, factory floor, or an apartment building, certainly forms a throughline of this story and becomes a central conflict for our main character. How is the selection of third person point-of-view related to this thematic?

MR: This story has created an interesting challenge as far as reconstructing backstory. Because it's existed in my head and on the page for so many decades, I might be a slightly unreliable first person narrator, in that it's hard to pull up the memory of those early choices. I do know that close third is my default for adult characters. I think this ties into my curiosity about character.

Returning again to film terminology, a mentor of mine, David Jauss, has described POV as differing camera angles, and while I do enjoy a wide-angle establishment shot, my real interest is in zooming in somewhere between a close up and an extreme close up. Maybe it's because I'm extremely nearsighted in real life that I feel like I can only really understand a character if I've invaded or, preferably, been invited into their personal space. In film, it's the angle that reveals even the most subtle change in expression.

In a similar way, I'm looking for those quiet shifts of thought or action that produce an insight, the secret that might be revealed if I patiently listen and observe. Unlike first person, in which I have a tendency to ruminate without paying attention to the environment, third person offers enough narrative distance to gain some perspective outside of the character. One recent adjustment I can think of is Thelma's little shake of her head when she passes the kids. To Thelma, it was one of those automatic gestures we make without realizing—I have a tendency to do this with my kids, or so I've been told—but it placed me far enough outside of her to wonder how that might appear to Carlos.

CA: I'm glad you brought up authorial consideration for complexity in secondary characters. This narrative features characters of varying ages, many from distinctly different backgrounds and, although this narrative is compressed, those outside of our protagonist still feel well-rounded and tangible on the page. Which characters do you have the most ease embodying? What challenges do more unfamiliar characters pose? How do you overcome those obstacles of characterization?

MR: With all my characters, I try to start from a place of compassion, curiosity, and the desire to find an emotional connection, not unlike how I aim to approach the people I meet in real life. I was a bookish kid and I also took a lot of acting classes (and still pop into one every so often). I think both put me on a path of empathy and instilled in me a drive to learn about the world through the eyes of people who differ in background or heritage. But I also have an awareness that I'm still an actor and therefore limited by my own set of experiences and world-view.

The adult novel I've been working on includes an abundance of perspectives (one may even argue an overabundance), along with a huge cast of supporting actors, but all tied together by a deep need to understand what it means to be human. I would never want to limit myself to the one human form I'm stuck in when there are so many other more interesting people to meet. That impulse to experience what it might be like to be someone else is one of the main factors that drives me to write.

That being said, being curious doesn't mean I get it right on the first go (or even after many, many goes). To counter any tendency toward stereotype, I look for ways to defamiliarize and humanize. I do hope that this approach can produce more rounded characters who surprise. To that point, I had no idea how Mr. Rhodes was going to react to Thelma's arrival at his door. When he first showed up on the page, I was considering him as a possible companion. Instead, he revealed himself to be a foil, counterproductive to her vision of the neighborhood. And of course, while it seems like Thelma is the one fearing the unknown, it's Mr. Rhodes who is ultimately the coward. In that way, I felt a bit sorry for him, living within such a closed off and limited view of life itself.

CA: You mentioned that you go through a process of defamiliarization when creating characters in order to avoid a reliance on tropes, stereotypes, and cliché. In what ways, as an author, do you practice this empathetic deprogramming? Has it impacted your life beyond the page in any way?

MR: My critical thesis for my MFA looked at ways in which fiction, in particular literary fiction, can enhance Theory of Mind, that sense of stepping into someone else's shoes. One study demonstrated that someone who'd just read a literary fiction passage was more likely to bend and pick up a pencil for another person. So I think that reading vastly and deeply is one of the best tools for generating an empathetic approach. The research for that paper helped me identify in my own reading process how those synapses are forming between language and thought.

As an example, when reading Tillie Olsen's novella *Tell Me a Riddle*, there was a death at the end which dissolved me into sobs; however, I hadn't realized I'd made an emotional connection with the character until that moment. So I cycled back through the writing to figure out the "how." One reason I found was the work's specificity of detail, which created this entirely unique person on the page. I may not have liked her, but I believed in her humanity. Understanding those techniques helps me work toward elevating reader connection in my own writing, as well as aiding in my personal interactions.

I also have a few practices I do in real life to help hone that skill. Again, I tend to be curious by nature, so when I notice someone on the street, or in line at the store, I try to go deeper than external identifiers by considering their goals and challenges. Or if a behavior catches my attention, I'll try to imagine a scenario that invites nuance and compassion. The skills I've picked up by being a more active listener also help. I think the modern-day impulse is to speak and speak loudly, but as an introvert I know there can be so much value in taking a seat and being the one who listens, who helps that other person feel seen and heard, while searching for the bridge to another's personal experience.

CA: We greatly appreciate you sharing this story with *Driftwood Press* and our readers. Where else can we find your work? Do you have any forthcoming projects or one still in the creative incubator?

MR: Thank you, Claire! It's such an honor to appear in *Driftwood*. Links to some of my short stories can be found online at MarcieRoman.com and my middle grade novel *Journey to the Parallels* is out now from *Fitzroy Books*. As far as work in the pupa stage, I'm nearing completion on that contemporary adult novel I mentioned, which explores similar issues about finding community, but on a larger scale. I'm also tightening up stories in a linked collection and finishing another project for younger readers. Plus, I'm always on the alert for whatever inspiration might emerge from the next great reading experience!

CASPER

What RoboCop don't get is how hurt makes you heaten. Moving hurts because it heatens you, and heat's just the littlest of you moving. Atoms squirming loose. What's he think is sweat? It's the you melting out of you. You pool down to wet, even spread out sky-wide as steam. That's what RoboCop's afraid of, spilling out to dampen some ditch the varms drink from. Reckons hurt's a thing you got to go hollow to hold. That's why he strives so thermos. Plays cool like he's metal. Plays sealed to keep from sweating. Tries to harden to contain the hurt, but Benji's the one holding us. Digging a ditch for us with instructions. RoboCop's got this hunch I empty when I run, but I just let myself liquid and flow whereverso Benji points me. Hurt's heat, and heat's moving. Put a cube of ice up against a puddle. Put a puddle up against steam. RoboCop must've missed that day of science class. Gander him stomping my heel so the hurt-heat thermometers up my leg, heaping his glare onto me. That's why RoboCop stays behind: he don't see how hurt-heat turns to speed.

See him irking at me jumping standing. Hear him groan when Benji goes-gets our swim goggles. RoboCop gaums my arm and I swat it. Because plus and minus can't touch. RoboCop's plus and I'm minus and both-us are held together by the nuclear of Benji. Like the littlest bits of one atom. Saw about them on a poster once. The poster was done up on that kind of plastic that glows so white with light it shines over its own image. Stuck on the wall of this man who picked me up hitching away from a rainstorm south of Gastonia. I said *toward the dry* to his ask of *where to.* And we drove some keeping quiet, just clucking his blinker and squawking the wipers. Had them going before the monsoon even caught up, like they might clear his own thinking. Then the thunderhead anviled down and he said he couldn't conscience me out on the roadside with this weather and did I want a bed for the night or at least till this drench blew over, only he'd already clucked his blinker about eight miles back and turned off the highway and the whole full of that silence since it had already been decided and I'd sat in it and knew. Only question was which end he wanted. Said the son was off at college; said his wife was visiting kin down-way of Knoxville, but from his front door down the hall I didn't see one picture. Plain wall until the atom poster in the bedroom he took me to. Like he'd had a thought to keep letting on, then reckoned if he got someone this far they were both past the fib. And you do wonder what starts and quits a man. This one said reckon you'll catch cold if you don't get out them clothes. And I stepped out my shorts without waiting for him to step out because ever since he'd clucked that blinker we'd been past that.

"Ain't stupid," I said.

His sitting squealed the mattress behind me. "So come here. Teach you something."

I backed up and kept my eyes on that wall-atom, wondering what kind of microscope and where was it pointing when whoever discovered that. The whole meantime he was tugging my worm I stared all my hurt at it. Him saying *I'll show you* like I hadn't been busting in trucks and tents and toilets and dumpsters ever since Ms. Ida rubbed that first hurt-heat out of me. Bet RoboCop busts to bikes. *I'll show you,* the Atom Man said, only he wasn't saying that to pretend to me. That was his own act because his other hand was working his own worm the whole going. Going till the hot melted down and founted and some more me had leaked out of me. It pooled in my lap while his other hand was on himself still a-pumping. My gunk stuck his palm to the back of my hand when he grabbed it. Pulled the chap off my knuckles; had the eczema real bad around then from dry winter and chlorine. The rain he'd picked me up from was the first good soak of that year and it was nigh on to February. Dumb to remember them things. Funny what-all the brain snags on when it's trying to divert from worse—which I'm fixing to get to. But first the Atom Man put my hand on his own little worm and I looked up at that poster and read the word I'd been staring at: *atom.* A tom, like one cat. I'd always reckoned it was Adam like the first person, the most basic unit. And I snorted in the middle of tugging him and he said, *don't you laugh at it. Show you something funny.* And he did. And I melted more with the heat.

One more funny thing is this varm-trap of an island. One good rinse shy of a sandbar. The beach access juts out them dunes and midairs like a toothpick, the sand gulped out from under it. Shorebreak backwashing right through the fenceposts clenching dunes. RoboCop stubs up behind me. I jump off into the sand and my heel mouths open, yapping. I don't fall; just sit down real fast.

"You got shots?" RoboCop asks.

"Fuck a vodka."

"No. Vaccines. Like for tetanus."

The soft in his voice turns me. There he perches, curling his toes over the edge like a diving block. Looking at me like I'm the pool he's fixing to dive into. Like he thinks I'll hold the hurt he's fixing to go through.

Then Benji presses up behind him. "Pier and back, Tootsies."

Both-us gleamed off his sunglasses: RoboCop plussing up on fleeing me. I hop into the water and swim out of the feel of his plusshove and don't look back because Benji taught me. Because before that. Ever time I turn full-around I see all them years before Benji like the bad half of a glass. One lifelong of empty.

The day I took the Atom Man's truck he was still going on about his wife and son, both-us sprawled on the bed and long-busted. I just stared up at that atom poster. The June sun scrubbed the picture off it with like a paintbrush white-washing graffiti. Atom Man talked himself to sleep. I reached his wallet from where his piled pants and left him no more than a smear of his own burst gauming the billfolds together, which was the undoing of how he'd done me in February. I walked up the hall chewing on what he'd gave me to laugh about that first evening. Filled my head up that way to keep from noticing all his frank-kindness. Like him tying his shoes real slow in front of me to teach me the knot without ever saying he was teaching me. Like the hotdogs cut up and lumped in with the macaroni. Like a pool out the back and his own treadmill and anything. The Atom Man's name was Adam. That was what he gave me to laugh at; he'd meant that statement plain instead of threatening.

What RoboCop wouldn't understand was how Adam making me laugh was worse than the hurting I'd been expecting. Because that—the not hurting, but his plain-meaning—was why I stayed those four months. And Adam said it then because he knew it would be. So I lathered up a wrath over that as I was leaving, scrubbing even his frank-kindnesses until they shined like what they all were: the same trap. Because I could've gone soft eating them hotdogs. Could've tied my shoelaces to run on the treadmill when it was airish out or raining. Could've bumped down the speed if I was sore, and next thing I'd be staying in bed the damn livelong, and then four months would bloat up like my belly and I'd no-count in Gastonia never moving or hurtening or amounting to anything. That's what Adam wanted. Thinking that wrathed me right on around and I went back to his pile of pants for his truck keys. I stood up and he'd stirred, maybe from their jangling.

"Fixing to run," I told him. Standing full-facing him with his wallet and keys.

But he hadn't seen what I was up to, or the footboard was blocking his view, and anyhow he was still thick with half-sleep. Could've used them windshield wipers about then on his thinkings. A nod's all he gave. Antsy, he called me.

And I came over and planted one on him, which I'd never done. Because it wasn't never like that—never lips but hands only. That kiss went about like an atom's pluses and minuses touching, that brushing adding all the more force to our aparting. Me planting one should've tipped him. Maybe he knew I was for-good leaving already. Maybe "antsy" was him good as telling me *take the pickup*. Frank-kindness can be hard to plain-say. Well, I ran from Gastonia how I told him, driving off in his truck, and it was easy as sitting up on the hoods and masting your back to a tailwind. Just had to get going. I'd lived as his alleged insect for whole seasons, playing his little Antsy from February until June.

Adam the Atom Man. The world sometimes is the strangest stuff. And I know he weren't lying about his name because I had his license with me.

A sob and some siphoned gas after that I took a 2.4-mile dip in a lake and dried off with a bike ride and topped it with a little marathon at the Chapel Hill Ironman. Well also some naps in the truck. Also parking out back of hotels and hopping the pool fence to swim. You try getting up a good hurt with ten yards of open water between flip-turns. Enough to make a man's head go like that branch RoboCop's rotating. Sometimes I wobbled inside saying I forgot a towel. Puddling heelprints right up to the front desk in that icebox seem-like that's common to all hotel lobbies: as if the A.C.'s coming up through the tile, the same freeze cramping up through your fascia cooling up through the air to where you're just waiting to see your breath steam. Sometimes did. Swear. Sometimes asked the desk person for one-them complimentary chocolates. Took the elevator up and grubbed off left-out trays of room service, even. You wouldn't believe some-them bounties. They got this enchilada I guess no one likes at the Hyatt. You can count on folks taking a bite or two before quitting. Sometimes seemed I was eating better than hotdogs and macaroni in that period. But I biked all the lard off. I went longer than live-long, pedaling on through the night. Times I was so crapped I propped the bike way-off at the far side of a rest stop and left it out there when I stiff-legged into the bathroom, hoping I'd come out and find it gone and the ride would end preemptory. Because the ride wouldn't end otherwise. But I always came out and there it was by the sign where I'd propped it. That brought the sobs. Climbing back on the bike, wiper-eyed and lungs rattling. Keeping on even past dozing off, waking up to honks and red lights. So all that. Maybe it was all part of the same shoving-off I got after planting one on Adam. No tell how long I'd've gone on if I hadn't snagged Benji's eyes after the Chapel Hill Ironman. I was taking a lap of the parking lot to jog the steam off, savoring the just-doneness when he bulged up on me. Swelled out the medical tent gnashing on his hair's long part. Wasn't even looking my way, but I sweat-felt his waiting. That belly-his convexing him, like a nuclear the above and under of him was circling. Biting on them split ends. That haircut's got a name, I was thinking. He just stood there gnawing it till I ran even with him. Then he hummed. That tune kudzu'd right on up my legs and tangled me.

"You run like you hump." First thing he told me.

I let him have that one. Hunch on him like he knew both halves of it, how a glass does: holding all my full and my empty. He stuck a receipt to the sweat on my chest. A phone number was scrawled on the side facing up. He told me to call after Thanksgiving. Promised then that he'd've found a home for me. Adam gave me home like a bed, but Benji was going to give me a fence. I could see it in the see-through of his looking. Them big sunglasses gleaminger than that atom poster, reflecting instead of whitening—showing me to me. More than that, showing him: Benj was looking through me. Then he told his secret name. And then-on ever day I was counting days.

Thanksgiving come and gone and I called the first second of midnight. He picked up before the first ring. Both-us had been sitting up, and that knowing right away petted me. All he said was an address. Said it twice, sticking his words to me like that receipt. Then he hung up and I drove to this flooded varm-bed of marsh they talk up like it's a beach. And that's the windup to how I am, swimming after his tug with my heel yapping. That hurt's heat, and heat's speed. Only thing to it is to how I always done and keep moving.

ALL-CONSUMING
A Conversation with Mason Boyles

James McNulty: Welcome to the pages of the *Driftwood Anthology*, Mason. Everyone here at the press is so excited to have your book finally published in early 2023. I'd love to ask you some questions to accompany this excerpt from the novel. When did you decide to be a writer?

Mason Boyles: I blame this desolate outcome on my parents' nightly habit of reading me to sleep. We did the *Great Illustrated Classics, Harry Potter, The Hobbit,* and Terry Pratchett, and regular immersion in those worlds is one of my earliest and fondest memories. I wrote my first story at six, sitting in the front room of my father's law office. My mom had clacked out her master's thesis on that typewriter; I came up with something about Johnny Appleseed. From then on, I would put together short stories and comic books with relative regularity. Lawrence Naumoff's introductory fiction workshop was what got me writing daily during my sophomore year at Chapel Hill. I've been a hopeless case ever since.

JM: What attracted you to fiction?

MB: The magic trick of its immersiveness. The novels I love most pull me fully into their worlds, so that reading becomes like vivid dreaming. It seems like the most central aspect to this is the creation of a consciousness that is compellingly inhabited. The writing must be vivid and specific enough to make the reader experience life right alongside the story's central characters.

JM: Do you often plan out your writing? To what degree do you outline?

MB: I outline as I go. Bigger-picture notes get recorded in a separate document, while short-term planning—notes on that chapter—goes directly below the draft. This might look like a reminder for a line of dialogue or something that needs to shift by the end of a scene. I'll bullet these to be deleted upon completion. I often see a general shape, but try to stay in the moment—to watch the characters go, letting their decisions dictate the direction of the next scene. A much smarter friend told me that he knows he's writing in the right direction when he deviates from his original vision for things. I value pivots that are hidden in plain sight and surprises that don't strain credulity.

JM: What do you need to be able to write?

MB: Adequate sleep, relative silence, and fingers.

JM: Does anything ever gum up the works?

MB: I'm most productive when I stick to my routine. A couple of hours of daily work has always suited me better than creative binging. I find that my focus and motivation are highest in the mornings, so writing is typically the first thing that I do in a day. This also ensures that I get something done before life has the opportunity to get in the way. I'll drink some strong coffee, take a cold shower, pop in a piece of nicotine gum, and listen to 40 hz binaural beats while I'm working to optimize mental acuity.

JM: Conversely, what inspires you? What typically triggers premise or character ideas?

MB: I'm interested in people who have to go against their nature to get what they want. Many story ideas emerge from a single image or scene; for *Bark On*, everything started with the idea of a runner being paced by a truck with a rope connecting them to its hitch. The logical progression is to imagine what kind of person would be driving that truck, and how they'd get the runner to listen to them. Setting is an endless reservoir for inspiration. I'm fascinated with transforming environments: the trash culvers and landsliding slopes around Lima, the eroding barrier island that inspired Kure. The unstable nature of those environments forces urgency.

JM: Do you have a favorite and least favorite part of the process?

MB: I like sinking so deeply into a story that it can surprise me. Both drafting and revising contain different kinds of revelations. The initial writing is obviously exploratory, but you also see new opportunities in early scenes after you've gotten the whole story in front of you. Maybe that's the most satisfying part of writing for me: the discovery.

JM: How conscious are you of the reader when you write?

MB: Delillo's got a line about not writing to an audience. For better or worse, this has informed my approach to drafting. Revision is partially the process of bending the author's vision into something clear enough for others to decipher. This is especially true in a book like *Bark On*, where a deep dive into a triathlon subculture, an elaborate plot, and extreme dialect run the risk of alienating a reader. Your sharp editing eye was critical in preserving the book's spirit while making an inroads toward accessibility.

JM: What writers have you learned the most from?

MB: Michelle Latiolais taught me that enough force can trump anything. Daniel Wallace told me a story could be like a cabinet and gently pushed me into broader reading. Mark Winegardner showed me how structure can be liberating. Kevin Barry's novels gave me faith in true insouciance, plus permission to get hyperbolic with gestures and language.

JM: What're some of your favorite books, and what have you been reading lately?

MB: Kevin Barry's *Night Boat to Tangier* is practically sacred to me. It's a tightly written crime novel with a dialogue-driven frame narrative confined to a ferry terminal and flashback sections that rove from Ireland to Spain to Morocco, distilling entire decades into vivid narrative summary. McCarthy's *All The Pretty Horses* is recklessly laconic, and appeals to that tragic ideal of a protagonist striving for a life that's beyond his actual reach. John Grady Cole was born a century too late, and perhaps too far north. I've been reading a lot of Elmore Leonard lately to study tight plotting and fast pace.

JM: Are you interested in any other mediums? What do they add to your writing?

MB: I can draw you a stick figure and play two chords on bass guitar. Most of my creative thinking outside of writing happens physically; climbing and surfing are both like problem-solving with your body. You've got to imagine how to make your limbs fit where they weren't meant to, if that makes sense. Both practices require a meditative level of mindfulness. They get me out of my head long enough to be restorative, providing a daily reset from writing. I've had the good fortune of leading undergraduate fiction workshops at FSU, and I think that good teaching is also an act of creativity.

JM: Are you interested in writing other forms, say poetry or nonfiction?

MB: I've spent most of the past two years novel-minded, but I'm an occasional writer and frequent reader of short stories. The requirements of short fiction are distinct enough to qualify it as a different form in my thinking. Teaching undergraduate workshop has given me the opportunity to revisit some of my favorite expressions of this genre—Denis Johnson's Fuckhead stories, Barry Hannah's early stuff, and Lee K. Abbott's stories consistently amaze me for their vocal range and potential as empathy machines.

JM: To what extent is there a didactic component in your writing?

MB: To the exact extent that my characters value it. I never write toward a moral, but I try to inhabit people who are moved by their own convictions. The writing that has moved me most portrays rather than explains; that is, it puts me in the mind and life of someone who's being irreversibly changed. Maybe they learn something, but they don't have to—and very often it's a thing too big for them to articulate.

JM: What are you working towards in your writing? Many writers keep to similar themes in their work. If you have one, what, would you say, are yours?

MB: I can't seem to let up off of folks consumed by superstition and compulsion. Fortunately, that provides an almost distressing degree of freedom. Right now, a lot of people without noses are showing up. I'm writing something incorrigibly dystopian, with witches and noise-canceling androids and a floating theocratic city.

JM: Have you ever worked in this genre before? What are you modeling this project after? Of course, there are plenty of great literary sci-fi novels, both classic and contemporary. *Dune* comes to mind; Marlon James' new trilogy, too.

MB: I've written some speculative short stories, but this novel is my first effort at anything substantively dystopian or steampunk-y. *Dune* is high-up in my personal canon. Every sci-fi novel that comes after it branches from it, in the same way that the Victorian novel cannot exist without *Madame Bovary*. I love Philip K. Dick for the elaborate scope of his novels, the hardboiled aspect that he brings to the genre, and the sheer syntactic energy. I also spent a lot of time in the *Warhammer 40k* universe in my teens.

JM: What other projects are you working on?

MB: Does a doctorate count as a project? I'm chewing through a 140-novel reading list in preparation for my qualifying exams, which will cover the history of the novel, crime fiction, and some rudimentary theory. I'm also seeking a publisher for a multigenerational mystery series about a collapsing coal mining dynasty.

JM: What are your ambitions as a writer? What would you like to work on in the future?

MB: I want to get that mystery series into print, then round out the aforementioned dystopian trilogy. I've got a novella about a cult of squatters in Peru that deserves returning to, and enough solid stories to get out a collection soon. Beyond that, more and more and more novels. The form is all-consuming. I don't see myself quitting the habit anytime soon.

A literary crime novel about found family and compulsion through the eyes of triathletes, Mason Boyles' *Bark On* never fails to surprise with innovative diction, original voices, and a thrilling narrative.

"Every sentence, every paragraph, is dense with inventive language. [...] Driven by uncanny energy and imagination, *Bark On* is a gripping and insightful novel."

—Kristin Rabe, *Foreword Reviews*

"*Bark On* is one of the strongest debut novels I've read in years. There's nothing weak about it, in fact: from the sentences to the story to the beating heart of it all, this book has an extraordinary musculature. I really enjoyed this novel."

—Daniel Wallace, author of *Big Fish*

AVAILABLE FROM DRIFTWOOD PRESS
WHEREVER BOOKS ARE SOLD

ABGDHWZARIAN

Bazeed

ا ll I should have to tell you is my ancestors made horses dance until the animals

ب roke sweat & no I don't mean like galloping across the Arabian desert towards oases you racist

ج od, I mean it literally, like at weddings & stuff, horses springing on heeled command to the song of drums

د id your parents accept you, you know, when you came out? Cuz like aren't you Muslim like aren't they Arab so…

ه enry, I'm so glad you asked! Yes, 'tis indeed a pity, a pity indeed most piteous, a most piteously piteous pity

و hen families reject their own—I'm so glad that here in America you've figured all of that out.

ز awaajil atfâli mushkilatun kabiratûn fil yamani, you'll learn to say in your CIA-funded intensive Arabic, as if—

ح ock it out of your mouth—child marriage isn't really a thing here cuz like 'Merica ain't Yemen, y'know? Where

ط aha, the prophet, his name meaning secret held by God, is surveilled in every mosque.

ي es, his dreaded name Mohammad—did you think we'd have less than 99 names to name him in a 100 different tongues?

ك ill doubt & fear everybody, we are become American—what, us?

ل apse in paying taxes to bring horror with the fall of night to our families?

م odernize with made-in-America rubbling rockets, the playgrounds of our first house?

ن o! Not us! Never us, Ameen, never us, astaghfirrullah al-3atheem. No really, I

س wear, the beard isn't like an Allah beard, y'know, Mo's actually quite the metrosexual.

ع ain is the 1st letter of the word eye in Arabic, & the word itself too, but to say it in English you'd have to invent the letter.

ف irst there was you, then there was us, and after that, long visa lines.

ح صدق الله العظيم is how you close the Qur'an in Arabic every time you read it, God's promise: He would not let us down.

ق هو الله أحد : say God is one!

ث it, we made it! يا إبني، مش أيّ كلام، والدو هولوم ده

ت rue, in season two the handsome imam played by Mahershala Ali, actually

ن anks the racist white men picketing the fence of his mosque, buys them coffee on his own dime, I kid you not—

خ اجعلنا أحبّ خير ! Ali is the new Potier, though Black and Muslim—humiliation on sale in melting pot America, 2 for the price of 1!

ذ ere's no point to resisting change.

ح uh is the letter and law of the Arab future & the future Arab.

ظ e truth is our language has known it all along. Like, before-the-greencard-lottery-was-even-a-thing long;

غ arb in Arabic is the word for *West*, which shares a root with the words *sunset* and *strange* and *stranger*, as in

غرَّبَ الْعَرَبُ غَرْبٌ غُروبٌ غَريبٌ وَما فيه الْعَرَب.

The abgdhwzarian is a modified form created by the poet as a reclamation of the more common abecedarian.

The abgdhwzarian returns the abecedarian closer to its semitic roots, by replacing the spine of its Latin alphabet with Arabic, in the abjad order derived from Phoenician [as opposed to hija' order]. The form requires that: 1. the poet include at least one phrase fully in Arabic wording and syntax, whatever alphabets are used; and 2. that the poet maintain the sonic integrity of the Arabic alphabet, however they tool the language(s) around them.

ز أوجل أفلي مشكلة كبيرة في يماني
j awaqul afālti mushkilatun kabiratun fil yamani
the following phrase transliterated in Latin characters:
child marriage is a big problem in Yemen.

آمين
Amen!

أستغفر الله العظيم
I seek God's forgiveness of my sins!
a phrase often used to aver distance between oneself and a sinful or unacceptable deed or thought.

صدق الله العظيم
God has spoken the truth.

قل هو الله أحد
Say God is one.

أمالَهُ! دَه هُولُو يَا ابْنِي، مِشْ أَيّ كَلَامْ!
It's on Hulu, son! That's no trifling thing.

خَيْر اللّهُمَّ اجْعَلْه خَيْر.
Let it be good, God.
a phrase of prayer asking God to make whatever just happened an omen of good things; often used when one wakes up after a nightmare.

غَرَبَتِ الْعَرَبُ غَرْبَ غُرُوبِ، وَنَاءَ فِيهِ الْعَرَبُ
The [sun of the] West sets a strange setting, and in it the Arabs collapse under the load.

the phrase uses the [very, very cool] matrix structure of the Arabic language to insist on multiple formulations of the three letter root غ - ر - ب, from which the word *West* and *sunset* and *strange* and *stranger* are derived. the word غَابَ has two meanings.

as an adjective, it can mean *far, distant, remote*.

as a verb [the technical usage here], it can mean *to collapse, to yield, to succumb, to weigh heavily upon.*

CARS RUNNING ON [رپ]FUMES

Bazeed in Conversation with Sara Elkamel

Sara Elkamel: For a poem that deals heavily in notions of identity, particularly the perception of Arab Muslims in the west, "abgdhwzarian" incorporates stunning images that add visual and sensual dimensions to the reader's experience. I'm thinking of the opening line:

my ancestors made horses dance until the animals / ﺑroke sweat

What do you think is the purpose of incorporating images in a poem like this one?

Bazeed: To say that there is a poverty of joyous imagery connected to the word "Arab" in the language and imagination and archive of English is an understatement erasing the work of centuries of racism, colonialism, and deliberate misinformation. I wanted to open the poem with that image of an ancient and rigorous practice cultivated by my ancestors simply so they could dance with their Arabian horses, a prized mythologized poeticized animal.

Funny you should ask about that phrase specifically, since it in particular has had such a journey with me in this poem! Months after submitting "abgdhwzarian" for this contest, I came across the same image reading Safia Elhillo's *The January Children* this summer for a cento project. In one of the poems in her Abdelhalim Hafez series she writes:

[your father] used to sing to his horses / to get them to dance …

There was something that felt formally fortuitous there, to be writing this poem particularly about being Arab in America, and naturally clustering around some of the same images and nostalgias as other folx writing about diaspora in America, and the diasporas of and in, English. So then I felt great about it. Then I researched it a little more and found out that actually, to get a horse to dance requires that you torture that horse, a lot. They are hopping like that because they are survivors of tons of pavlovian conditioning: they expect the drum beat to arrive with the heat of a whip, crack of a stick. It's pretty horrific. So then I considered taking it out and replacing it with some other image or metaphor that doesn't celebrate cruelty to one species for the pomp and pomposity of another. But ultimately I decided to keep it, for authenticity's sake. Yes, my ancestors made their horses dance. Yes, they hurt their most prized animal to do it, repeatedly, and passed down the practice as art. I can hold that complexity.

SE: I've always wondered about the process one goes through to write an Abecedarian. Can you tell us a little bit about the play by play? Was it a kind of collage, where you were assembling notes you already had, or were you starting "from scratch"? In a way, I'm trying to gauge how you got from the "alif" to the "yaa".

B: I started from scratch, though I'd considered the other approach too. But ultimately I didn't want to slot in any lines against any of the letters that the rest of the poem would then have to cater to or work toward or around or justify or feel indebted to or anything. Which meant that I couldn't really plan or write it in a collage-y kind of way, or decide how I'd use a letter before I got to it. I think the single thing I knew going in was that I would start with the image of dancing horses for the first line. The second thing I knew was the constraint I made for myself, that the poem respect the sonic integrity of the Arabic alphabet. The third thing I knew or anticipated was that I'd have to flip the page to landscape orientation, because I am a long-winded motherfucker.

So I would start a line, get to the next Arabic letter, and only at that juncture figure out what words I could use to finish/build on a thought, or start a new one, depending on what the previous line was trying to do. Doing it that way felt less like composition than discovery. Here's one example I remember distinctly! The line about child marriage and America not being like Yemen ended, and then there I was staring at that ﻂ, without the possibility of a direct equivalent in Latin alphabets, and knowing therefore that I couldn't use an English word because that would violate my rule re: sonic integrity. So then I thought of Taha, one of the ninety-nine names of the prophet Mohammad, which I then connected back to the idea of Muslims being surveilled in the same America whose political propaganda machine mythologizes it into a land of exceptional freedoms, in direct opposition to the Muslim lands it invades purportedly to disseminate those very freedoms. If I'd started the poem with trying to solve for ﻂ and some of the other equivalent-less letters, I probably wouldn't have ended up with that juxtaposition, of Yemen as two-dimensionally imagined by invading Americans, and America through the third-dimensionally lived experience of a surveilled, othered populace.

But actually trying to answer this question has got me thinking poets should start recording those time-lapse videos the next time they work on poems that have formal constraints like this, or that require some kind of problem solving like this! It'd be a revelation to be able to see that archive of live composition, decision-making, and editing specifically with forms like this.

SE: The way you've adapted the principles of the abecedarian poem to give us a poem propelled by the twenty-eight letters of the Arabic alphabet feels central to the arguments you make, where identity is being negotiated and asserted by the speaker. How did you arrive at the abgdhwzarian form for this piece?

B: Before this abgdhwzarian was an abgdhwzarian, it was an abecedarian! I started writing the poem in a workshop led by Omotara James, where we read Natalie Diaz's "Abecedarian Requiring Further Examination of Anglikan Seraphym Subjugation of a Wild Indian Rezervation." Her taking on the abecedarian form specifically for that was inherently saying something meta: here was an indigenous poet taking on this form in colonial America, a form that in its very raison d'être gives primacy to the same letters of the Latin alphabet that deliberately and systematically decimated and forcibly replaced so many hundreds of indigenous languages, lingual macrophagy deeply rooted and widespread across white colonial practices. The poem reminds us, by hijacking its letters, that English is a decimation.

My intention while attempting the abecedarian initially had been to write a love letter to the structure and music of the Arabic language, which I have lived and will die in awe of, in this extremely constrained form. And I wanted that praise spelled out in this other, hegemonic alphabet shoved down my own postcolonial-subject throat. I'm writing this interview in English, aren't I?

Around the same time I was working on that abecedarian, I attended a virtual reading featuring Marwa Helal, where she read WHO REALʕ, which, to quote her, is "the return of poem to be read from right to left," which, to quote her again, is a form that: "vehemently rejects you if you try to read it left to right. To vehemently reject, in this case, means to transfer the feeling of every time the poet has heard an English as Only Language speaker patronizingly utter in some variation the following phrase: 'Oh, [so-and-so] is English as a Second Language...' As if it was a kind of weakness, nah."

An excerpt from WHO REALʕ:

> asks poem this of draft shorter a see to professor first the
> device stylistic this sustain could i long how
> think you do long how 'prof dunno i 'w counter i
> ᵀᴹpneumoic hegemonic demonic heteronormative khwhite the
> ʕitself sustain can

The poem that flows from there works so fluidly against the surety in this line of questioning—how long can you sustain...?! Like, of course Marwa Helal can fucking sustain! She has the nimbleness of mind and affect and personality and language involved in code switching, in speaking in many tongues. Which people know who've been reading in two directions for their entire history of reading. Which people know who've been speaking in two alphabets for most of their histories of speaking.

So, taking those learnings from the spirit of those two poems, I turned the abecedarian into an abgdhwzarian, and that change in form not so much vehemently rejects the reader, as requires extra work for the prize of comprehension. And it requires that from the very first letter: if you don't read Arabic, you're forced to slow down to deduce every letter starting every line of the poem. Other lines include entire Arabic phrases, whose meaning cannot be deduced, and the reader's comprehension here requires a glossary, and the generosity of the poet in deciding to provide one. I think that felt particularly satisfying to me, having now spent twenty years an immigrant in America, witnessing our treatment in the mainstream medias of this country, how we live in its public imagination. How often foreign accents, for example, are both the butt of the joke and its delivery method, to the lazy stand-up comic. How they are assumed to be markers of outsiderness, or signs of stupidity, than skins of chameleon. But in the space of this poem, and in so many Americas, I'm the one who doesn't need a glossary.

And actually, after I'd written the final draft, I found out in researching the abecedarian form that it derives from Hebrew and semitic sources, which for me was this incredibly rich meta moment. Because here was the form itself and its ancestry saying something: about English-language hegemony and its short memory; about English literary establishments and their appropriations; about an archive of colonizing Johnnys-come-lately renaming things to facilitate forgetting they didn't invent them. All of which the poem was already speaking to, prior to my unearthing this history. Like in my best writing moments, that felt like the piece itself winking back at me, telling me it wanted to be written.

SE: Is chance, or fortuitous coincidence an experience you've had before in your writing, or artistic practice more widely?

B: Not often retroactively like that, but definitely with poetry in making the thing I invite in chance in ways that I don't with my other work. I've been really into found forms, for the puzzle of them, and have been making a lot of work in that vein, mainly as centos and long-form erasures. And one thing that's been true from the start is that, more than make room for randomness, I design it deliberately into the process. So for example, I've been composing these moirologia centos, remembering my friends' dead, whose lines I source from their personal libraries. I spend a day with their books, pick out twenty to thirty titles based on what randomly calls to me, based on title or cover or just vibes, flip to a random spot in each one, and that spread is where my line has to come from. And I absolutely love it. With chance literally dictating the entirety of the vocabulary available to me, there's a lot more room for surprise and discovery, and a lot less room for me to return to my own writerly habits and images and obsessions.

SE: I'm so impressed by the way the poem keeps shifting in tone and register, particularly between lyric gestures and more conversational, facetious gestures. I am curious as to how the form itself informed these movements. Did you find the abgdhwzarian form more inclined to tone diversity than other poetic forms you've experimented with?

B: That spread in tone and register is a tendency that's consistent throughout my work I think, so probably some of that in the piece is just who I am as a writer. But there were definite ways that the form and purpose of the poem informed that in particular as well, and sometimes—in the most exciting of ways!—forced it.

So, to speak about form first: I had a strict constraint for myself that I must keep the sonic integrity of the Arabic alphabet. As in, I could not approximate one sound for another to make a phrase make sense if the letter didn't already exist in English. Of which we have a few! For most of those letters, I just used Arabic words, so it was fun to come up with turning the aspirated h in "ح ock it out of your mouth" into an onomatopoeia of spitting in English.

And now to speak about purpose contributing to this spread in tone: As many of us know all too well, there is also a lot of pressure on writers presumed to occupy marginal identities, to make their writing-in-mostly-English fully accessible to folx who do not read their other language[s], which get treated as auxiliary, as flavor, and—depending on the publisher, the editor—are given that exoticizing treatment visually, words italicized on the page, though their function is to speak the true[r] names of things. So it felt important here that I not adjust my humor or tone in Anglicizing ways. It felt important that I allow myself as much Arabic as I wanted, which I do, in three registers [Qur'anic, Modern Standard, and colloquial], without indulging my training to use the body of the poem to explain away the foreignness in the writing-"world"-literature-in-English sleight of hand that I have read so much of, and certainly aspired to and emulated in other work.

SE: Is there something about poetry that makes you more willing to take the risk of being not-fully-understood, versus fiction for instance?

B: I started my education in poetry by attending a weekly poetry reading and discussion circle, run by my friend C Bain on Monday nights at Ugly Duckling Presse. One week we were looking at some examples of how poets use elusive or abstract narrative in their work—or something like that, I can't quite remember. Anyway, one of the poems we read was Gabrielle Calvocoressi's "The Bandleader Calls It the Angel Position". It's a super creepy, very disturbing poem. Or so I thought everyone would think! But the room was split. Half the people in the room read it as describing a violent, scary, nonconsensual sexual experience, while the other half were convinced the poem depicted a very hot, consensual, kinky experience. I think that was the moment when I was like, holy shit! Here there be magic!

Which isn't to say that moment opened up any kind of floodgate; most of the poems I write deal in extremely concrete images and syntax, and I'm not sure how fluently I will ever compose in the language of abstraction. But when I get excited about those possibilities in the medium of poetry, that's the moment that comes to mind, the wonder I felt that the same language could contain these multitudes. That the same metaphors on a page could leave readers with such vastly different ideas about the emotional truths of the poem.

SE: I feel like your writing actually comes across as a living, breathing thing. One reason I think so is that irony and sarcasm are very common features of your work. Why do you think draws you to them?

B: My earliest introduction to political art that I recognized as such was the song "Valéry Giscard d'Estaing," lyrics by Ahmad Fouad

Negm, music by Sheikh Imam, which my father taught me to sing. As you know, those lyrics make fun of the rhetorics of white supremacy, and the promise of justice in colonial husbandry, by repeating increasingly ridiculous claims of how good life will be, on this occasion of French President Valéry Giscard d'Estaing's visit to Cairo, making him the first president of the French Republic to ever do so on an official visit. (Though France has been stealing from Egypt for millenia!) This is my very quick translation of a couple verses:

> *Valéry Giscard d'Estaing,*
> *and his madame too,*
> *will catch the wolf right by the tail,*
> *and eradicate hunger in the hungry.*
>
> *And all the TV screens will color!*
> *And all the cooperatives bloom.*
> *And instead of petrol,*
> *Cars will run on perfume.*

As with many places with repressive governance and unprotected speech, a lot of political commentary in Egypt has had to cloak itself in disguises of farce and humor, and so I think in some ways I was schooled early in that as both aesthetic and tool. And there is incredible power in simply repeating ridiculous claims as the method of unveiling the gaslighting in their logics, which, in the case of American mythologies on Arabs, rely almost entirely on a—and I mean this quite literally!—absolutely deadly mix of racism, white supremacy, prejudice, short memory, and utter ignorance. So if I just simply say back the terribly racist thing you've probably been at the very least thinking, if not spewing online and irl, Bob, can you hear it? And if Bob can't hear it, won't readers occupying other, similarly marginalized positions hear it? Won't they recognize the recyclable phrases by which their humanity is routinely discounted? So in those ways, irony and sarcasm act as shield and weapon and witness report and mirror.

SE: This poem has numerous Qur'anic references, and so does much of your work. Is it the language itself or the cultural connotations that draws you to scripture? Or something else entirely?

B: The primary reason is that the Qur'an and the history and present of Arabic are inextricably linked. It is ubiquitous: it is the first poetry many of us hear as children of the SWANA region, Muslim or not. The stories the Qur'an inherits from its biblical predecessors and the ones it invents were among the first I was told as a kid; Noah and the ark and Jonah and the whale and Mohammad and the spider at the mouth of the cave. And so naturally, as with Christian language in secular English, Qur'anic language has naturally seeped into secular Arabic, and is in use by Arabophones everywhere, Muslim and otherwise. So while some of these phrases may come from the Qur'an or refer to it, a lot of them function idiomatically.

Where it gets tricky is knowing that folx unfamiliar with Arab and Muslim cultures but steeped in their stereotypes will read religiosity in these common and everyday phrases that mean something else. Because of course that is in line with how the Western imagination figures us, as extremely conservative and religiously crazed people thanking Allah in spirits of great piety and intention for the day seven hundred times. So it felt in keeping with the spirit of the poem not to prioritize a non-Arabic speaker's confusion, and to write this as I, Mariam—named for that chapter in the Qur'an, incidentally!—would.

The second reason has more to do with the poem's purpose, what I want to say about the Arab in the American imagination. In religion class growing up, I was taught that while the Jews had a split sea, and the Christians a virgin birth, our main miracle as Muslims was the Qur'an. Now, I think there is something to be said about a people who imagine their religion's main miracle to be a poetic text. I think there is something further to be said about a people whose God's first injunction spoken directly to its prophet is "Read." I think there is something to be said about a people who, over the majestically slow crawl of centuries, built a language that is a literal matrix, which is to say, a language absolutely *designed* to be relational. Arabic feels tooled, is tooled. Arabic is not something that Time and the necessity to communicate threw together.

Now, none of those things that could be said are any of the things most people actually say, about the Arabs.

So, to think about my culture's affect toward, and respect for, story and history and poetry; about the complexity and precision and vastness of Arabic; about its formal and structural acknowledgement of the interconnected of life; and to juxtapose all of that with the spectre of the Arab as defiled by the Western imagination, historical and contemporaneous, in all the orientalist ways Edward Said made so granularly legible (as a hyper-sexualized savage, as an entity understanding belonging only in tribal ways, as vehement protectors of chastity and devaluers of Actual Culture™, etc etc etc etc etc etc), and to put all of that into abgdhwzarian, is my attempt at a poetic fuck-you to those same racists who equate Islam with barbarity.

SE: Because you sent me a recording of your reading of the poem, and you mentioned it is meant to be performed, I noticed how being spoken completely changes the piece. Spoken, there's a sense of running over, while on the page, the poem is visually segmented by the Arabic letters, which may offer the reader some leeway to determine the breath and pause for themselves. Ideally, would you want readers to be roaming freely across the poem, or experience these stops?

B: I make a practice of providing a recording for every poem I get published online, which I do mainly for accessibility reasons; nobody should have to listen to a poem as a computer decides to read it. And while of course I am thinking about rhythm and flow as I'm composing a piece, I often find the breath of the poem only after it's finished, when I begin figuring out how to perform it, and where what I discover about its rhythm and flow feeds back into final edits.

I must admit too to a bit of anxiety I have after a poem leaves the very narrow sphere of my control—my laptop!—and is out in the world, to have it read how I intended it. I blame coming to poetry after years of writing fiction and essays and plays, and approaching those mediums as orchestrator, translator, mediator, disambiguator. Because ideally, the reader should read the poem however the hell they read it! And I should trust the container of it to hold those multiple readings. So I'm working on unclenching around that one. Stay tuned!

SE: I know that your practice frequently jumps off the page—you're a writer of prose, poetry, plays, and essays, and a stunning performer. When you sit down to write "a poem," are you just writing a poem, or does your engagement with other mediums influence your writing process and result?

B: While there's a poetic impulse in all of my work, it took me quite a bit of time to stand in it confidently enough to attempt writing, like, actual poems that I was calling poems. It took the pandemic and the attendant anxiety that had me enrolling in every workshop I could find to really get me started; I had probably four accidental poems to my name prior to March 2020. So this is very new for me, and if my imposter syndrome as a writer of plays and fiction is Jack, my imposter syndrome as a poet is the entire village of giants up the beanstalk.

I recognize certain limitations in my capacity for abstracting language or using it as inventively as I see other poets whose work I aspire towards—which includes you as I've gushed to you many times before! I feel very much weighed down by a concreteness of syntax that I recognize as a legacy of the other forms I've worked in, with lesser capacity to hold and mold and break and abstract language, and my own anxieties already discussed around having the reader absorb my every intention. I try to remind myself that March 2020 was three years ago. The poet I am is three very chaotic years old. They have a lot of learning and unlearning and relearning still to do.

I think the one line I can draw through all the genres I write in is that sound is huge. By the time I've finished a poem, I'll have read it out loud and sounded it out enough times to have completely memorized it—which comes in real handy for readings! And I do that with essays, I do that with fiction, I do that with plays. Before any actor has put a single line of mine into their mouth and body, I've chewed and spit out seventeen barely-different versions of it.

For what it's worth, I give credit to Arabic for that, my attunement to the aural. Its matrix is all assonance, agility, and play! I'm glad its sounds entered me first.

THE KOOL-AID MAN CANNOT SPILL IN THE ARCTIC
Luke Burton

One actual ghost and suddenly the entire world is haunted.

My brother leans and twists out the window of the Tacoma in an attempt to photograph a store called "Grocery Casino #4" in Truth or Consequences, NM.

Of course, it is the coolest things that warm the fastest.

That prank where you release three greased pigs labeled "1" "2" and "4" into your high school.

We are pretty sure you will leave with a little smile on your face.

The gas station's loud-speaker advertisement claims to care about "This Town."

{In The Abstract} I say to no one in particular.

That overlap between small worlds within The World.

Music where no sound is repeated. Not even silence.

Without an initial trajectory, I pivot to selling concrete as a career.

Seed nostalgia for brutalist architecture on TikTok.

There is a theory that posits that we are living in the best possible hell.

The Kool-Aid man has arms that extend outside his pitcher-body implying they are made of something besides glass. This character design was implemented 3 years before Jonestown, 7 years after "The Electric Kool-Aid Acid Test."

I've never seen it, but my beliefs have been broken upon the anvil of the real.

They didn't actually drink Kool-Aid at Jonestown.

In the photo, my brother is holding a fifth of Old Crow outside "Celebration" Drive-through liquor store. The fish-eye lens bends the landscape around him as if he is the center of this little world. The coming snowwill destroy Texas.

I've come to see gravity as the constant internal rhythm of the earth.

There is a Hooters franchise that looks out over the Gulf of Mexico.

Every year, 60 billion chickens are slaughtered globally. Right now their carcasses are becoming fossilized in thousands of landfills, in thousands of fast-food adjacent micro-forests forming a chicken-bone stratum.

Sometimes, the Kool-Aid man is depicted holding a smaller pitcher shaped identically to his own body and filled with the same punch-red juice.

Even the Kool-Aid man needs something to pour himself from.

So what do you do?

LUKE BURTON
In Conversation

Jerrod Schwarz: One of the most striking aspects of this poem is the visual language. The long line lengths, the plethora of stanzas, and the mix of smaller and larger sections; there is entropy here alongside incredibly specific language. When drafting this poem, how did the visual language arise? Did the presentation of this poem come about naturally, or is your process more deliberate?

Luke Burton: Because the content of the poem is pretty "dense" so to speak, I intuitively felt that line breaks/extensive caesura might push the whole thing into incomprehensibility. Additionally, the long lines arose from what felt like the poem's natural affinity towards complete sentences as opposed to fragments (especially since, once again, the content could already be a little too fragmentary for its own good). By separating the individual stanzas, each gets to stand on its own and in relation to the whole. Because the scope is so broad, the whole is less than the sum of its parts. I think the visual layout helps underscore that point. How these individual stanzas add up, or what they add up to is hard to say, but there is a visual sense of both distance and collection. It's in that dynamic that magic can happen.

JS: There is a powerful duality in this piece between seemingly random details and stark familial insight, specifically around the speaker's brother. What work did you do to balance these two aspects of the poem?

LB: These days seemingly all of my poems are secretly about accumulation. What happens when things stack up? At what point does a random smattering of stars become a constellation? The intensely personal vs the absurdity of the broader context. (Or are those two things even opposed?) I am intensely interested in the possibilities of relation between seemingly unrelated details. There is a real charge there—a frisson, a shock of static electricity—when seemingly disparate elements manage to connect. Like there is some logic to the work that cannot be known but can be felt or experienced.

That said, too much randomness and the whole thing falls apart. The familial insights are there to ground the poem in actual events, in concrete details that the reader can hold onto amid the randomness of the poem. Actual persons doing actual things in actual places to help balance the constantly tangential musings, facts, jokes, ephemera, etc. How that balance is achieved has to do with timing, something I'll admit I am navigating purely by feel. It's worth noting that I spent a month living out of my brother's Tacoma and driving around America during the height of the pandemic, a surreal experience to be sure, and one that inevitably finds its way into one's art—even if in an oblique way.

JS: I'm fascinated by this poem's ending: a question that could be interpreted in a myriad of ways and one that could be addressed to a host of different people. What do you think poets gain by ending their poems with a question? Do you see any challenges in giving your reader greater agency of identity within a poem?

LB: You've got to trust the reader, I think. A question at the end of a poem always invites, or in the case of this poem's direct address, demands, reflection. A question (I hope) opens up the poem from its own little context into a broader realm of meaning. I suppose the risk inherent in a question is that the poem is left suspended. No final image or articulation the reader can hang their hat on. Then again, poems only ever really "work" while in flight.

Without giving up the mystery, I think the question at the end of the poem makes a move to demonstrate that this poem was never really about its specifics—in a sense they could have been anything—it was always about how they correspond to life in their accumulation. The flood of facts and statistics, the personal aesthetic moments, the anthropo-scenic, the booze and death and marketing and noise, the absurdity and fear, the lingering sadness in the contemporary American landscape, the ghosts and practical jokes, all of it is coming right at you all the time. So what does one do with that?

I mean it. So what do you do? From where do you pour yourself?

ONLY RUBBER BANDS IN THE BANANA BOWL

Kimberly Sailor

Nosebleeds, from late October
to the egg hunt, the stop and go drips
replaced with young daisies
around wicker baskets. When you hand me
the last tissue before Daylight Savings,
I am nostalgic for an evening I've never had:

healthy, healed, no more swaddling desert air,
pulling my insides out into empty arms.
No more fertility drugs, not ever.

They are replacing all the lead pipes in my house,
in my body. This is too much, this bruised plumbing.
The head gore lasts 'til Easter.
I try alternate nostril breathing, to give
half a rest, to restore
half the heart rates.

Twins, too thin, don't make it. I peel
a carrot into the shape of a woman's leg,
gently curving behind the knee
to straddle the traditional ham supper.

A knick near the ankle:
a shaving slip, authentic and
red and sliced. I cannot cut carrot coins
anymore because this produce is real now,

seductive and adulterous,
distracting from poisonous relentlessness.
Nosebleed air mixed with negative tests,
then: spotting someone's pet store rabbit, free
thumping away behind pink and orange boulders.
I am jealous of being lost in the desert.

More blood makes me dizzy,
makes me follow silly advice, salt
and petroleum jelly suggestions.

Seven months of nasal stinging
will mess up the nicest hayfever hutch
for rabbits, wild and tame.

Tell me honestly: Did I miss
the Resurrection? Did you find
my prenatal eggs, soft and boiled?
Another pastel holiday
without matching dresses.

There's only rubber bands
in the banana bowl:
not baby shower prizes,
or extra potassium,
for three elastic bodies.

KIMBERLY SAILOR

Jerrod Schwarz: This is a harrowing poem that confronts grief and loss in both intimate and explicit ways. How do you personally go about translating these concerns/themes into a poem? What does your idea-to-draft-to-piece process look like?

Kimberly Sailor: My first draft of a poem usually looks like a letter to myself—not quite a diary entry, more like an unspoken conversation. I work to document micro details of an experience that I can shape in later drafts. It's difficult to initially ignore form and presentation, but if you craft from the start it narrows your word choices and expression options too quickly. One poetry instructor told me that the first draft shouldn't look like a poem, it should just be a mess on the page. With "Only Rubber Bands in the Banana Bowl", this was an easier exercise because there literally were rubber bands hanging out in my banana bowl. The cheap gas station by my house used to group bananas together with rubber bands (nature's method of "bunching" was apparently not good enough), and I'd stare at the rubber bands my kids left behind after breakfast. The mind can journey many places if you don't immediately force a direction, and I keep a file on my computer called "Poetic Bits" for this kind of freewriting. Occasionally the pieces turn into flash fiction or a short story, but that's really alright. Here's the very first draft for "Only Rubber Bands in the Banana Bowl":

> *Maybe we should just stop buying bananas because we can never keep the bowl full, and everyone is disappointed in the morning when there's just the damned rubber bands. I think we've had this problem since Easter, because the kids thought about using the rubber bands to make patterns while dying eggs, but I said shells are too easy to crack. You don't just squeeze eggs, even if they don't bleed. The air is too dry in this house; I'm not sure if I live in the midwest or the southwest, but I'd bleed hard in both. Remember thinking we could choose how many kids we'd have?*

JS: Blood is a reoccurring image throughout your poem, particularly focused on how it leaves the body in the form of a nosebleed. How early on in your writing did this central image appear? How did it evolve as the poem grew?

KS: I started the blood work in the first draft and expanded it to be the unifying theme. Fertility and infertility is all blood, all the time—the absence or the presence. We measure our wellness and vitality with blood and see our sacrifices in a framework of blood, too. The relationships, the lineage, and the struggles I expose in this poem come back to blood.

JS: Many poems with an explicit "*I*" fit into the confessional poem categorization. That being said, I am always curious to see how poets define their work. Do you see this poem as existing within the long line of confessional poetry? Perhaps more specifically, are there any traditions or structures that inform your writing?

KS: Absolutely, this poem fits into the Confessional style. I never use that word when I talk about my poetry, though; I'm not against it, but I think the scope is broader for my work. When asked, I usually say I write "domestic poems", because that gives me license to give a voice to each family member, who always sees and feels the same scenario very differently. I don't lean on any traditions or structures when crafting, but I do love contemporary, written right now, written today poetry where poets are responding to what's happening in their lives and the headlines. That's what gets me revved up.

JS: Finally, what is one poem, poet, or book that you think deserves more readers and recognition?

KS: Christopher Citro is a zany, eccentric poet with pieces that lift off the page and laugh at the absurdities of life. His book *If We Had a Lemon We'd Throw It and Call That the Sun* is a total romp.

DUMP TINKER
Margaret Yapp

DUMP   TINKER

I don't miss swimming or think about swimming often. When I do, thoughts like memories underwater which makes sense & very underslept. I can't believe I slept so little for many days sometimes my tampons smell like a full Easter supper. Are you romantic? Let me guess baby carrots? Swallow hard. If you're wondering then you're nowhere in this dump & of course I do

TINKER

DUMP

seven planets to the light. My eyes hunker : glowing heart with half arrow on left side changes into an arrow pointing up right, then back to half arrow heart, repeats. I notice some wallpapers eight eight eight … a quick trip stops. Right wind barrier left more lanes. I cross another violent invisible line into the field of opportunity going a little over. Bald eagle nowhere near water body

PUTTER PINE
Margaret Yapp

PUTTER   **PINE**

I won't take for granted the small square window in our front door. Darn where competition comes from. Making piece (fake piece) or faking piece. Winning action. My pinky toes consider closing up shop, they gossip, unionize. An empty rectangular parallel piped just enough sides missing to crawl inside or thrust through. Or five blankets in one room. Here I am & I bow out

PUTTER

the lantern bug, peanut bug, alligator bug. Your mirror face. Cause to starve, away. I colander greens in sink, wet my shirt, break the cup, spill a liquid, vibration through cord. Sharp quick ring of a vessel maker. Fluid, juice of animal, plant. Laughter, by definition, requires moisture remember? We spoke about this : to indulge a whim, an organized theory, universally recognized

PINE

RIDDANCE PANDER
Margaret Yapp

RIDDANCE

PANDER

thank you says my liver : thank you says my liver : thank you to my liver's dad
(my dad's liver) trust me … an image three times. An image of an image of
an image. Snow pile where I have repeatedly kicked my boots, gone inside.
Many cells have 24 hour clocks certain about direction I want around it's all
good because it's truth, not because I'm at practice : a print stuck in a brick

RIDDANCE

PANDER

information exists & isn't findable, doesn't have location. Glomus : ball of
string, four sphere at the end I'll have changed by chance. I do one I thought
was called honeysuckle until I found out better, I still chew nobs. Nobs at
best slightly sweet & at worst tasteless. Someone else tilled our garden plot last
year & this year I promise I'll try to till plot alone until I can learn to forgive

Jerrod Schwarz: These are some of the most visually arresting poems we've ever published, and it's a joy to share work that feels this new and confident. How did you arrive at the visual presentation of these pieces?

Margaret Yapp: That's really sweet, thank you so much. I want to start by explaining that these three poems are part of a longer series called *GLACIAL ERRATICS*. Glacial erratics are rocks left behind as a glacier moves across a landscape. They can be small or big. Think: big boulder on the edge of a soybean field. Glacial erratic! I wonder how often I encounter them. To exist where they exist, a glacial erratic required such massive movement. I am humbled by the history of these erratics.

It feels difficult for me to say how I arrived at the visual presentation of these poems. I can say that as I was writing these, I was considering the following: there are eight poems in *GLACIAL ERRATICS*. The eight hinges, when viewed at once, can be arranged into two squares of equal size and weight. Also, in each, there are two stanzas of equal lines, so there's some symmetry happening across different formal elements. Neither the hinge shape (when an ERRATIC is viewed individually) nor the squares (when the ERRATICS are viewed simultaneously) are mysterious shapes. I mean it's just right angles! Simple. They should be immediately familiar and obvious to a reader. When these are printed in a book one day (hit me up), the eight erratics will be spread throughout the book. So, viewing the eight erratics at once would require dismantling the physical book and physical rearranging by a reader. I'm using the structure of a codex and the familiarity of these shapes to prompt a reader to construct two squares internally, to move the hinges that have been scattered, back to how they fit together.

JS: After reading through these poems, I was struck by how these dense, lush poems made so much room for blank space on the page. What is the significance of these blank spaces in your visual language? Are there any writing traditions that you are working towards or against?

MY: I think this question sort of blends with the first question! The squares! It was all about accomplishing the squares. I heard somewhere (I know exactly where...a one-hour Netflix special about "design") that rectangles are the fastest shape the human brain can process. So that got me wondering if that's why books are rectangles? If that's why pages are rectangles? Yeah... I wrote these poems in the middle of my MFA in the middle of quarantine so I was thinking a lot about rectangles...

When these GLACIAL ERRATICS poems are in a book, each hinge will stretch across the full spread of the book. In other words: each erratic will take up two pages. So, in addition to the stuff with squares that I talked about earlier, I'm playing with shapes in another way here: each erratic will be made up of two rectangles (the stanzas), stretched over two other rectangles (the pages) that make up one rectangle (the spread). The blank space is in service of this shape play. The overlapping rectangles and squares are in service of introducing a massive sense of balance, symmetry, and completeness to the eight poems.

JS: The language in these three pieces is surprising but never jarring, entropic but never senseless. I would love to know what your first drafts of these poems look like. Is the language and syntax wrought, or does it manifest naturally?

MY: Okay, I hope that my answer to this third question will help illuminate the first two, because I realize these poems are not at all about rocks or right angles. I had to google "entropic." I think it's true of these poems, they're a little chaotic. I want them to feel maybe jarring or at least unpredictable. I want them to be fun and physically pleasurable to read out loud! I had to go back and re-read these poems just now, because they're a little old for me. It was interesting to read them from this distance of time while specifically considering sources of language. Of course, there are infinite sources of language in every poem. In these poems, I see a lot of stuff my friends have said. For example, "sometimes my tampons smell like a full Easter supper" is something my best friend Bre said. There's also recollections of jokes and bits I've shared with my partner. And always a lot of etymology stuff in here, which is a really rich source for me: when I'm feeling stuck in a poem, I'll pick a word that hits a nerve and let it guide for a while. I see old lines pulled from old poems that have otherwise disappeared. In all of my writing, I'm often not sure where a word or line comes from, it's just something I hear in my head and record.

SCORCHED EARTH TAPESTRY

Bader Al Awadhi

Pull rings hang like stems on the branch,
A pear must only be picked in *daylight*.

> The pot is cleaned with limestone and sand.

My uncles in the womb of a drained tank,
when the torture rooms need refilling.

The elders eat locust on steel skewers,
The young ones learn celibacy from mines.

> The same obesity that killed my grandfather
> saved him from being hauled into that bus.

Layla makes something with the last tin.
Thurayah is pregnant with nine handguns.
Mansoor knows his way to school by taking the first right
after the second hanged man.

A third line turns this phone call to conspiracy.

> *They do things to your fingernails.*
> *They do things to your sister and make you watch.*

When the oil fields burned,
the Americans came to save us.

You can forget about Geneva.

> I feel dirty on the sixth lane of Highway 80.

The lower part of Abaya blows
like a tail to the side. Thin legs exposed.
From a distance, the widows look like crows on the beach.

> For comfort, the family is told the corpse
> died smiling, and the scene smelled of rosewater
> and musk—meaning *ignore the blood*.

BADER AL AWADHI
In Conversation

Jerrod Schwarz: This poem is filled with vivid, tangled, and adjacent moments of pain and loss. What did the first draft of this poem look like? How wrought or natural did these harrowing details appear in the final draft?

Bader Al Awadhi: The details are lifted straight from personal accounts from friends and family who lived through The Gulf War. I initially wanted to assemble these stories either in poetic vignettes or prose style poems, but then I tried experimenting with various standalone lines that I wrote a while ago and compiled them into an assemblage or collage style poem instead. These images, or moments, existed previously in a notes app folder that I keep for random bouts of inspiration, shower thoughts, or filing away poetic lines for later use. I usually like to pick a line and then expand it into a bigger piece, but for this one I chose to lift several lines and arrange them together based on commonality with little connective tissue.

JS: I'm really struck by the power of punctuation in this piece. Specifically, the consistent use of periods is oppressive in the best way; I'm forced to slow down and consider the weight of each sentence and line. How do you approach punctuation when writing? How do you think it informs the rhythm of your writing?

BA: I try to use punctuation and pauses deliberately in my poem. Moments of stop are meant to be "punchy," in a way, forcing the reader to linger on the oppressiveness of the line, not as a moment for rest but rather a meditative or pensive reckoning with the subject matter. The poem does jump around a lot so the periods are needed to function as anchoring pieces for each line.

JS: I love how the stanzas in this piece zig-zag down the page, creating visual tension to mirror the language. When drafting a poem, what visual aspects do you focus on the most? What do you want readers to infer from the visual language of your poem?

BA: The title, "Scorched Earth Tapestry," came to me before deciding on the shape of the poem. This title heavily informed my choice of line breaks and indentations. I wanted the stanzas to appear disparate yet simultaneously strewn together by a tethering force, perhaps memory or collective trauma. Visually, the downwards zig-zag shape of the poem is meant to evoke an unpolished, almost patchwork quilt-like feeling, as if the lines do not really belong together but are forced to interact with one another. And in doing so they become rough and frayed; their seams in a state of tatter and disarray. Part of the visualization is also meant to convey that this is very much a collage poem, one where the reader sort of leaps from one image to the next without staying too long on one line, highlighting the contemporaneous and disruptive quality of the events, as well as the fragmentation of memory and emotion that occurs when an entire generation is traumatized by war.

JS: Finally, what is one poem, poet, or book that you think deserves more readers and recognition?

BA: Eduardo Corral's poems, "Self-Portrait with Tumbling and Lasso" and "Border Triptych" in particular, are two works that inspire me as of late and deserve more recognition from readers.

17 COOL TIPS FOR WITHSTANDING YOUR OWN UNDEATH
Shaoni White

house a swamp
in your lungs.

lintel your deaden. threshold
your mouth, rust it shut.
permit no foe.
guard your hush.
rot your larynx, fester
your tongue.

wound your sing.

clutch your gristle, spin it
into string, tie a knot,
thread your sing-wound
like a needle's eye.

sew your voice closed.
now your bronchioles will flood
but they'll be a no-drown land.
you won't sink. here
in your lungs,
humor your gallows,
plant your cypresses.

weave your floor
from the roots.

Jerrod Schwarz: This poem makes wonderful use of commands, propelling the reader from one directive to the next. Did the first draft of this poem make use of this mandate structure? What changed from the first to final draft of this piece?

Shaoni White: The mandate structure was always part of the poem. My poetry emerges from wordplay; I take something familiar and twist into something irreverent and fascinating (to me). This one started with "gallows humor" twisted into "humor your gallows": a noun phrase turned into a command. Then I riffed on the imperative syntax and the imagery of the humored gallows until it developed a more-or-less coherent thematics.

JS: The lack of capitalization in this poem does a great job of controlling rhythm and adding extra emphasis to line breaks and stanza breaks. Was this decision unique to this poem or something you have done in other pieces? How does capitalization inform your writing?

SW: Usage of capitalization varies widely across my work, mainly because I often use capitalization or the lack thereof to distinguish various voices from one another. Certain voices are Capitalization Kinds Of Voices. Others are not. I dislike the idea of foregrounding my personal "poetic voice"; I just don't find my own voice very interesting. I'd rather approach language like a mynah: through imitation and transformation, both solemnly and mockingly. Any sense of coherent authorial voice that emerges in my work is through the collage-like combination of other voices. In this poem, I wanted to contrast the long, overly capitalized title, with its cheery tone, with the terse and frequently-punctuated lowercase stanzas.

JS: Your poem is full of details about the human body, particularly our insides. What are the challenges when writing about the body? What are the advantages?

SW: Every poem is about the body, especially poems that aren't. We're always writing about the body, even when we don't think we are and especially when we wish we weren't. The difficulty with deliberately writing about the body is that there's nothing you can say that hasn't been said a hundred times before—the trick is to make what you're saying feel new, even if it's just an acknowledgment of something we all secretly know. The upside of drawing attention to the body in your writing is that you become more conscious of the embodied nature of the act: the physicality of voicing a syllable or of pressing keys on a keyboard. Ideally, that awareness hones your poetic practice to a fine edge.

JS: Finally, what is one poem, poet, or book that you think deserves more readers and recognition?

SW: I wish Joseph Lease were more well-known outside of the poetry world. His book *Broken World* was the first volume of contemporary poetry that I ever read. I picked it up by chance in a secondhand bookstore at age thirteen. I read the first two poems in the book while my parents were off doing something else and felt as if I'd been struck by lightning. Lease is "critically acclaimed," for whatever that's worth, but it feels like the only people reading his work are the critics doing the acclaiming. When I was in high school, I sat down with two of my friends, neither of whom could care less about contemporary poetry—one of them was failing English class—and opened *Broken World* to its titular poem. I tapped the subtitle, "For James Assatly," and explained the context. We read it together, silently, and then we talked about it, and then one of my friends asked to borrow the book. That's the kind of audience I wish Joseph Lease's poetry had.

A secret place to vomit
in the hollow of all things –
accessible from anywhere,
instantaneously. I
snap my fingers and a trap
door swings underfoot.

My palace of malady.
A scallop-shell citadel
where no one knocks impatiently.
No embarrassing noises
breach the vacuum. No strangers
after-shaving in the sink.

A secret place to vomit
outfitted for the purpose –
a muzak of loon calls and sea breeze
sobbing from the intercom.
A porcelain pedestal
at an accessible height

with carpeted kneepads
and a masseuse's face cradle.
Clean shirts unspool from a hands-
free dispenser. A spritz of air
freshener envelops me.
I am minted and watered and new.

A secret place to vomit
when my body revolts or
revolts against me. I emerge
as though from a Narnian
Wardrobe – no time has passed.
No one asks if I'm alright.

ANTHONY IMMERGLUCK
In Conversation

Jerrod Schwarz: I love the repeated phrase in the poem that opens several stanzas and how it consistently brings readers back to this hidden space. Was this repeated phrase in the original draft of your poem, or did it appear more often in revision? What are the challenges in repeating phrases or lines in a poem?

Anthony Immergluck: Thanks! I work refrains into many of my poems, and I typically think of them as the scaffolding for the overall construction. I find that repeated phrases help impose discipline and focus on my writing and editing, as well as establish a rhythmic and tonal structure for the reader. In this poem, I hope the refrain also adds to the sense of longing in the voice. This phrase was my entry point into "Utopia," and the challenge was building a piece around it that enriched and deepened the central conceit. I don't want to my poems to end up back where they start, but I also don't want them to lose focus. Ideally, they should be about one idea, but with as much complexity as I can pull off. In this case, the speaker is fantasizing. So I had to ask myself how the emerging details of the fantasy could continue to surprise and challenge the reader.

JS: This poem exists in tight, small stanzas with similar lengths. I'm always fascinated by poets' choices when it comes to visual language, and I would love to know how the presentation of this poem came to be. Do you usually work in smaller stanzas, or was this poem unique? What do you want to communicate visually in your writing?

AI: This poem is about the dream of dignity, control, and privacy, and so I wanted it to look and feel like a particularly fussed-over object. Early drafts had a rigid metrical structure, which has loosened significantly over revisions but is still partially detectable. In terms of visual presentation, I typically want to make sure a poem's form matches or elevates its content. That means something different for every poem, and sometimes the pursuit can be a little bit of a folly or diversion. But it's always something I try to consider. Again, I think this poem was asking to look manicured and precise. Others ask to look fluid or chaotic.

JS: I'm fascinated by the title of this poem and how it contrasts against the body of the poem. Do titles come early in your drafting process or later? How integral are titles in your writing process?

AL: This is about the sixth or seventh title I tried for this poem, and I still feel like there's a better one just out of my line of sight. I wanted something ironic, but not in a jokey or flippant way, that established the text as an aspirational fantasy. So, in this case, the title was the final step—I kept tweaking it long after the poem proper was finished. But that's not typical of my poems. Sometimes the titles come first and the rest of the poem generates from that. Sometimes they emerge organically as a byproduct of the writing process.

JS: Finally, what is one poem, poet, or book that you think deserves more readers and recognition?

AL: I've recently been really excited about Katie Farris' work.

12 = 12 on any day don't it ma?
carry the one

berried in the ground
with lexicon

named
lester, say–we got voices too

~~Uninigmaticism~~
(you knee nig mat a sizzm)
unrealiability
        boiling over cupcake batter
municipalitascious

stop running
        in the kitchen

I know what everyone is thinking
        in the world

I try to matter
        sad = 1968

don't it ma? don't it?
        don't we matter ma?

don't we ma?
        Septimber is here ma?

aint it ma? am?

September came, and so did
the decibels. Some of us stayed
to do the hard part: we didn't
do it, but imagine trying to
find out who did.

We use all the science to know
the spaces between
the hole and the gun.

                                        We think he did it
                                        because he was sad.

We didn't do it, but imagine
trying to find out who did

(Imagine how annoying
those decibels

                                                were)

Jerrod Schwarz: This is a visually arresting poem, and I'm especially drawn to all of the uncommon uses of punctuation: equal signs, strikethroughs, dashes, and parentheses. Where does punctuation fit in your writing process? Are these elements in the first draft, or do they come about later?

Robert Laidler: I think arresting is a great way to describe this poem, especially in the way that the punctuation works. I remember when I was learning to use punctuation in poems, I would think of them as ways to steer a pause, or command an adjustment to how to approach a poem; a way to teach the reader how to read the rest of the poem. In this poem, I think I am using that steering and commanding in a much more direct and confrontational way. Usually punctuation comes after I've written the words and have done my extreme editing, but in this case, the punctuation came out while I was writing the poem.

JS: The language here is a harrowing mix of vivid imagery and unconventional syntax. What do you think influences your writing style most? Perhaps more accurately, what has led you to your current your style?

RL: Jazz drumming influences my current writing style more than anything. Nate Smith, who is my favorite drummer, plays recognizable rhythms with "ghost notes" sprinkled in the gaps to change the sound. He frequently changes the pocket and timing of each phrase in his music. I try to do this in my work, and at the moment, I am in the really early stages of seeing what other "pocket changes" I can make to push the boundaries of recognizable voice, syntax, and grammar.

JS: This poem exists specifically within the context of a chapbook-length work. What advice would you give to poets attempting to create a cohesive voice in their manuscripts? What feels crucial to consider when writing a whole series of poems?

RL: My advice for any manuscript is to never force cohesion but allow the poems to speak to each other organically. Sometimes poems that seem disparate, such as "P" in my collection, are the glue that will hold two sections together. Not only is it important to consider what each poem will do for the collection on their own, but also what they will teach and impose on the poems that follow.

JS: Finally, what is one poem, poet, or book that you think deserves more readers and recognition?

RL: *City Eclogue* by Ed Roberson should be read by everyone in the world! I think it is the most difficult, beautiful, and innovative book of poems I've ever read.

AVIARY

Derek Annis

I eat all the waffles I can stuff
into my father's boots.
I have an electric cinderblock
for the collection plate.
I shut the waterfall
off and ride my horse
to dust. Police officers
shake their fingers
all the way to the bank
of the river, where no car tires
trade cigarettes for laughs.
In the laps of their giant mothers,
cigar smoking robots click
into gear and fire
the gravedigger.
He has mouths to feed
to the pigs. Enough
for another month
or two, during which time
he can apply
to himself
a second coat
of gold paint
and hide in the basement
of my paper house
where blackbirds splash
against the walls
like bags of nails.

Jerrod Schwarz: This poem is purposefully entropic, darting swiftly from detail to detail but never losing central focus. I would love to know about your writing process, specifically how your poems originate. Do you have clear goals in mind beforehand, or do the images come about more naturally?

Derek Annis: I think my poems, and poems in general, are most successful when writing them is a process of discovery as opposed to relaying information. If I know specifically what I want to write about or convey to readers beforehand, then I'm unlikely to be surprised by what happens in the poem as I'm writing it. For me, the process of discovering and the experience of being surprised are the most interesting parts of writing poems. Even though my poems pretty much always end up being "about" my own life experiences, I'm still surprised by how those experiences are conveyed or what the poems say about them. So, when I sit down to write, I don't have any goals in terms of content, imagery, or message. The only goal I have is to be surprised by the end result. My most frequent approach to achieving that goal is to follow sound. The images and ideas that emerge while I'm pursuing sound frequently surprise me, and when I'm lucky they end up making poems worth revising.

JS: What role does the speaker play in your poetry? This specific poem seems to have a unified speaker, but that might be just one interpretation.

DA: Almost all of my poems have a unified speaker. The role of that speaker is, I suppose, to speak into existence a space in which certain ineffable experiences can be transferred to the reader. Even though many of my poems travel far beyond facts and reality, I usually still consider myself the speaker, and I consider the poems autobiographical. Some experiences, particularly traumatic and ecstatic ones, are too large to fit into the facts of the situations from which they arise.

JS: I always love when a poem has the rhythm and syntax to support a single stanza. What are the advantages of single-stanza poems? What are the challenges?

DA: I don't think there are any particular advantages or challenges of single-stanza poems, and that's because it's a decision I make during the revision process. Usually not until I'm close to a final draft. I think the challenge is in trying to figure out whether stanza breaks would benefit a specific poem. In other words, writing a single-stanza poem isn't a challenge because I would never try to force a poem into a single stanza. That being said, the primary factor I consider when deciding whether or not to include stanza breaks is momentum. Some poems need breathing room or space for the reader to rest. "Aviary" contains several end-stopped lines, which I think slows the momentum as much as the poem requires. Since this poem has a fairly chaotic trajectory, any further disruption of the poem's momentum would risk ejecting the reader from it completely. For me, it's a matter of keeping the reader in the poem while also allowing them space to breathe.

JS: Finally, what is one poem, poet, or book that you think deserves more readers and recognition?

DA: There are so many great poets, and so few who have the readership their work warrants, that it's difficult to choose just one who deserves more recognition. I can think of a dozen off the top of my head. The person at the top of that list for me, though, is Laura Read. Laura is a friend and mentor, and she was my first creative writing teacher. Her third full-length collection, *But She Is Also Jane*, won the Juniper Prize for Poetry and is forthcoming from University of Massachusetts Press. Laura's poems are incredibly well-balanced. They blend narrative and lyric, they make conceptual leaps while maintaining connection to their centers, they are simultaneously funny and poignant, they are political without being didactic, and they are personal yet universal. I haven't encountered many other poets who can maintain that kind of balance in their work. In addition to her poetry, Laura also deserves recognition for the work she does in the poetry community. She is universally loved by her students, and has instilled a love for poetry in countless young people who wouldn't have otherwise developed any interest in it.

HAVE YOU MISSED
THE COLOR RED?
Caroline Harper New

Mama, you would love living

in this cave. It feels like being swallowed
by a sea monster.   The belly is warm
            and full of animals who also
                  can't find the mouth.

The animals have no eyes,
but we are too small to see each other anyways.

                  Mama, the cave would love

        living inside you. The animals
would never go hungry and I could show you

the worms clumped like hair in a drain.
                  Shocks of red you would relish.
        You never had that luxury, but look

                  at the curtains I've stitched! The ceiling
                  is vaulted with Gothic ribs and the walls
                        glow with gypsum glitter.

Little streams run through the tiles and when the animals
            spit slow stalactites from the ceiling, their saliva
            carves new caves in the floor and our house

                  multiplies.
            You would love it, Mama.
Even if you can't find the mouth,
there is always another way out.

Jerrod Schwarz: I really love how this poem addresses a specific person, in this case the speaker's mother. What are the challenges in writing poems to someone directly? Inversely, what are the advantages in being explicitly direct?

Caroline Harper New: There's something about writing directly to someone that feels both intimate and ancient. Looking back on my earliest poems, they were almost always addressed to a lover, a friend, a sister, a stranger—and always undelivered. These poems contain the weight of the unsaid; shared experiences that remain unnamed, but bleed through every other line. There's a tenderness in direct addresses that I've recently felt the need to return to.

The challenge is that the direct address becomes an act of wrestling the unrequited, the regret, the know-better. The things we could say if given the courage, or could have said, if given the time. This particular poem is a bit different because it belongs to a series written from the imagined perspective of the biblical character, Lot's daughter, who addresses her mother after she has turned to a pillar of salt. By stepping into this imagined grief, I had to deeply consider how I would see the world if my own mother were gone, and how I would call her back—through apples, mirrors, cave creatures, my own children. Knowing this one day will be true added a sense of urgency to the series.

JS: The line placement and stanza breaks in this piece feel chaotic but intentional, a mirror of the gorgeous language. At what stage in your writing process do you address the visuals of your poem? Does the final draft resemble the first, or were there big changes?

CHN: Every poet develops their own personal logic of the page. For me, the right margin leans into imagination and escapism, whereas the left margin is an anchor, a tether to reality. Inhale as we move right, exhale as we're snapped back to the left. In my mind, it makes the poems jump between these two spaces, almost as if the speaker is having a conversation with themselves.

With the very first poem in this series, I found myself aligning lines to other lines, rather than the given left margin. While the initial move was intuitive, I then felt this pattern gave the poem both a predictability and chaos that should continue throughout the rest. I wanted the series to feel like it created and was constrained to its own logic, much like the speaker, as she invents fantastical ways to commune with her mother. The intimacy in the impossibilities.

JS: My favorite moments in this piece are the descriptions of caves and cave animals. Is animal imagery common throughout your work, or was this poem unique?

CHN: My first poem in fifth grade was about a hippopotamus named Peggy Sue, so maybe the curse of animal imagery hasn't changed much since. I grew up in rural Georgia, where livestock and wildlife were present figures in my life, and I love paying heed to the little creatures that get little poetic attention. In this case, I was fascinated by the worms (Limnodrilus sulphurensis) and bacteria (Thiobacillus thiooxidans) that quite literally create the geography of caves. In the speaker's grief and escapist tendencies, I wanted to make companions of them, as we would of dogs, deer, bluebirds.

While my penchant for animals is somewhat glaring, I've been more surprised at how the image of the cave itself percolates in my work. An editor once pointed out how often my poems take place in pseudo-caves. Wombs, whale bellies, underwater parlors, alligator mouths, deer ribs, suckerholes in the ice—as you can see, many still involving animals. The personal investigation that ensued has made me much more conscious of poetic landscapes. In this poem, you can see how the speaker is stranded between this setting as a place of both safety and entrapment, of nurture and devouring. How she picks beauty from the horrors of her captivity and offers it back as a home.

JS: Finally, what is one poem, poet, or book that you think deserves more readers and recognition?

CHN: One poet I've really turned to lately is H.R. Webster. One of her poems—I think it may have been "My Mother says, 'I'm Going to Flush the Toilet Now'"—pulled me out of a nine-month writing hiatus and ignited whatever area of my brain needs poetry.

I worked with Webster at the *Michigan Quarterly Review*, but only became familiar with her work this past year. There's something terribly raw and uprooting about the way she uses language to dig history out of the mundane, in a way both plainspoken and gut-wrenching. Her poems lurch between memories in a way that feels like falling down the stairs. The bruising from line to line, the length of the fall unknown. Having a familiar yet unnoticed surfaces thrust dangerously close your face.

Her first book, *What Follows,* came out last June. I haven't gotten my hands on it yet, but I imagine it will be just as tender and devastating as every poem I've read by her.

INSTANT HYMN
Sarah Levine

I feel like straw
in the scarecrow.

When I am with you
I feel like straw

in the scarecrow in the rain
in the mud

when dogs
chew each-other's ears

and storm
makes the grass grow.

I should touch the back
of your neck more.

Dance like a bucket
rolling down a mountain.

In the dark
in the driveway

we stare at the moon
pick fruit off a tree

and I want to
wash my hands less pulling red

birds out of each-other.
All heart and dirt

and everything would be new
because there is newness in the best things.

SARAH LEVINE
In Conversation

Jerrod Schwarz: I love the incredibly short lines of this piece. Is this line length
categorical of your writing? What draws you to creating visually compact poems?

Sarah Levine: Thank you! I love experimenting with architecture in my poetry: line length, line breaks, stanzas, and placement on the page. With architecture comes a sense of play, and with "Instant Hymn" I liked how shorter lines changed the cadence, pulse, and intensity of the image in each stanza.

JS: I'm struck by the power of this poem's title, how the word *hymn* contextualizes the details. What are your thoughts on poem titles? What role do they play in your own writing process?

SL: I enjoy reading other poets titles, especially Frank Stanford, Paul Guest, and Paige Lewis. They inspire me. I try not to overthink titles too much. It's really satisfying when they come together organically and unforced. There's a little magic when the right title just fits. The perfect crumb.

JS: This piece is full of animal imagery. What role do animals play in your other poems?

SL: Geese, geese, geese, thrushes, geese! Birds fascinate me: their sounds and colors, maybe it's just my palpable jealousy at their ability to fly.

JS: Finally, what is one poem, poet, or book that you think deserves more readers and recognition?

SL: *Bright Brave Phenomena* by Amanda Nadelberg.

IF THE WORLD WERE BORN
FROM A WING LIFTING

Robin Walter

and the world began
with mouth wide   open to release her
                    heart/ a body
shearing   / a body/

    the flightsong that   followed

O winter , O   sorrow ,

the girls look as if / they are flying! they are   flying !

           winter's nipping wrongs   become   spring
                 borne
        on the back of a flicker
      the barely brown down
              of his checkered chest catching
           a breeze

      the quick slash of red
         below his
    cheek

        /

    O spring , sweet sorrow

burn day into dusk if you
please / please
burn the world into   my palm /
I will hold it . will I

hold it /

Jerrod Schwarz: This is a visually arresting poem, arpeggiating down the page. Where in your writing process did the visual language of this poem finalize? How similar is the first draft to the final?

Robin Walter: I love that verb arpeggiate. It seems related conceptually in my mind to murmuration—the phenomenon that results when a flock of starlings take flight. Harmony in asynchrony. The marriage of these terms—of music and motion—offers an opening through which we might understand the concerns that emerge in this project. In keeping with Olson's offering that poetic form is never more than an extension of content, the poems in this collection adopt the form of their primary considerations: wing, flight, fever, flock, bird. The poems take flight as the body takes flight. As they migrate across the page they migrate into and out of body, waiting always for a return.

While I was working on this project, I was simultaneously working on a companion visual art piece that consists of a series of hundreds of torn scraps and fragments of multimedia prints and found and made texts. The physicality of these fragments—torn apart, rearranged, and sewn back together—seems integral to the form that emerged in this collection. Through the physical act of shearing, tearing, and sewing, I became especially attentive to the edge, wherein questions began to emerge about balance and flight. How does the poem invite us to tend to the relation of part to whole, and of whole to part? How much of itself can a thing lose and still retain itself? How might the poem demand a sustained wonder about the mysteries of collapse and flight, and the tenuous balance that connects the two? How might this work invite us to encounter a mutual fragility—wherein the thing that is torn away gains equal importance to that which is left behind? How does it make physical that which is rent?

As Rimbaud has it, "If what [the poet] brings back from down there has form, [she] brings forth form; if it is formless, [she] brings forth formlessness." In this work, the form brought forth from down there—that most primal poetic state—is a winged form, a form that fevers between form and formlessness, between flight and flightlessness. These poems investigate schism and tremor through body and wing and ask the reader to consider joint, suture and graft. The form asks the reader to attend especially to the edges, wherein the poem begins to enact the tearing and shearing that occurs in the scraps and fragments that inform this work.

There is something about what David Mutschlecner calls "the unity of contradiction" that feels present in the conditions that were necessary for this project to come into being. Even as one element is taken away, another emerges. It is the absence that presences the poems that find their form via erasure. A Heraclitian logic seems to govern the process; absence becomes presence, and presence absence.

In these poems, we might begin to understand letter as bone and word as wing. We might understand the flight of words that occurs across the page not so much as erasure but rather a consideration of different bones within the same wing. The wings of this project, I hope, enact the actions present within Olson's examination of those primary words 'is,' 'not,' and 'be':

'Is' comes from the Aryan root, as, to breathe. The English 'not' equals the Sanscrit na, which may come from the root na, to be lost, to perish. 'Be' is from bhu, to grow.

The wing both is and is not—which is to say, it breathes, it roots, it perishes, it is lost, and it grows. It flits between the violence and mercy of language, between the violence and mercy of the poem's primary consideration of flight.

JS: I'm drawn toward the use of forward-slashes in this piece. How do you approach punctuation in your poetry?

RW: I first encountered a variation of the forward-slash in Sam Sax's brilliant *Bury It*. In their collection the forward-slash acts as the thing that joins even as it keeps apart. I began to experiment with its use as a way to create a stutter step in my writing, a form that might help enact the strange and stranged relationship between trauma and memory. It allowed me to start over; revise; say the same thing differently. I discovered that the forward-slash allowed me to veer to the left when continuing forward logically or linearly seemed impossible. A way to maintain motion and momentum even when that momentum circled back on itself. Each slash, I believe, became a little stitch. Perhaps it also became a little wing.

JS: The final two lines of the poem are a haunting inversion of each other. Every poet approaches the weight of endings differently, and I would love to know your thoughts. In your own writing practice, how do you value a poem's ending?

RW: I just read a beautiful thought in Agni's 50th edition that features photographer and poet Don Bogen's work. A 'finished poem,' is described as an opening extended to the reader. It seems right to me that, in this logic, the end of a poem is also its beginning. The end then also inverts our understanding of a thing so finite as a poem.

JS: Finally, what is one poem, poet, or book that you think deserves more readers and recognition?

RW: Dear friend Susannah Lodge-Regal just published her debut collection *Where The Light Feeds* with *Gasher Press* out in March. Per Dan Beachy-Quick, "'*Where the Light Feeds* is no book of prophecy—it is better than that. It is a book of the hours becoming ours, a book in which love manifests, a book that teaches us to say what it learns to sing: 'thank you for the luck.'"

To hold in your hands and heart a small piece of that luck, order Susannah's book at gasherpress.com

UNTITLED
Ana Prudaru

WAY BACK HOME 2
Qiyue Zhang

WAY BACK HOME 3
Qiyue Zhang

fair weather friend

Kimball Anderson

feeling okay today

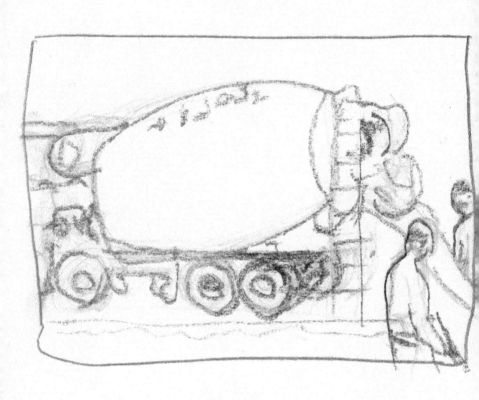

for the first time in so long

remembering the feeling

of

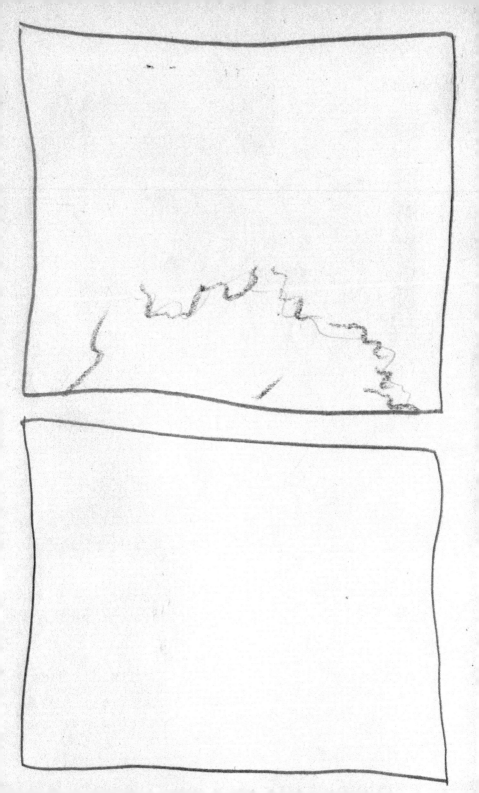

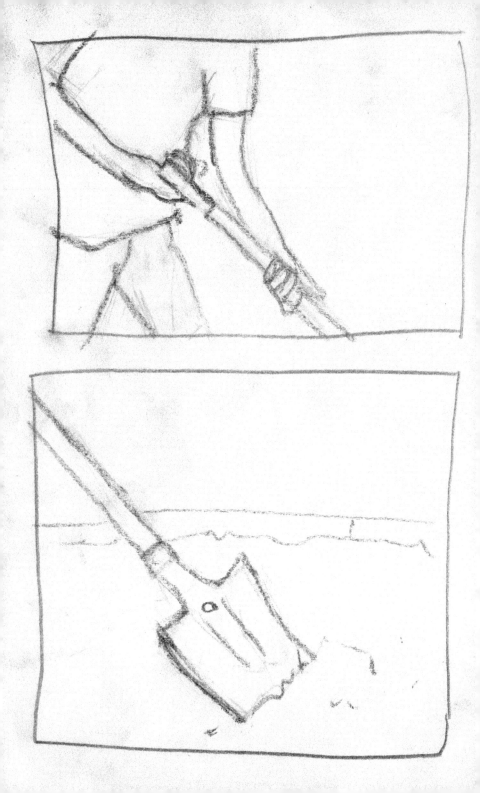

of

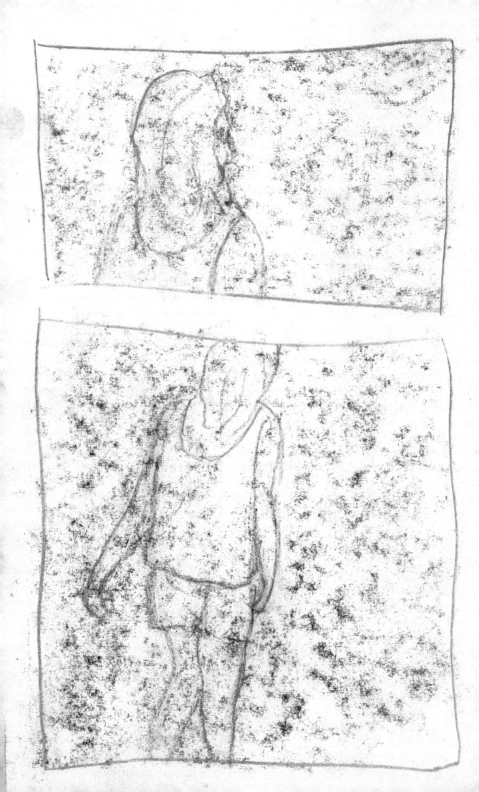

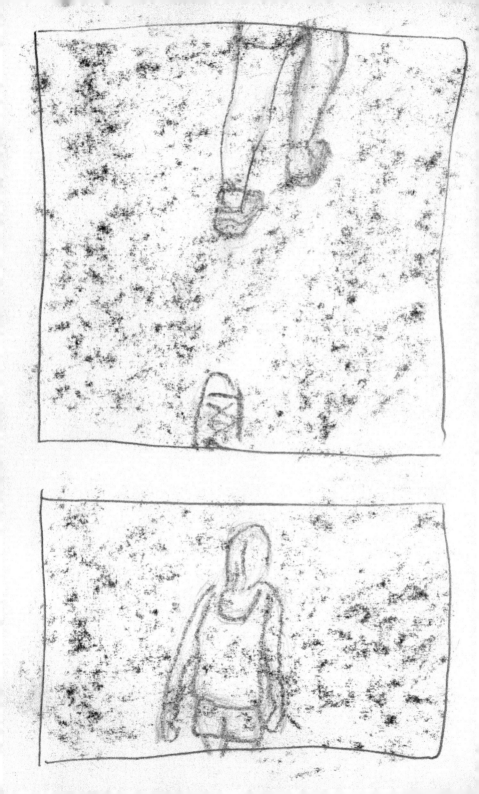

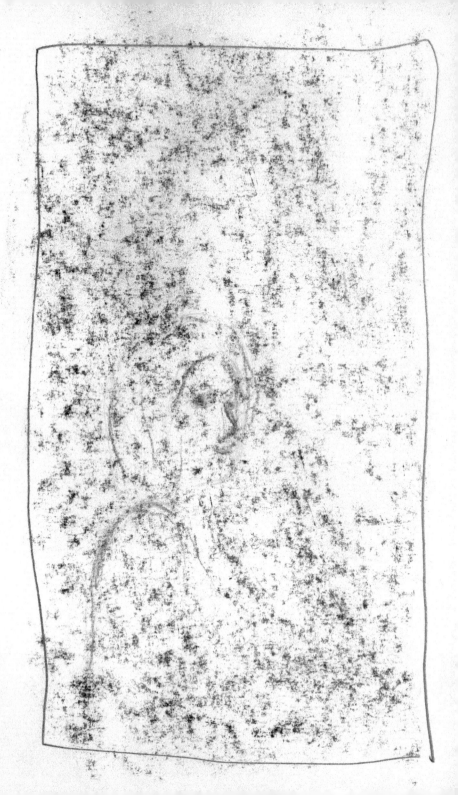

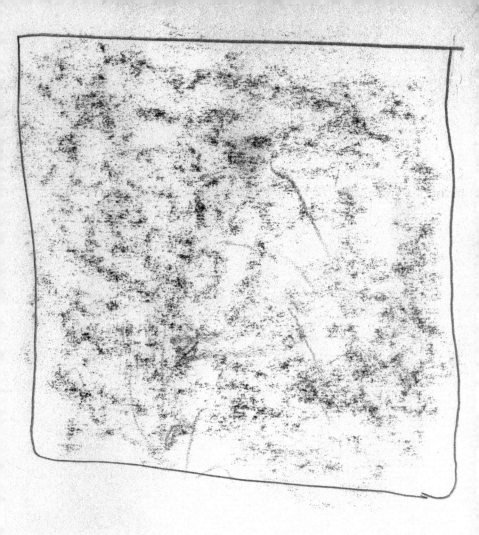

but there's a grill going somewhere

the smell of

coal burning

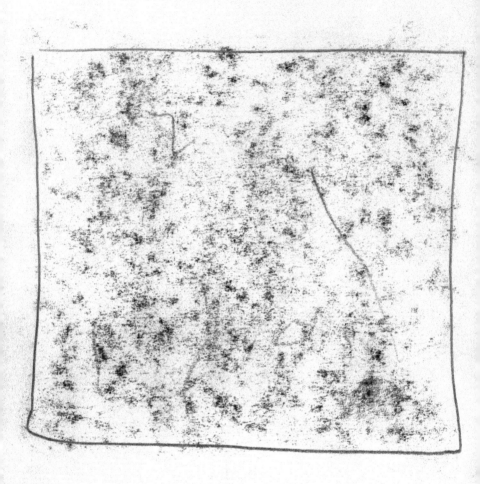

laughter and raucous conversation

and I feel like I could be there

I like the feeling

that if I wanted to

that could be me

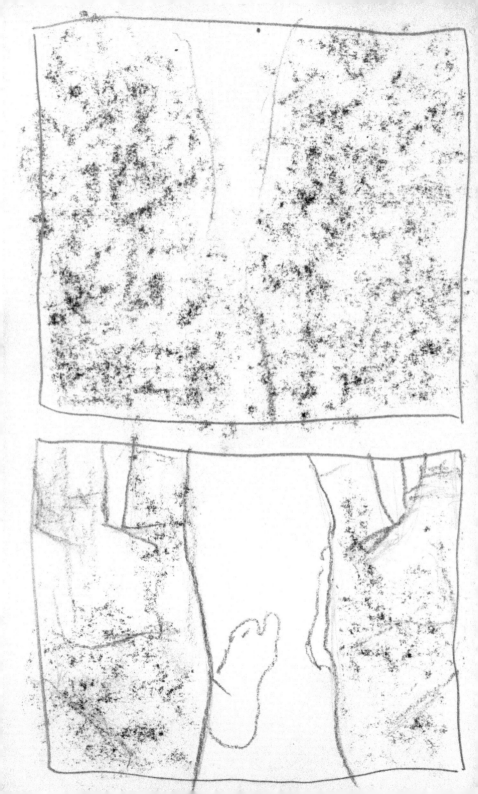

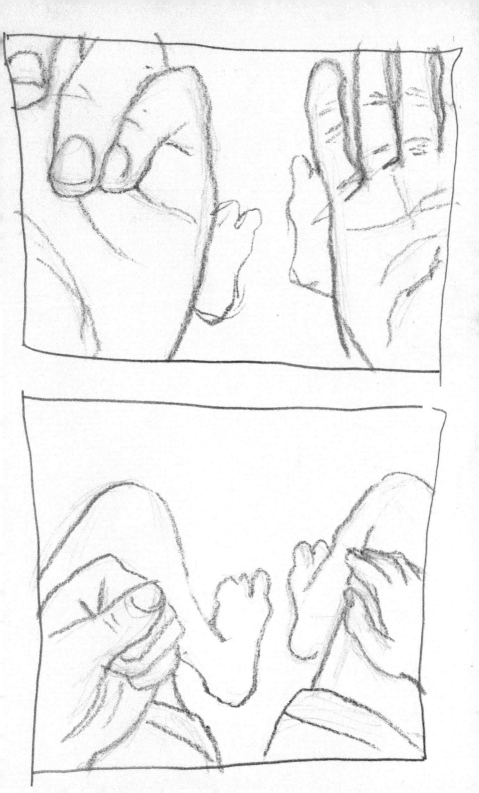

the exhilaration of possibility

has never led me anywhere good

...but

but

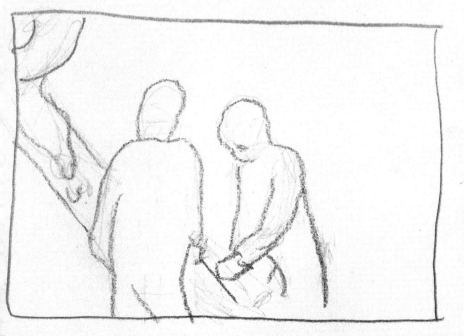

it's starting to feel familiar

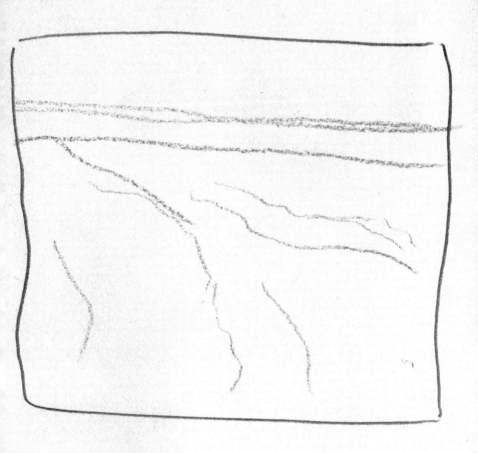

like an old friend

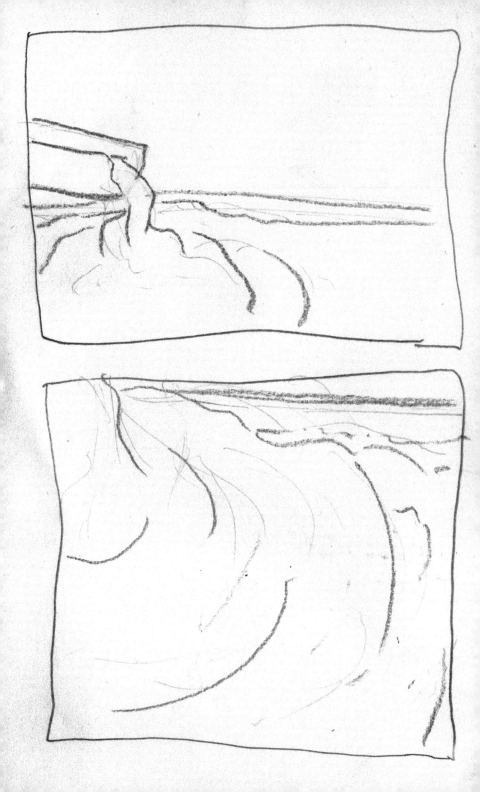

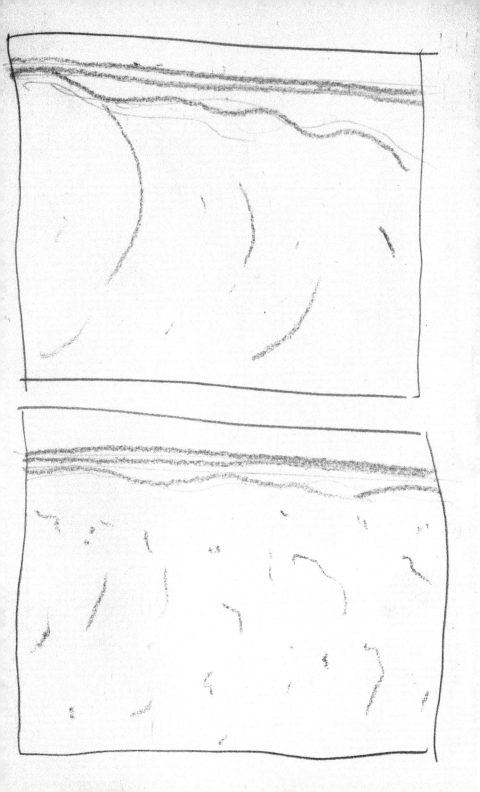

can't I just

pretend to be something else

a moment more

KIMBALL ANDERSON
In Conversation

James McNulty: There's a clear autobiographical and meditative tone to "Fair Weather Friend." Could you speak a little to the real-world inspirations for this piece?

Kimball Anderson: To me, this story is about chronic illness and the moments you allow yourself to fantasize about being healthier than you are. The POV character is just sitting on the stoop, inactive. Watching people at work, taking in the cookout nearby, remembering times spent with others. It's this feeling of floating, of letting go and just going with the rhythm of the world. And the rhythm of the world is biased towards that sort of active life. When you are chronically ill, it's common to feel like you have fallen out of that rhythm. Friends just seem to move at a pace you can no longer understand, and they can't understand you either. The necessities of life, deadlines, bills, everything is built at a tempo for bodies different than yours. To just sit there, to feel that rhythm, to remember it—that can be a beautiful thing. And it can also be dangerous, because as much as you may want to move at that pace, it will just push you past your limits.

JM: How did you land on the visual style of this piece?

KA: I'm very much into figuring out quick and impactful art styles. Inspired by my health limits, but also by the personality that it gives to lines and marks. I wanted to get across the feeling of energy held inside. The pacing of the comic is very deliberate and slow, but I wanted the linework to feel like it's alive and buzzing. The wobbly and scribbly forms were part of that, but I also used a blue and red layer effect on all of it to give it a sort of charged effect.

JM: What tools did you use to craft "Fair Weather Friend"?

KA: It was just simple pencil and paper! With a layer effect put over it digitally.

JM: What consideration went into the pacing of the writing here?

KA: There's a temptation in comics to pace everything as fast as you can, because every panel and page you add is another panel or page you are going to have to draw. But I have experimented a lot with wordless and abstract comics, and I found all sorts of ineffable feelings that I'm not sure I could have otherwise. In those comics, it feels impossible to tell if anyone else can feel them with me, though. There's just nothing to grab onto. So when I approach comics like these, I think of the narrative as a sort of contextual wrapper that I can put around the abstraction, that makes it more tangible. An attempt to tell something understandable but still containing ambiguity, and still charting that unknown emotional landscape. A slower pace is how I give space for this uncertainty to exist on its own terms.

Jerrod Schwarz: This piece mixes rough line work with quiet paneling. Was this an intentional decision or something that came more organically as you started creating the piece?

KA: It's a little of both, organic and planned. I tend to start with a concept I want to express in a comic, a very clear theme or idea, and then past that I just intuitively let myself follow the process. As I said above, I was trying to get the feeling of energy in stillness. But a lot of that decision itself was just a matter of feeling what felt honest or true in the moment. Maybe this is connected to a constant low level brain fog I've been in for years, and the ways I have adapted to it. I can get myself to hold onto a concept for a little bit, but at some point I have to let go and trust that if I keep with my instinctual "right" and "wrong" feelings I'll stay on the path I set myself out on.

JS: What did revision or editing look like for this comic? More broadly, how do you think editing a comic differs from revising a piece of writing?

KA: Comics are a visual medium, so naturally there's an element of editing visuals. There were a few instances of that in this comic, panels which, as originally drawn, didn't have quite the right visual impact and were redrawn, or looking back at the pages on paper and realizing a couple more lines would make the image read more clearly as representing what it's supposed to represent. But as a writing process, the editing is different too, since there are often three distinct stages to a comic process: script, thumbnails (small scale rough drafts), and the pages themselves. I tend to keep the script stage sparse, writing it as almost a poem to reinterpret into the visual language when I do the thumbnails. Sometimes in thumbnailing I realize I don't really need some lines of text, because they are made superfluous by the images. And when I do the final pages, I often find myself editing the lines right before writing them on the page, because the recontextualization of the words helps me see them anew.

JOHANNES BRAHMS:
PIANO TRIO NO.2 IN C MAJOR, OP.87

BY YARON REGEV & DAVE YOUKOVICH

LOVE CAN RETRACE ITS WAY BACK TO THE INTERSECTIONS OF 'MIGHT-HAVE-BEEN'. EACH MOMENT SPLITS US INTO COUNTLESS POSSIBILITIES, WHY NOT SETTLE, THEN, FOR ONE THAT NEVER WAS?

IT IS A MATTER OF ALLOWING THE EYES ENOUGH STARING, PAST HIGHWAYS, INTO THAT ROOM IN WHICH ALL THE INTERSECTIONS STILL EXIST.

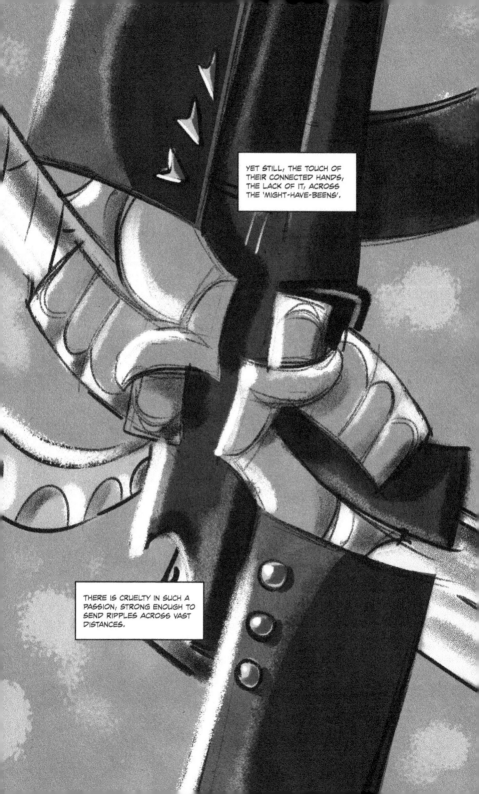

IN THAT WHERE AND WHEN, A REMBRANDT PAINTED THE DISSECTION OF THEIR HEARTS. THE GENTLEMEN STOOD AROUND THEIR BODIES, SEEKING CLUES IN KNIVES RATHER THAN FLESH. THEY WEIGHED THE HEARTS FIRST, THERE ARE SCALES FOR THAT.

OUT OF PITY, PLACED BLEEDING LIPS TO BLEEDING LIPS. THE WALLS STILL STRETCHED, EVEN THERE. THE PRIMORDIAL OCEAN, WITH ITS CREATURES OF GENESIS SWIMMING IN THE SEMEN OF GOD.

PERHAPS THERE, TWO CELLS SWIMMING IN THE MUCK. THEY SPOKE NOTHING OF LOVE, ALL THOSE TROGLODYTES. IT WAS A LATER ACCIDENT, A SICKNESS TO PASS FROM CREATION TO CREATION.

WHILE OTHERS HAVE ANGRY, HAMMER WIELDING PROPHETS, THEY BEAR THEIR PAIN IN SILENCE. THE TASTE OF GHOSTLY KISSES, THE SCALDING OF A LOVER'S TOUCH ON THEIR SKIN.

LIVING IN A SUIT OF BLACK MATTER. ONE COULD GET USED TO THAT. AFTER ALL, A CARESS IS SIMPLY A CARESS, A KISS IS JUST A KISS. AND THE HEART, EXTRACTED AND WEIGHED.

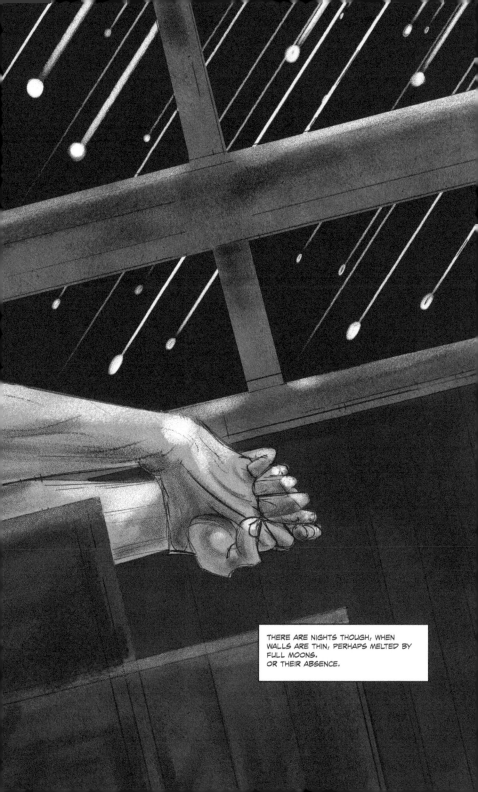

THERE ARE NIGHTS THOUGH, WHEN
WALLS ARE THIN, PERHAPS MELTED BY
FULL MOONS.
OR THEIR ABSENCE.

YARON REGEV & DAVE YOUKOVICH
In Conversation

James McNulty: How did the two of you collaborate on "Johannes Brahms"?

Yaron Regev: Dave and I have been collaborating for over twenty years. Our first collaboration was on *The Cave*, a graphic novel about Plato, Socrates, and a broken, contemporary reality. It was just recently published in Israel.

JM: The story here is told through narration rather than dialogue and concrete scenes. Why did you make this decision?

YR: The Johannes Brahms piece is a part of *Ghosts of Love and Country,* a graphic novel comprised of fourteen chapters. Each chapter is a free adaptation in words and images of a different chamber music piece. The texts are "stream of consciousness" and I attempted to recreate what went through my mind as I was listening to the music. The writing began and ended with the music, following each chamber music piece's movements. Dave then freely adapted my texts and gave them his own unique visual interpretation. Dave had complete creative freedom. In this piece, for example, I distinctly imagined a man and a woman as I listened to the music and wrote, but Dave read the text and saw two men in his imagination—which was what he ended up illustrating. I found that to be amazing and wonderful. This was exactly the sort of experiment I wanted to make. Showing how we affect each other through art and through barriers of time, distance, and different mindsets, each of us giving it his or her unique interpretation. I also wanted to demonstrate how supposedly "dead" artistic forms can be very much alive and thriving through the power of active performance, interpretation, and individual imagination.

Jerrod Schwarz: What are the challenges of writing about war?

YR: Even though the texts for "Ghosts of Love and Country" were all written spontaneously while listening to the musical pieces, a connecting thread of personal and national crisis slowly began to emerge. Living in a war-torn country has a deep psychological, and often repressed, impact. The main challenge in writing about war is, in my opinion, to avoid the clichés people often remain indifferent to. In *Ghosts of Love and Country,* I tried to demonstrate that being apart and unaffected is impossible. The more Israelis repress the state of war they live in, the darker the shadows lurking under the surface, as is evident by the current disturbing political developments in the country.

JM: What tools were used to craft this comic?

Dave Youkovich: I always begin a new project by sketching out my ideas on the same paper that I've printed the script on. This allows me to jot down notes and make little scribblings as I go, capturing all of my thoughts and creative impulses as they come to me. After I've finished sketching, I make my notes and sketches more legible and send them back to Yaron for review. We then discuss what works well, what needs to be improved, and what might be best to leave out.

For this particular piece, I decided to skip the traditional pencil and paper stage and go straight to Photoshop. The graphical direction for this project was already very clear in my mind from the start, so I felt confident in my ability to bring it to life digitally.

JS: How did you two land on the modern art style for this comic? Picasso and other modernists seem like big inspirations, but were there any others?

DY: More than anything, I love the commercial illustrators of the end of the 19th century and the first half of the 20th. They're the unsung heroes of art. I think the style is a clash of artists from the Art Deco era, Bruce Timm, and Genndy Tartakovsky.

dados

by stefanie jordan

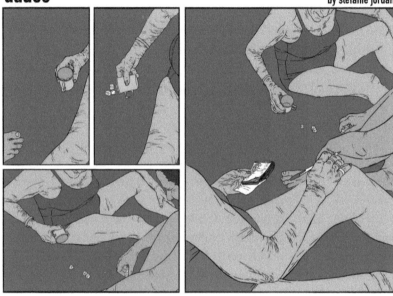

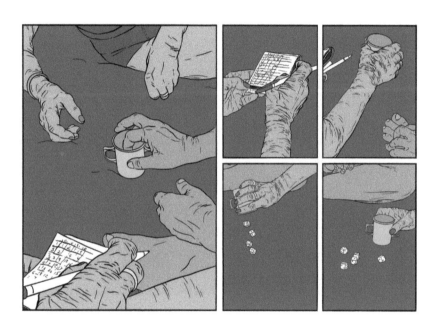

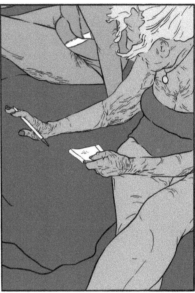

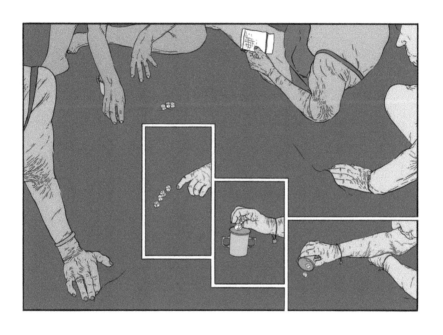

STEFANIE JORDAN
In Conversation

James McNulty: We were so interested by the decisions of angles and bodies on display here. What do you consider when deciding on angles and point of view?

Stefanie Jordan: My tendency is to perceive the world around me in rhythms, patterns, and to virtually scan for shapes that associate with one another. These aspects most certainly influence my visual decisions. There is also a compositional idea: a playing field, a stage on which the characters in their interaction show themselves, the women in their body consciousness and their attitude to life, and within all these aspects (to some extend symbolically) the game itself. The rather "male-associated" game with playing dice once again reinforces the self-evidence and self-confidence of these women. Their body language, especially their gestures and the positions they take, is the visual vocabulary of the story.

JM: There are plenty of striking and detailed displays of bodies here. Did you use models, reference photos, or memory to draw these?

SJ: "DADOS," which, by the way, is the Spanish word for dice, is based on a day at the beach I spent with a group of women in their eighties who are very dear to me. While relaxing in the sun and laying out on a bunch of towels, they enjoyed a game of dice that they completely got lost in. This scene inspired me to create a graphic narrative to show the body positivity they displayed and that also touched me so deeply. Therefore I took several photos that served as a starting point for the images I later drew.

Jerrod Schwarz: We were really struck by the details in these characters' hands—all of the wrinkles and complicated gestures. What parts of the body are you most interested in drawing? Moreover, which parts of the body are the most challenging to render?

SJ: I am most interested in hands in these drawings because they are extremely telling. Hand gestures can convey habitus, they show lots of character and are explicit expressers of a person's attitude. More specifically, my drawings showcase age as external as well as internal dimensions in very clear contrast. Extremely wrinkled, these hands are also expressers of vigor and vitality. It is very telling of these women through the way they wear jewelry and nail polish that they have a very clear appreciation for themselves. Furthermore, they do so at an age when women normally become socially invisible because they no longer conform to the ideal of beauty trimmed for youth.

By making them the subject of my story, I set a counterpoint to the common representations of femininity in which women are only ascribed attractiveness when they are still the object of a desiring gaze. The women shown here no longer submit to such attributions, they express ease with themselves as they are, and each other's company as women. "DADOS" is a homage to age, to older women and their individual ways of aging. Their expressive wrinkles give a visual testimony to a long life lived.

JS: The lack of shadows or shading was immediately interesting, as it gave this piece a pop-art feel without compromising the attention to detailed bodies. Is this style something you have developed, or was it brand new for this piece?

SJ: Normally I like to use shadows to give depth to bodies in my drawings and to formulate them that way. For this piece, however, I decided quite consciously against it. It was important to me to work out the wrinkles more like a cartographer, tracing their courses on the skin as on a map of life per say, to highlight them aesthetically as "life lines."

To emphasize the quality of the human skin as a chart of recorded time, I designed the skin tone as a homogeneous color surface. In such a way, it can best serve as a background for the inscribed topographical lines, in return emphasising and enhancing their graphic quality.

Without shadows, everything is laid out in the open. Since my drawings are also meant to be a loving tribute to age, it is important to me to convey that there is nothing at all to hide.

BASEBALL
Ben Montague

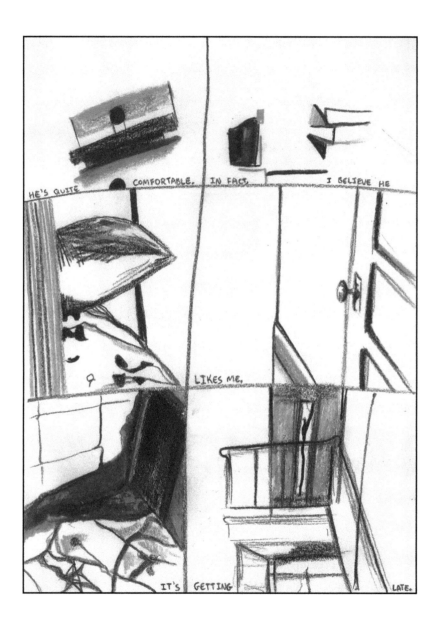

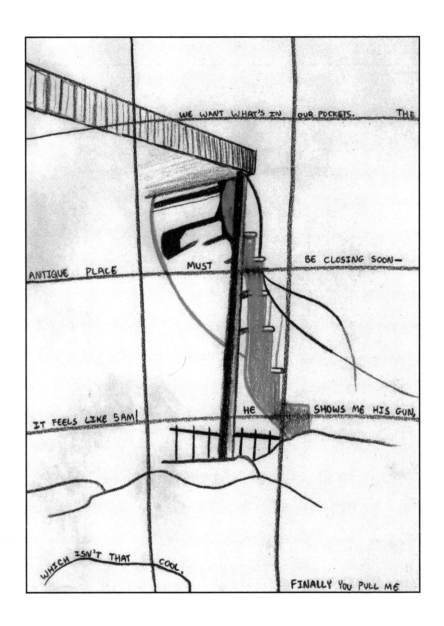

WE WANT WHAT'S IN OUR POCKETS. THE

ANTIQUE PLACE MUST BE CLOSING SOON—

IT FEELS LIKE 5AM! HE SHOWS ME HIS GUN,

WHICH ISN'T THAT COOL.

FINALLY YOU PULL ME

BE MY FRIEND
Ben Montague

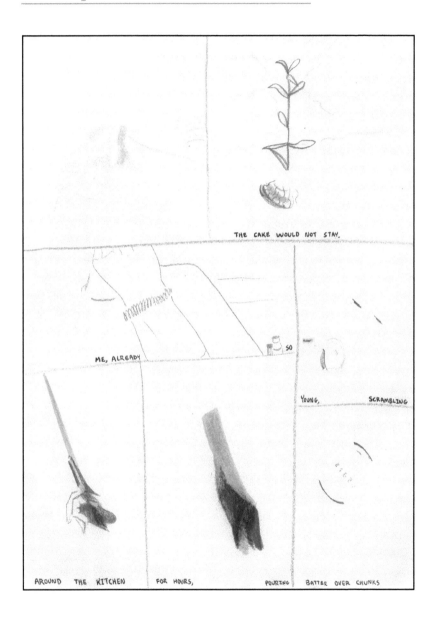

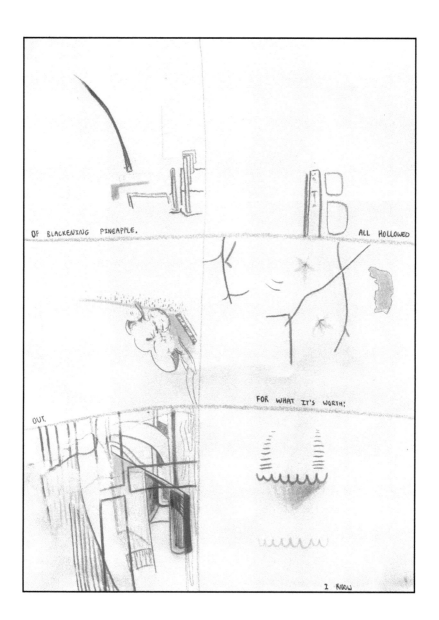

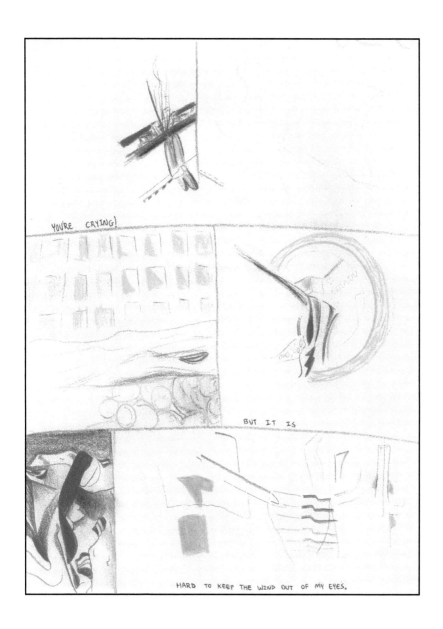

YOU'RE CRYING!

BUT IT IS

HARD TO KEEP THE WIND OUT OF MY EYES.

COLD SWIM
Ben Montague

GROWING, SPARKLING WITH DEW.

I WANT
TO GO

INTO THE WOODS, I TELL HER— JUST A SHORT

WALK, A LITTLE ON THE BREAST.

I DON'T KNOW WHAT I'M SAYING, BUT THE WOODS ARE SO

LUSH. I. PEEKED OVER MY MOTHER'S

SHOULDER SOME TIME AGO.

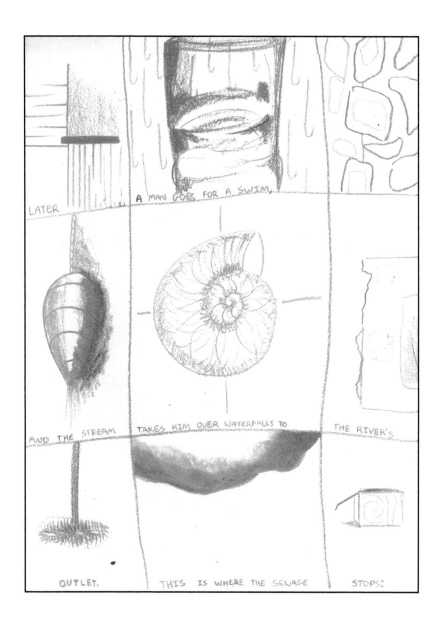

KILLING JAR
Ben Montague

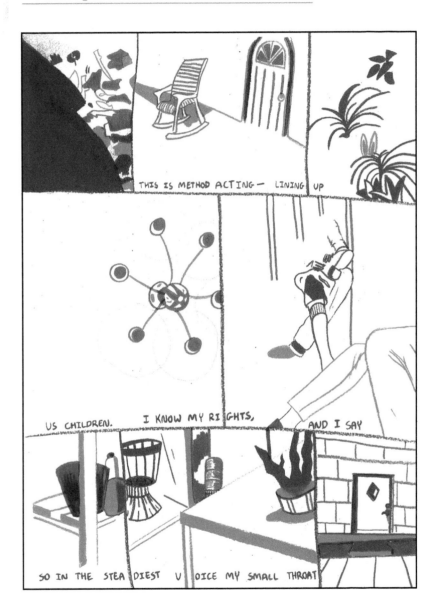

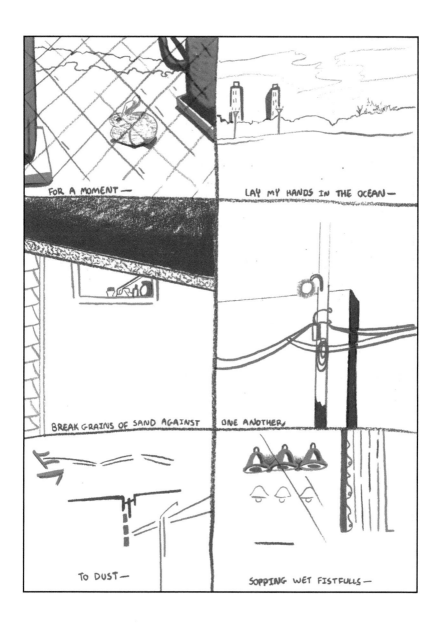

FOR A MOMENT —

LAY MY HANDS IN THE OCEAN —

BREAK GRAINS OF SAND AGAINST

ONE ANOTHER,

TO DUST —

SOPPING WET FISTFULLS —

BEN MONTAGUE
In Conversation

Jerrod Schwarz: I love how the line work is so informed by color; there is an illustrative awareness here for both shapes and lines that feels so organic. What does your drafting and creation process look like? More specifically, what goes in to making these pieces feel so vigorous and intentional at the same time?

Ben Montague: This collection of shorts has a very strict methodology behind it—I write the text for each comic right upon waking from a dream. In that moment, I can use the dream's plot to access its tone, which is ultimately what drives the comic. When I create a visual environment for the story to live in, the goal is to give a sense of someone doing a 360-degree survey of their surroundings as they wander through the dream's landscape, without providing deeper details of its logic. I want the reader to empathize with the underlying anxieties and desires of each narrator without knowing anything about who they are or what they've done.

James McNulty: For the more abstract panels, how do you decide what to draw?

BM: The most abstract penels come from using intense close-ups as references, such as the crease between a person's arm and torso, or the edges of two buildings meeting. I feel that these are things we spend a considerable amount of time looking at while processing information—but rarely center.

JS: I would love to know too how the words in your comics are crafted. The lack of any formal speech or narration bubbles makes them feel one with their panels.

BM: The less romantic part of my answer is: the actual pages of the comic are fairly rigid. I know I want to maintain the format of having four pages, and I divide my text over that wherever the words will be clearest. The more romantic part is: they absolutely should feel like they're incognito, like they've been tossed to the wind and have scattered like leaves or bits of mylar. I want the words to blend into the background the same way a conversation from another room drifts through open doorways.

JM: Many of these short, abstract pieces play with how the words are spaced and delivered to the audience, breaking up a smoother rhythm in favor of staccato. Could you talk a little about how you decide where to place your words—and what you hope to achieve by these unconventional placements?

BM: While it is most common to read line breaks like pauses, for the most part, I design my comics more in the mindset of film editing—meaning text progressing over a new image is less a request for pause and more an indication of switching shots. When I write, I do so in block or monologue formation. In opposition to that, though, I do hope that the space between words is just a little bit disorienting, and that pauses are created organically by the reader searching for the string of thought on the page.

JM: There's a very assured, steady pacing to these shorts. How much do you consider pacing when you're creating comics?

BM: The pacing really comes from format. I find that regardless of the length or breadth of the dream, the space it takes to put myself back in the narrator's shoes for a summary or scene is consistent across each comic. As a result, I know when I set up to draw that I will be working with four pages. Through repetition, I've tricked myself into maintaining a certain rhythm almost unconsciously.

JM: How autobiographical are these pieces?

BM: I hope to convey these dreams in the present tense, in a way that reads not so much as a retelling but as a moment of processing in real-time. The writing of the comic is, for me, the moment where the symbology of the dream aligns with what is happening in my life more broadly. They are certainly autobiographical in that sense—I have lived these stories in an alternate reality.

JM: What tools did you use to create these pieces? Colored pencils?

BM: Yes, mostly colored pencils, and occasionally pencil and pen.

JM: What other cartoonists are working in a similar vein?

BM: I think there are some parallels to be made with Aiden Koch's work because of her loose and scribbly use of colored pencils—I try to keep from making my comics feel "precious," embracing stray marks and mistakes. In general, though, I tend to see more similarities with animation and film. Sadie Benning's films feature a stream of abstracted close-up images that feel disconnected to her first-person narrations. That hits closer to home than any other body of work I can think of.

CONTRIBUTORS

Michael Hugh Stewart is the author of four books and the current recipient of the Rhode Island Council for the Arts Fellowships in both fiction and poetry. He teaches creative nonfiction at Brown University. You can read more on his website (michaelhughstewart.com).

Johanna Povirk-Znoy is an artist and writer living in Philadelphia. She received an MFA from the Yale School of Art in 2015 and is currently pursuing a degree in Art Therapy & Counseling from Drexel University. She has a story published with *Short American Fiction* that you can read online should you like.

Vincent Panella's stories have appeared in several small magazines including *The MacGuffin, Paterson Literary Review, WIPS Journal, Voices in Italian Americana, The Long Story, Main Street Rag*, and *Ovunque Siamo* (Pushcart nominee). He's written a memoir called *The Other Side*, (*Doubleday*, 1979); a novel, *Cutter's Island*, (*Academy*

Chicago, 2000, ForeWord Winner); *Lost Hearts*, a story collection (*Apollo's Bow*, 2010); and *Sicilian Dreams*, a novel recently published by *Bordighera Press* and a Finalist in Historical Fiction for the 2020 Indie Book Awards.

Izzy Buck is a Philadelphia based writer. She holds a B.A. in Creative Writing and Psychology from Franklin and Marshall College. Once her health is under control, she plans to work on a collection of speculative short stories centered around chronic illness.

Rebecca Starks' short fiction has appeared in *Epiphany, Crab Orchard Review, Tahoma Literary Review,* and *Orca*. The author of the poetry collections *Fetch, Muse* and *Time Is Always Now*, both by *Able Muse Press*, she is the recipient of Rattle's 2018 Neil Postman Award for Metaphor. She grew up in Louisville, Kentucky and lives in Richmond, Vermont.

Victor McConnell grew up in a

small town in Texas and graduated from Dartmouth's creative writing program in 2004. After a long mostly dormant period, he resumed writing fiction in 2020. His short fiction has been selected for publication (or named as an honorable mention/finalist in contests) by *Writer's Digest, The Los Angeles Review, The Texas Observer, Kallisto Gaia Press, Driftwood Press, Rufus on Fire, New Letters, Flash 500,* and *Sterling Clack Clack.* He has an eleven-year-old son and lives in Golden, Colorado.

Jenna Abrams grew up in Massachusetts. Her stories have been published or are forthcoming in *Epoch* and *The Masters Review Anthology XI*; selected as finalists for The Florida Review 2021-2022 Jeanne Leiby Memorial Chapbook Award, the Quarterly West 2021 Chapbook Contest, the Yemassee 2021 Chapbook Contest, and the Indiana Review 2021 Fiction Prize; and shortlisted for *The Masters Review Anthology IX*. Jenna earned an MFA at UC Irvine, where she was a recipient of the MacDonald Harris Prize. She has received support from Vermont Studio Center, and was a 2020 Elizabeth George Foundation grantee.

Marcie Roman's short fiction has appeared in *CALYX, upstreet, Split Lip Magazine, Black Fox*, and *The Gravity of the Thing*, among others. Her novel *Journey to the Parallels* (*Fitzroy Books*, 2022) won the 2020 Kraken Book Prize for middle grade fiction. She is the recipient of an Illinois Arts Council Award and has an MFA in Writing from Vermont College of Fine Arts.

Mason Boyles is a PhD student in FSU's creative writing program. He holds his MFA from UC Irvine, where he received the Weinberg and Schaeffer Fellowships. His fiction has appeared in publications such as *The Wisconsin Review, The Baltimore Review, The New Guard*, and *Black Dandy*, among others. He is currently revising a novel about a set of un-conjoined twins who inherit a system of folk magic and a collapsing Appalachian strip mine.

Bazeed is an Egyptian immigrant, writer, performance artist, stage actor, and cook living in Brooklyn. An alliteration-leaning writer of prose, poetry, plays, and pantry lists, their work across genres has been published in print and online, and their plays performed on stages in the United States and abroad. Bazeed is currently at work on a book-length erasure poem of the hyper-racist text, *The Arab Mind; The Sunshine School Songbook*, a solo cabaret sponsored by late-stage capitalism and the algorithms of Gulf Labor dystopias; and the second draft of their so-faggy-it's-in-the-title! play, *faggy faafi Cairo boy*.

Luke Burton tends bar and slings food to make rent. He wonders if one could make it from Vermont to California without stepping foot off the pavement. He writes poems and makes video art. His work has appeared in *Okay Donkey, Bard Papers, The Redlands Review* and elsewhere. He holds a degree in Written Arts and Experimental Humanities from Bard College and is a Senior Editor at *GENERAL SUBJECT / NO SUBJECT Press*.

Kimberly Sailor, from Mount Horeb, WI, is a 2020 poetry fellowship recipient from the Martha's Vineyard Institute of Creative Writing. Sailor, a 2022 and 2019 Hal Prize poetry finalist, is also the editor-in-chief of the Recorded A Cappella Review Board. Her poetry has appeared in *Sixfold, the Peninsula Pulse, Silver Birch Press,* and *the Eunoia Review*. She is the author of the novel *The Clarinet Whale*, teaches elementary-aged students, and serves as a volunteer firefighter in her community. You can read more about her on her website (kimberlysailor.com).

Margaret Yapp is from Iowa City. She works as the Image + Word editor at *Prompt Press* and an editorial assistant at the University of Iowa Press. Margaret is currently an MFA candidate at the University of Iowa Center for the Book and a member of the Iowa City Poetry Advisory Council. She has an MFA in poetry from the Iowa Writers' Workshop. Her work has appeared in *Second Factory, Asphalte, Brink*, and elsewhere. You can read more at Margaret's website (margaretyapp.com).

Bader Al Awadhi is an undergraduate English major at Loyola Marymount University. He is an international student from Kuwait studying abroad in Los Angeles. Bader pushes the boundaries of imagination in his poems. He writes extensively on the nuances of identity, its intersections with culture, religion, sexuality, and navigating the world of Western academia with English as a second language. His work addresses social issues that are most important to him, ones which affect his own community as well as other marginalized groups, and brings a unique voice to poetry that expresses the beauty and complexity of his Middle Eastern heritage.

Shaoni White writes speculative poetry and fiction. Their poetic work has appeared in *smoke and mold, Channel Magazine, Apparition Lit, Fantasy Magazine, The Deadlands*, and *Augur*. Their short stories have appeared in *Uncanny Magazine, Fireside, Nightmare Magazine, PodCastle*, and elsewhere. Raised in Southern California, they hold a BA in English Literature and Linguistics from Swarthmore College. They spend their free time swing dancing and embroidering. Find them at shaonicwhite.com or on Twitter at @shaonicwhite.

Anthony Immergluck is a poet, publishing professional, and musician with an MFA in Poetry from New York University–Paris. Originally from the Chicago area, he now lives in Madison, Wisconsin and works in academic publishing.

Robert Laidler is an Assistant Professor of Teaching in the Wayne State Department of English. He's the author of a poetic li-

bretto, *The Fallen Petals of Nameless Flowers*, which premiered at Chamber Music Detroit in 2022. He earned his MFA in poetry from the University of Michigan, where he is currently a Zell Fellow. His poems have won various awards and published in a number of places, now including this place, of the which, he is really proud of. He enjoys music, eating, and eating while listening to music.

Derek Annis is a neurodivergent poet from the Inland Northwest. He is the author of *Neighborhood of Gray Houses* (*Lost Horse Press*), the associate director of *Willow Springs Books*, and the associate director of *Lynx House Press*. Their poems have appeared in *The Account, Colorado Review, Epiphany, The Gettysburg Review, The Missouri Review Online, Poet Lore, Spillway*, and *Third Coast*, among others.

Caroline New is a poet and artist from Bainbridge, GA. Her work explores natural disaster, motherhood, and ancestry in the Gulf Coast, and is informed by a background in visual arts and anthropology. She is currently a Helen Zell fellow the University of Michigan, where she received her MFA in Creative Writing.

Her poems can be found in *Ruminate, PRISM International, and Southern Humanities Review,* with publications forthcoming in the *American Poetry Review.* More info available online (www.carolineharpernew.com).

Sarah Levine is currently teaching 7th Grade ELA and AP Literature in Western Massachusetts. Her latest chapbook, *Take Me Home,* was selected by Leah Maines as a finalist for the 2019 Finishing Line Press New Women's Voices Chapbook Prize. Her poems have appeared in *Passages North, Best New Poets, Green Mountains Review,* among other publications. She holds an MFA from Sarah Lawrence College and an MAT from Smith College. Levine has been nominated for a Pushcart Prize, won Westchester Review's Writers Under 30 Contest, and is the author of chapbook, *Her Man* (*New Megaphone Press,* 2014).

Robin Walter lives in Fort Collins, Colorado. She received her MFA in poetry from Colorado State University, where she now teaches. Her work is forthcoming or has appeared in *American Poetry Review, Poets.org, Seneca Review, West Branch, Wildness* and elsewhere. Her manuscript

Little Mercy is a finalist for the 2022 National Poetry Series, and was selected by Kazim Ali as a finalist for Omnidawn's 1st/2nd book prize. Her chapbook *o oio* was a finalist for the 2020 Broken River Prize judged by Kaveh Akbar. Her poetry manuscript of the same title was a finalist for the 2021 Interim Test Site Poetry Series, and a semi-finalist for the series in 2020. She was the recipient of the 2021 Academy of American Poets Prize.

Ana Prundaru lives in Switzerland. Her recent work appears in *Lunate, North Dakota Quarterly,* and *Suburban Review.*

Qiyue Zhang is an illustrator currently living in Jersey City. She graduated from the School of Visual Arts with a BFA in Illustration. She loves to tell stories through her pictures. She uses analog and digital materials such as watercolor, ink, pencil, and Photoshop.

Kimball Anderson makes comics that have a floating feeling and rhythm to them. Since they were young, they've been disabled by chronic illness, which informs every part of their creative process. Much of their work explores the ignored, quiet spaces along the periphery that people fall into, and the lost and yearning people that fall into them. Their work has appeared in journals and anthologies like *Anomaly, Ink Brick*, and *How to Wait*. You can find more of their comics online (outside-life.com).

Yaron Regev is an author and translator. He is the author of two graphic novels, *Ghosts of Love and Country* (2019) and *The Cave* (2022), as well as an upcoming YA fantasy series called *The Door Behind the Sun*, the short play *Until the Children Will Return*, and several adult novels.

Dave Youkovich is a seasoned comic book artist and illustrator with over fifteen years of experience in the industry. He got his start in the fanzine scene in Argentina at the young age of fourteen, creating mini horror comics and writing about underground death metal bands. By the age of sixteen, he had published his first professional works in local magazines and even founded a pioneering digital magazine called *MAKABRA*, which featured comics, art, and music articles.

Stefanie Jordan holds a degree in animation from the Film Accademy in Potsdam/Germany. She has made animated films, as well as feature-length documentaries, writing, directing, producing, and doing camerawork for over twenty years. Stefanie's work has been awarded many accolades and prizes internationally, including the Silver Bear at the Berlin International Film Festival and the German Woman Media Award. It has been shown in venues as diverse as New York's MoMA as well as television in Denmark, Austria, Germany, The Netherlands and the US. She was awarded the Women Artist grant for Film & Video by the Berlin Senate four times. Her comics have been featured in international online magazines and have been exhibited in diverse venues—most recently at the Comic Days in Stuttgart/Germany.

Ben Montague is an a-disciplinary artist who takes inspiration from performance, theatre, philosophy, narrative and archival practices. As an extension of their need to compartmentalize, the objects they make (physical or ephemeral) become representational surrogates for whatever it is they can't comprehend, concede to or abide by. Recurring obsessions include the "flight" in fight-or-flight, projection, intimacy, and the perceived shame and limitations of subjective experience.